Isotype.

Plantae Occidentales Selectae

NO. 3429.   FLORA. Nevadensis.

NOMEN. Cymopterus Ripleyi Barneby
  var. saniculoides Barneby, Leafl.
  W. Bot. III, 82 (1941).
LOC. Base of Spotted Range towards
  Frenchman Flat, S. Nye County.
HABITAT denuded white alkaline-calcar.
  hills, rare.
                    ALT. 3200 p.s.m.

DIE 13/V ANNO 1941 LEGERUNT

H. D. RIPLEY & R. C. BARNEBY.

Both

Both

A PORTRAIT IN TWO PARTS

Douglas Crase

PANTHEON BOOKS

NEW YORK

Library of Congress Cataloging-in-Publication Data

Crase, Douglas.
Both : a portrait in two parts / Douglas Crase.
p.   cm.
Includes bibliographical references.
ISBN 0-375-42266-8
1. Barneby, Rupert C.   2. Ripley, Dwight.   3. Botanists—United
States—Biography.   4. Plant collectors—United States—Biography.
5. Artists—United States—Biography.   I. Title.

QK31.B29C73 2004   580'92'2—dc22   [B]   2003061184

FOR FRANK POLACH

poetae dilectissimo

Contents

Rupert

A LTHOUGH DR. RUPERT C. BARNEBY was apparently the most accomplished legume taxonomist since Bentham, and had prepared himself since childhood to that end, his work was a subject that I as a nonscientist could not readily discuss. This did not disappoint him. It was enough in 1975 that I came along as the partner of his new friend, Frank Polach. Frank and I had arrived in New York the year before, when we both were thirty, and Frank had begun work soon after as a plant information officer at the New York Botanical Garden. There, bearing an unrecognizable leaf sent by some anxious gardener, he approached the celebrated elder figure who was known, instantly and by everyone, it seems, as Rupert. The leaf was identified, and now Frank and I were on our way to the Botanical Garden where we had been invited to Rupert's for dinner so that I too might be presented for inspection. A visiting botanist will reach the garden today, I suppose, by cab from the airport or by car from the suburbs. I wonder how to convey the impact, on a provincial newcomer, of this dinner excursion that began, by contrast, with descent to the IND local at Twenty-third Street, change to the D train, and exit fifty minutes later to street-level air on Bedford Park Boulevard in the unfamiliar Bronx. Down the hill and across the railroad tracks stood the Mosholu Gate to the Botanical Garden beyond. Frank had told me that the garden once was part of the Lorillard estate; never, despite his description, could I have foreseen the freedom of ground and sky, the splendid if threatened optimism of the Museum Building, the acres of primeval hemlock (the woolly adelgid had not begun its destruction), or the precipitous river gorge we had to cross in order to arrive at the side door of Pierre Lorillard's old stone stable, its ground floor occupied by the garden security headquarters, its loft by Rupert Barneby. Here, at the head of the narrow stairs, we were welcomed to a room that fit beneath its pitched roof like the nave of a small Gothic chapel, stone walls exposed, deep casement windows encrusted with grime. On the floors were antique Bijar rugs, on the walls an oil by Miró, two drawings by Jackson Pollock, foxed prints of *Astragalus* (the legume genus, aSTRAGGalus, as we were later to learn, that was Rupert's lifelong taxonomic passion), and, lined up wherever there was an available shelf or ledge, the books that included rare floras, first-edition poetry, travel guides in French, German, Spanish, Portuguese. It was hard to believe, while seated at a refectory table on eighteenth-century Portuguese chairs, when served a gentle curry on hand-painted Spode, or while smoking after dinner the smuggled cigars, that we were destined ever to get back on the subway. Instead we soaked up the gossip, delivered in an English accent that was both unassuming and lyrically at odds with the occasional squawk from the two-way radio downstairs: firsthand gossip about Auden and Isherwood, Peggy Guggenheim and Marcel Duchamp (figures as otherwise legendary to me as Bentham and Hooker, George Forrest, or Redouté may be to botanists), and gossip, too, about a figure whose name we did not recognize but whose portrait, in the lightly Surrealist manner of a vanished era, hung in the bedroom—our host's own partner of forty-eight years, the late Dwight Ripley.

My reaction to that evening was not original: greedy to learn and at the same time bristling with pride so as not to be influenced. The aesthetics of Surrealism, the habits of a discipline so foreign as taxonomy, had little, I thought, to offer me. Besides, like every other potential mentor, the sixty-three-year-old Rupert Barneby was inconsistent. He warned us, perhaps that very evening, against making "a deep plan" for our lives; if you have a deep plan, he said, you set yourselves up for disaster. It was advice that seemed congruent with his personality. Years later we discovered a description of Rupert in the diaries of Judith Malina, actress and founder of the avant-garde Living Theatre, who knew him in his forties. "Rupert, the gentle one," she wrote, "submits to fate, seems to be part of an eternal process, like the bud, blossom and withering of one of his plants." And yet this gentle one, at the very moment he was warning us to avoid deep plans, was himself finishing work on "Daleae Imagines," the illustrated revision of the genus *Dalea* that had occupied him then for at least ten years. Was this no plan? At a memorial tribute that would be held at the garden in 2001, after Rupert died, we heard Gwilym Lewis, from the Royal Botanic Gardens at Kew, emphasize that Rupert's published output could be calculated at one new page of taxonomic text every third day for fifty-nine consecutive years. Perhaps the deepest plan of all had been the one that inspired his "Atlas of North American *Astragalus*," published in 1964 and still the standard in its field, an achievement that was not ten but twenty years in the making, had a long foreground before that, and continued to claim his interest thereafter. Clearly Rupert did have lessons to teach, though he did so by such unexpected example that what I chiefly value from our early years with him is surprise: surprise when this thoroughly achieved figure insisted on being as alive in the present as we were, when he reached across time, nationality, and (let's face it) social class to provide a sudden moral poke. How could I forget the day I was feeling so justly sorry for myself, and he asked what was wrong? Oh nothing, I said, just my life is over. And Rupert's response, so swift it nearly felled me, was "How dare you say that to *me!*"

Only later did I fully grasp that Frank and I had come to dinner not two years after Rupert's own partner, he of the portrait, had died. The story of their partnered lives, the way those lives blended productively into the worlds of botany and art, cannot truly be told without a look back to their beginnings. Rupert had been born at Trewyn (he pronounced it treWIN), a brooding pile of a country house built in the late seventeenth century on still more ancient foundations at the foot of the Black Mountains, just barely across the border from England, in Wales. It was here in the uplands, along Offa's Dyke, around the ruins of Llanthony Priory, that he discovered as a boy his affinity for the forms and identities of plants. Frank and I were to see this special area one rainy October 6 after pitching and sliding our rental car up a lane so deep we could not see where we were until, cresting the hill, we came perilously close to the back door of Trewyn itself. This was not a polite arrival. Certainly it astonished the owner, the Lady Telford, who in her yellow slicker climbed down from the bulldozer she had rented for the day and offered to show us inside; she could scarcely believe that word of the bed-and-breakfast she intended to open had reached so soon across the Atlantic. Shamelessly I exploited the misunderstanding, and a few minutes later we were standing in the upstairs room (it's behind the second-floor front window at far left) where Rupert Charles Barneby was born. Rupert too was astonished when he learned of our visit. We had been there, uncannily, on his birthday. Whether he was delighted or appalled by our effrontery I couldn't tell, but he studied raptly the brochure we brought him: Trewyn Court, Bed & Breakfast. "It was never a *court!*" he said indignantly. In 1911, the year he was born, Trewyn comprised several thousand acres; he remembered riding with his mother in a carriage at Christmas to deliver presents in the village. In New York he devised traditions of his own. Each year a Christmas poinsettia would appear, delivered personally by Rupert to the lobby of our building. He never announced himself on these occasions but went on his way, dispensing gifts, perhaps, to his other villagers.

Trewyn

The young Rupert did not live continuously at Trewyn. During World War I his mother, born Louisa Geraldine Ingham, was so fearful of being left alone in the country that his father, Philip Bartholomew Barneby, rented something even more substantial to house his family while he was away: Ludlow Castle. All of it. Rupert's earliest botanical memory, which will explain perhaps his fondness for yellow, was of a cowslip in the Ludlow Castle moat. Not far to the southeast stood Saltmarshe Castle, the crenellated and dramatic, not to say melodramatic residence in Herefordshire of his grandfather William Barneby. And east of that, near Bromyard, was the historic family seat of Lower Brockhampton, a crooked, half-timbered manor house built in the fourteenth century, preserved and now opened to visitors by the National Trust. Rupert had two older brothers, Edmund and Tom, and a younger sister, Geraldine. When he was nine, the fourteen-year-old Edmund was killed in a riding accident at Trewyn; his mother again grew fearful of the country, and the family retreated to Wilcroft, a second Georgian landmark they maintained near Hereford in the village of Bartestree. Budd Myers, a friend who knew Rupert during the 1960s, once heard that he was secretly a Plantagenet, in a direct though illegitimate line from Richard, Duke of York. Surely this was a tale for gullible Americans. So, being Americans, Frank and I looked in *Burke's Landed Gentry*, where the original Barneby is identified, suggestively, as among York's retinue and as treasurer in 1461 to York's legitimate son, Edward IV. We were not surprised to learn that Rupert had a family coat of arms. On the shield are lions, rampant, and below is the motto VIRTUTE NON VI.

Like his father before him, Rupert was sent to an exclusive, or, as

Rupert at Harrow   *Dwight at Harrow*

the English call it, a "public" school. His father had attended Eton; Rupert followed his brother Tom to Harrow. Unlike father or brother, he soon was sent home again. At Harrow the fourteen-year-old Rupert Barneby had met the sixteen-year-old Dwight Ripley, and the result was a sudden boyhood romance. Ripley, whose full name was Harry Dwight Dillon Ripley, was an only child born in London in 1908. His Anglo-Irish mother was an actress whose name Rupert couldn't remember (it was Alice Louise), and his American father, Harry, was a grandson of Sidney Dillon—one of those organizers of the Union Pacific Railroad who can be seen, waiting to drive the golden spike, in a famous photograph that was taken at Promontory Point, Utah, in 1869. And there was the rub. Harrow was alarmed, not because a schoolboy crush was unusual, but because young Ripley was not English. The elder Ripley had died from the effects of alcoholism when Dwight was only four; his fortune, which included two American trust funds in addition to his Sussex estate, the Spinney, had been willed in part to his widow and in part, as he came of age, to Dwight. The relatives in America refused to release the funds. Dwight's mother litigated her claim unsuccessfully in London and then, with Dwight in tow, successfully in New York. There she entered so wholeheartedly into the available nightlife that on one occasion she misplaced her son. The ensuing three-day search by police ended only when friends called to ask why she had not retrieved the boy she left in their apartment. She died, also broken by alcohol, a few years after returning to England. Dwight's upbringing was supervised thereafter by his solicitor, and by the time he reached Harrow he was rich, precocious, and eccentric. At the Spinney he had built already a rock garden and an alpine house of his own, and his Harrow School notebooks are filled with lists of desired plants, in Latin. This was Rupert's first and perhaps last encounter with a contemporary whose Latin was better than his own. Rupert at times proudly recalled the childhood self-reliance he himself had shown in the Woolhope Club, an association of amateur naturalists in Herefordshire whose officers challenged the taxonomic determinations in his herbarium and were proved, by the twelve-year-old Rupert, to be wrong. But his botanical independence met its match in his new friend's horticultural independence. At nine years of age Dwight grew a garden at the Spinney that was nothing but parsleys; now he was making plans for a "Contrary Garden," in which the species would be chosen for flower colors that were *not* as advertised. It was inevitable, or at least predictable, that when Barneby senior returned his son to school the two boys would resume, where they left off, the progress of their affair.

From Harrow, Rupert went in 1929 to Trinity College, Cambridge, to read not botany but modern languages. His father thought it unsuitable for a man to study flowers, and intended his son to be a diplomat. Dwight had gone the year before to Oxford, and he too studied languages. During his final year there, in 1931, the prestigious firm of Elkin Mathews & Marrot published Dwight's collection of thirty-one poems, called simply *Poems*. (Mathews was the first publisher of Yeats, James Joyce, and Ezra Pound.) Of the thirty-one poems, only one is in English. Eventually Dwight was fluent in fifteen languages, and able to read and write in perhaps thirty. The library at the New York Botanical Garden has the manuscript of his *Etymological Dictionary of Vernacular Plant Names*, the massive multilingual project he had nearly completed before he died. I have a copy of his *Poems*. When Rupert mailed it, he enclosed for me a delicate explanation of Dwight's aesthetics, but there is not much that needs explaining about the book's dedication: *Ruperto Barneby, poetae dilectissimo,* the poet's most beloved. Rupert completed his own curriculum at Cambridge in 1932 and persuaded his father to send him to the university at Grenoble, in France, for further training in languages. He did not explain to his father that Dwight was already there. The two young men spent a memorable year learning, carousing, and also botanizing to the south, where Dwight filled the endpapers of H. Stuart Thompson's *Flowering Plants of the Riviera* with lists of species destined for the gardens back at the Spinney. By now those gardens were regarded as "theirs." I do not know how long Barneby senior waited, once the pair had returned to England, to deliver the ultimatum that Rupert described to us so vividly. Philip Barneby would not meet his son at the Spinney, nor would he allow him home. He summoned him to Hyde Park instead. Relinquish the attachment, he said, and come home as before. Otherwise never return. It would be romantic to think it was love for Dwight alone, but more likely it was a combination of love, his future in botany, and his native personality that motivated Rupert Barneby to give fate no second thought. He never saw his father again.

Although disinherited, Rupert had the advantage of class, plus Dwight's money, and he might have dabbled in amateur botany most of his life. Where did he get the idea to be a great taxonomist instead? Sometime in the early 1930s, at Cambridge, on a visit to Kew, or at Walter Ingwersen's alpine plant nursery in Sussex, he met Noel Sandwith, ten years his senior and an assistant then in the herbarium at Kew. Sandwith concentrated on the flora of Mexico and later became an authority on tropical flora throughout the Americas, in particular that family of showy and sometimes odd ornamentals, the Bignoniaceae. But it was an omission in his resumé that made Sandwith, to the younger man, a compelling example: like Rupert, he had no academic training in botany. His degree was in classics. By the time Rupert met him, Sandwith had made three botanical expeditions to Spain and had deposited more than sixteen hundred specimens at Kew. When Rupert and Dwight themselves collected in Spain, they followed frequently in Sandwith's footsteps, going to the Cabo de Gata, for instance, to find *Antirrhinum charidemi,* a snapdragon he had described and named. Named!— without a botany degree. Here was an approachable model that would encourage the future Dr. Barneby to turn his aspirations, too, into habits of practical size. At the same time it was Sandwith who prompted in Rupert his lasting engagement with the multivolume novel by Marcel Proust, *À la recherche du temps perdu*, the final volumes of which were just then being published in English. The botanist James Grimes has related how eagerly Rupert guided him, when they were in Paris together in 1991, to the places intimately associated with the life of Proust. Over the years I myself heard Rupert and Frank so frequently mix Proust with their botanical gossip that I could easily believe Swann, Jim Grimes and Albertine, the Guermantes, the Maguires, and the Holmgrens must wander the halls at the Botanical Garden together. Proust's immense novel, Sandwith told Rupert, is "a work of stupendous, mysterious genius." It is not all mysterious, however. Maxims are sometimes isolated from the narrative, and some of these had appeared in 1948 in *The Maxims of Marcel Proust*, a book that Rupert used thereafter as a way to bring the master to unread friends. One especially Barnebian lesson was this: "It is not the desire for fame but the habit of work which allows us to produce a masterpiece." Sandwith, who died unexpectedly in 1965, willed his set of Proust to Rupert. For Dwight and Rupert both, the example of the older botanist was never exhausted and his name became a kind of compliment. Said Dwight of one new acquaintance: "He's like an extrovert, versatile Noel S., and what could be better than that?"

The sustained, enabling influence on Rupert's early direction as a botanist was supplied, of course, by none other than Dwight himself. Dwight's wealth provided the means, his affection the latitude, and his gardens the focus for Rupert's increasingly learned, plant's-eye view of collecting, horticulture, and taxonomy. Years later, in an article in the *Bulletin of the American Rock Garden Society*, Rupert

would recall their early garden enthusiasms, and characterize them
(not quite succinctly) as "excesses of what a doctrinaire Marxist
might well condemn as bourgeois eclecticism, though they might as
accurately and more charitably be described as symptoms of collector's mania." To support their mania, the two young men mounted
the annual collecting expeditions that took them eventually throughout the Mediterranean area, and repeatedly to Algeria and Spain. For
the rest of their lives Spain would claim a special place in their
affections. In Spain, Rupert discovered the profusion of species,
soon to prove taxonomically irresistible, in the genus *Astragalus*.
There, as he later told botanist Stanley Welsh, he received his "bap-
tism" as a collector. But it was on the coast of Algeria that he and
Dwight located the sea lavender *Limonium asparagoides*, which he
had tracked via a lithograph published in Paris in 1896, and which
they proudly brought back from the village of Nemours for cultivation in England. Rupert's account of their expedition has the pun-
gent hauteur that so frequently marked his style. "Nemours," he
wrote, "though teeming with human life, looked from a distance like
a vast ruined pigsty, and I recall with still vivid discomfort the panic
of curiosity that Dwight and I aroused in our passage through it.
The narrow pebble beach below the town, when we fought our way
to it, turned out to be the municipal latrine, and it was in this improbable and squalid setting that we found *L. asparagoides* draped over
the mud cliffs."

At the Spinney the sea lavender *L. asparagoides* became the star of
the garden, and its glamour was confirmed when it received an
Award of Merit from the Royal Horticultural Society in the autumn
of 1938. It was called *Statice asparagoides* then. "Mr. Ripley created

quite a furore," reported the nurseryman Ingwersen, "when he brought to the Alpine Garden Society Show a wonderful specimen plant of the delightfully graceful *Statice asparagoides.*" The suffix *oides* in a species epithet means "like" or "resembling," so Dwight's glamorous entry at the garden show must have resembled *Asparagus* (not the spear, we may trust, but the mature asparagus, which is feathery as it goes to seed). At the Spinney the two men grew their star specimen on a pile of rock and tufa that was meant to provide the conditions of a modest cliff. The rocks had been propped against an existing kitchen-garden wall, then sheltered with glass as if by a partial, unheated greenhouse. The result, a "cliff house," was considered novel enough to be a model for alpine gardeners throughout England. Botanist Peter Davis, who met Rupert and Dwight at Ingwersen's nursery when he was still an apprentice there in 1937, described this cliff house for a festschrift in *Brittonia,* the New York Botanical Garden's journal of systematic botany, which honored Rupert in his seventieth year. "Those were exciting days," wrote Davis. "Purring through the deep country lanes in Dwight's chauffeur-driven Packard, I wondered not only what was for lunch (always delicious) but what new rarities had been added from their west Mediterranean journeys, and were now flowering in cultivation for the first time." In addition to the cliff house, the Spinney included three greenhouses, a sand garden for seashore plants, a water garden, herbaceous borders, and an area solely for plants of bizarre aspect; a new rarity would find its place, not just in one of these, but also pressed, mounted, and classified in the private herbarium of Rupert Barneby. In retrospect, it is possible to discern in this sequence the unfolding of an education unusual in both its breadth and intensity. Rupert saw each plant ecologically in place where he and Dwight collected it, watched it assert its horticultural needs in their gardens, examined beneath his microscope its structures of evolutionary response, and felt in his own hand the drawings he made of it. The continuum could be retraced in his mind at will, a practice that must have strengthened his ability to extrapolate in less familiar situations, and that gave him, perhaps, his famous "nose" for collecting: it seemed Rupert could tell where a plant might be found by the way it looked as a specimen in a distant herbarium. Surely it was this practice that lay behind his abiding regard for the herbarium as an intimate model, complex and perhaps so far unexcelled, of the worldwide life of plants. In 1939 he compiled with Dwight a taxonomically ordered, annotated list of species being grown at the Spinney; it was published in a fine-press edition as *A List of Plants Cultivated or Native at The Spinney, Waldron, Sussex*. There is a copy in the library of the Botanical Garden. The *List* records a total of 1,138 species, 385 of which had been collected personally by Dwight and Rupert, 74 by Davis, and 25 by Ingwersen. Reflecting on the Spinney's gardens some thirty-five years later, the *Quarterly Bulletin of the Alpine Garden Society* observed that "one is amazed at the number of plants unknown to us today," and went on to mention specifically the sea lavender from Nemours, still stubbornly calling it *Statice asparagoides*. Eventually the collection at the Spinney was dispersed to Kew, Cambridge, and private gardeners; it was due solely to this, wrote the *Quarterly Bulletin*, "that many fine plants like *Diosphaera asperuloides* and *Trachelium lanceolatum* are in cultivation today, for they have never been re-introduced."

As the scale of the Spinney makes plain, the Rupert who advised us to make no "deep plan" was accustomed by life with Dwight to making no small plans either. He was accustomed likewise to ambitious friends. Dwight kept a residence in London, and the two men mixed in circles that included Dwight's fellow Oxonians Wystan Auden and Stephen Spender, as well as Christopher Isherwood, the Huxleys, the Sitwells, Cyril Connolly and his American wife, Jean Connolly: circles in which the admired standards were for satire in literature and, in society, sarcasm and wit. Jean Connolly, who became one of Dwight's closer friends, was at the center of avant-garde sets on both sides of the Atlantic; she was the only woman, said Auden, who could keep him up all night. Because of her connections in the art world, she was to play a pivotal role in the lives of Rupert and Dwight. Once, while I was turning pages in the Clive Fisher biography of Cyril Connolly (the English writer, critic, and editor of the standard-setting journal *Horizon*), I scanned the photo inserts; there next to Jean Connolly at a house party in England was a younger version of the face that looked out from the portrait in Rupert's bedroom. Indeed, verified Rupert, I had spotted Dwight. The party occurred in 1935 at Richard Wyndham's house, the Tickerage (it was not far from the Spinney), and the others grouped beside Dwight and Jean Connolly in the photograph are Patrick Balfour (later Lord Kinross), Constant Lambert (the composer), Angela Culme-Seymour (who was to marry Balfour), Wyndham (a soldier, writer, and finally photographer who was killed covering the Arab-Israeli war in 1948), Tom Driberg (the columnist "William Hickey" at the *Daily Express* and later member of Parliament), Connolly, Spender, Tony Hyndman (Spender's boyfriend),

Mamaine Paget (later the second wife of Arthur Koestler), and John
Rayner (also of the *Daily Express*). Joan Eyres-Monsell (later Leigh-
Fermor) was taking the picture. Rupert, who disliked Spender, is
not part of the group—which is a shame, because Frank and I
know only two photographs, of much later date, in which he and
Dwight appear together. Rupert, five feet ten inches, always slen-
der, was blond, blue-eyed, and aquiline in a classic English manner;
Dwight, the same height but more muscular, was dark, brown-
eyed, and Celtic. Together when young they must have looked like
ideal casting for *Brideshead Revisited*. On board ship from Marseilles to Cairo in 1937 they met Peter Markham Scott, artist, later
founder of the Slimbridge Refuge and cofounder of the World
Wildlife Fund, fresh then from a bronze-medal performance as a
single yachtsman in the Olympics. Scott made a pencil sketch of
Rupert. The sketch, which surfaced years later in Rupert's loft, is of
a sulky, eye-catching twenty-six-year-old. Judith Malina, on a visit
to Rupert and Dwight in the 1950s, described to her diary the paintings, books, and other objects in their house. "There are photo
albums full of castles on the Riviera," she wrote, "and there we see
the dashing boys, the millionaire from America and his English pal,
as chic as they come."

When the impending civil war made it impossible to collect in
their beloved Spain, Rupert and Dwight decided on a substitute destination where the language was also Spanish and the conditions
semiarid: Mexico. They arrived in 1936 in Los Angeles and readied
themselves for an expedition south. In the literature so far published
about Rupert's career, there is a nagging inconsistency in the dates
given for their arrival in the United States. This was because, from

1936 until their permanent arrival (which they believed temporary) in 1939, they came and went. The Rupert of later years, blithely modest, seemed to think biography unimportant, and he casually volunteered whichever date was relevant to the story being told at the moment. Other times he supplied dates that simply were wrong. The adventure of 1936, at any rate, was not auspicious for his future in botany. He and Dwight, heading south in a Packard with non-botanist friends, Hope and Harold Chown, intended to travel six hundred miles beyond the border to La Paz in Baja California. Rupert's "nose" had told them what discoveries should be waiting along the way. His nose failed to tell them about the road. By nine o'clock on their first night beyond Ensenada they were stuck in a ravine-sized ditch with a shredded front tire (*tyre*, as they still spelled it), no jack, and were forced to spend the night with their married friends in the car—"a memory," wrote Dwight, "over which I prefer to draw the veil." They never got to La Paz, but stayed the next two weeks at a ranch ten miles beyond the abandoned Packard. There they saw their first *Phacelia* (a genus of bluebell-like plants that does not occur in Europe), and decided to regard it as a harbinger of better things to come. In 1938 they were back in California. This time the live plants they collected were established temporarily in a holding garden at 330 North Bristol, the imposing Spanish-style residence they rented in the Brentwood section of Los Angeles. From "330" they mounted expeditions eastward to Death Valley and Titus Canyon, hoping to find the unusual, yellow-flowered *Maurandya petrophila*. The *Maurandya* was so narrowly endemic—its range so limited—that it had been discovered in Titus Canyon only in 1932 and not named until

1935, a mere three years before. Rupert's attention, deep plan or no, was riveted. If a species could go undiscovered within the boundaries of the Death Valley National Monument, visited every year by waves of tourists with cameras, what might be undiscovered in remoter areas? Dwight's attention was fixed on the prickly *Maurandya* itself, its flowers, he said, a chill sulphur, its form like a "primrose wrapped in a thistle boa." They longed to collect it, but

Rupert in Death Valley

the *Maurandya* was too rare for the vasculum, a frustration Dwight could recall years afterward: "She can't be picked, she can't be picked, she can't be *touched*."

The patterns of life centered on collecting for the Spinney might have continued indefinitely, except, as Rupert put it so characteristically, "Mars had other plans." At first the two men ignored the ominous signs. Dwight financed a trip to Crete so that Rupert, along with Peter Davis, could search for *Senecio gnaphalodes,* a rare shrublike groundsel that had gone unlocated so long it was virtually legend. Here too there was no decent road; Rupert wisely selected transport by mule instead of Packard. The expedition was a success, and Rupert's collector-oriented observations appear in the first published article of his career, "Plants from Eastern Crete," in the *New Flora and Silva* of April 1939. Colleagues who were to witness Rupert's facility for moving seamlessly from the historical record to life, and back again, would have recognized the mounting excitement in his account. "As the path reaches high ground it skirts a west-facing limestone cliff which should be famous in botanical literature, for this is almost certainly the *locus classicus* from which Sieber two hundred years ago described his *Senecio gnaphalodes*." The groundsel is present and accounted for in *A List of Plants,* but it was barely established at the Spinney before the ominous signs of war became dreadful events. Auden and Isherwood had left England in January 1939. Auden stayed in New York, but Isherwood went on to Los Angeles, where he joined Dwight's still closer friends, Chris Wood and Gerald Heard, who had emigrated along with Aldous, Maria, and son Matthew Huxley two years before. In August, Germany and the Soviet Union signed a nonaggression pact; Poland was invaded on September 1, and Britain two days later was at war. Frank and I never learned exactly when Rupert and Dwight left to follow their friends. We know Rupert obtained a new passport in June, and by October 1939 the two men were in New York. There, Dwight settled in for a series of visits to an American dentist. Rupert, however, could hardly wait. He left Dwight to the dentist and boarded a train for Chicago and San Antonio. For four weeks he botanized alone in a Dodge (he was a terrible driver!) through New Mexico, Arizona, and California, until he arrived finally at the Hotel Padre on Cahuenga Boulevard in Hollywood. When Dwight joined him they became part of the wartime colony of English expatriates that soon flourished along the southern California coast. Huxley was now a disciple of Swami Prabhavananda, had finished his California novel *After Many a Summer Dies the Swan*, and would begin later the experiments with mescaline and LSD that he recorded in *The Doors of Perception*. Heard, the science commentator and popular philosopher, was a nonstop talker who nonetheless meditated, was a novitiate yogi (*"yo-gee!"* observed Dwight), and later was to feed the UFO rumors with his book *Is Another World Watching?* Wood was heir to a canned-goods fortune, flew his own plane, yet refused to travel on the ground except by bicycle. Jean Connolly, shortly to arrive from London by way of Ireland, was bringing her close friend Denham Fouts, a storied young American who was the lover then of Peter Watson, the wealthy publisher of *Horizon*, and was widely assumed to have been, before that, the lover of Prince Paul of Greece. These are the figures satirized by Isherwood in his novel *Down There on a Visit*—a novel in which the portrayal of Jean Connolly as "Ruthie" is so rude that it confirmed, said Rupert,

Dwight's longstanding opinion that Isherwood was a "snit." These are the same figures (all can be found in Dwight's old address books) who made up the improbably sophisticated base from which the two botanists with English accents readied their Dodge to hunt for plants in the North American desert.

Rupert's mature career as a taxonomist began in a Death Valley motel on the long night of April 18, 1940, with a drawing. Two weeks earlier, in the Spotted Range of Nye County, Nevada, he and Dwight had found a plant he did not quite recognize; by the time they found it again on the cliffs of Titus Canyon, in California, Rupert was convinced it was an unidentified *Gilia*—his first new species, a find so exciting he stayed up all night sketching it. "To this region belong memorable species," he wrote later, "relicts of a mesophytic vegetation of immense antiquity, and it is believed that the *Gilia* is an unrecognized member of this august and ancient company." Like Noel Sandwith, he would name a plant, and the name was ready: *ripleyi*. Unfortunately, *G. ripleyi* was not cooperating. The brittle stems, the prickly holly-like leaves, the inflorescences left over from the preceding year, were unmistakable, but in mid-April the plant had not come back to life. Even when he returned in June, this year's panicles were barely rising from among the leaves. He had his drawing (it hung, fifty-eight years later, just inside the door of his final apartment), but he had no complete specimen, and he could not describe a new species without seeing its flower. Publication of the new name—provided he could find a place to publish it—would have to wait. Back in Los Angeles, he was further disappointed when he took his specimens for study to the herbarium at the University of California at Los Angeles and was turned unceremoniously away; he lacked the appropriate degree. Resilient, maybe naive, he headed north to the California Academy of Sciences in San Francisco. "Mr. Barneby, an Englishman sojourning in Los Angeles, has been studying with us for several days," wrote the botanist John Thomas Howell in his journal there on November 12. "He's especially interested in desert flora." The confident curator of the academy, Alice Eastwood, welcomed visitors who loved, as she did, plants. She had hired the young Howell in 1929 shortly after Susanna Bixby Bryant dismissed him from his position at the Rancho Santa Ana Botanic Garden, which was located then on the Bryant ranch in Santa Ana Canyon, south of Los Angeles. Eastwood had been a councillor of Rancho Santa Ana; both she and Howell remained friends of taxonomist Philip Munz, a frequent visitor to the Rancho herbarium. It was natural for them to provide Rupert with his introduction to Munz. It was fateful, too, for Munz was a dean and professor of botany at Pomona College, east of Los Angeles in Claremont, and there in the Pomona College herbarium lay the historic collections of Marcus Eugene Jones, the eccentric explorer-botanist whose "Revision of North American species of *Astragalus*," privately published in 1923, was the last word so far on the complex genus *Astragalus*.

"Our halcyon spring" was the way Rupert would remember the collecting season of the following May, 1941, when he and Dwight embarked on their first extended plant hunt in the American West. They headed straight for Nevada in the track of Marcus Jones. Like many adventures, theirs ratified the best of precursor habits: in this case, the division of labor whereby Rupert would concentrate on the taxonomy while Dwight focused on the rock-gardening poten-

tial of their finds. From 1942 to 1950, Dwight sent twelve accounts
of their expeditions to the *Quarterly Bulletin of the Alpine Garden
Society* back in Britain. The botanist Margaret Williams later compiled a truncated selection for the Northern Nevada Native Plant
Society; it was published as *Impressions of Nevada,* by H. Dwight
Ripley, in 1978. It was only through reading these accounts, wrote
Williams for Rupert's *Brittonia* festschrift, that she had become
aware of her own state's native plants. "Dwight Ripley described
these plants so vividly and Rupert Barneby photographed them
with such clarity," she recalled, "that I felt I had to see them for
myself and attempt to establish them in my garden." Dwight's
reports are spirited and convincing. Some of his descriptions are
cited even today by alpine plant growers. (Look under *Lepidium
nanum* in the Arrowhead Alpines catalog or under *Arctomecon
humilis* in Jim & Jenny Archibald's 'Bryn Collen' seed list.) Dwight's
reports demonstrate, too, how keenly he and Rupert understood
their project. "It was the tireless Marcus Jones who found and
named so many of the rare species of the district," he wrote of
Nevada. "His only means of travel was his bicycle, on which one
may imagine him swooping and skimming like some exotic bird
over the valleys scorched by summer sun, or toiling up dusty roads
that led, tedious, yet arrow-straight, into the flaming mountains."
The two men dubbed their predecessor the Knight of the Burning
Bicycle. Despite the Knight's prior labors, Ripley & Barneby (as
they would be known from their collection labels) located in just
one month eleven previously unidentified species. Six were in the
genus *Astragalus.* In Connor's Pass they discovered a new *Castilleja,*
a three-inch Indian paintbrush that "burns in all the rock fissures,"

Dwight on Frenchman Flat

wrote Dwight, "with wads of pure vermilion." At Frenchman Flat
they encountered an unidentified *Cymopterus,* a parsley-like plant
noticed first by parsley aficionado Dwight for its unusually dark
flower heads, reminders, he thought, "of chocolate truffles from
some pre-war *confiserie.*" At Yucca Flat the two men found the same
Cymopterus, but this time the flower heads were apple green. Rupert,
even through his camera lens, suspected this must be the species
type and the truffle-flowered one a variety. "The *Cymopterus* photo
was the most perfect you've yet managed," wrote Sandwith from
Kew that August, referring to the type photograph that would hang

at the New York Botanical Garden, a half century later, on Rupert's office wall behind his desk. Rupert also photographed Dwight crouched next to a *Phacelia* on Frenchman Flat. Nevada was austere, but Dwight, in his report to the *Quarterly Bulletin,* made clear the reason for its appeal: "one might well be in south-eastern Spain."

Perhaps the most surprising feature of the trip to Nevada that halcyon spring is that Rupert and Dwight did not intend to make it. They intended to go to Mexico. Neither was a United States citizen, and because of the war in Europe it was difficult to cross the border and return. Dwight had been born with dual citizenship but at twenty-one was required to choose, and he had chosen Britain. Now they were given to understand that it would be easier to negotiate the border if one of the pair was American. Dwight went to New York to enlist the aid of his lawyer and his influential American family (a cousin was S. Dillon Ripley, ornithologist and later longtime secretary of the Smithsonian Institution; Dwight called him "Bird-Boy"). It was an unusual naturalization—a measure made its way through Congress to restore Dwight Ripley's citizenship—but it was not good enough to get Rupert into Mexico. "We should never have mentioned the camera," wrote Dwight the previous year. "They're spy-mad just now, and if we'd claimed to be plain tourists it might have been O.K." Meanwhile a bomb meant for London had fallen short in Sussex and damaged the greenhouses at the Spinney; there would be no safe destination for the seeds they hoped to collect. "We keep them from now on for that nook in Napa," wrote Dwight, "or if you will, that moon-drenched rose-garden in Culver City." The prospect of a lengthier stay in America meant that Rupert, thirty years old with no profession and no projected employment, had to become a legal resident too. The *Cymopterus* in the Nevada desert would prove, in this regard, his unexpected ally. The two men, thrilled with their "haul" of new species, arranged to deposit specimens at the California Academy of Sciences. Eastwood and Howell, who understandably might have been taken aback, recognized instead what was being offered, encouraged Rupert to publish as a taxonomist himself, and made room for his first paper to appear that November in their privately published *Leaflets of Western Botany*. In this, his taxonomic debut, Rupert described the discovery from Yucca Flat and named it *Cymopterus ripleyi*. The truffle-flowered version from Frenchman Flat he described as a variety, *Cymopterus ripleyi* var. *saniculoides*. Here was the first species (the uncooperative *Gilia* was not yet described) to be named for his friend. A vernacular name I have seen for the *Cymopterus* today is Ripley's spring-parsley, an unknowing tribute to the nine-year-old parsley gardener of long ago. To Eastwood and Howell, Rupert wrote: "As you

Cymopterus ripleyi, *Yucca Flat, 1941*

know, this is my first taxonomic paper, so you can imagine how excited I was to receive it." He must have been likewise excited to see that Eastwood, in the same issue, had described the new paintbrush from Connor's Pass as *Castilleja barnebyana*, the first species to be named for *him*. Dwight was excited and relieved; the November *Leaflets* could not have come at a better time. That same month he and Rupert moved from a hotel in Santa Monica to a more satisfactorily residential address, 9921 Robbins Drive in Beverly Hills, and invited to dinner Miss Dicky Bonaparte, an immigration counselor who was skilled at getting alien actors and actresses into the country, and who had arranged earlier a legal arrival for Isherwood. As publishing author for *Cymopterus ripleyi*, Rupert had a claim to useful employment in the United States. Miss Bonaparte came to dinner on December 6, the night before Pearl Harbor. Two weeks later she drove Rupert across the Mexican border to Ensenada, and on December 23, 1941, Rupert C. Barneby, of 9921 Robbins Drive, Beverly Hills, arrived in the United States of America—"on foot," according to the immigration inspector's report—at San Ysidro, California, a legal alien.

Rupert once told an interviewer from the *New York Times* that he was an autodidact, self-taught, and added "that doesn't mean I don't know." But those who admire and seek to emulate him should not believe, as I'm afraid I once did, that his career materialized as a natural reward. James Grimes, in a tribute to Rupert in the journal *Systematic Botany*, suggested the sterner truth: "In an age where the Ph.D. is the ticket to the profession, it is incredible, literally, that Rupert has succeeded as he has." In fact, the pattern that emerges from the early history traced by Rupert and Dwight in the United

States is a pattern of determination, which, if not deeply planned, was skillfully managed. Dwight, at least, was crafty on his friend's behalf. From New York, where he was pressing his case for citizenship, he reported early in 1941 his discovery of a botanical supply store on West Fourth Street; he is sending Rupert a new vasculum. "Angel mine:" he writes, "if Munz is as good as he sounds, a few more visits to Pomona won't be amiss, & I shall come along too next time." Munz was indeed as good as he sounds, but in due course. He did not open the Marcus Jones collections to the self-taught taxonomist on his doorstep quite so spontaneously as the later accounts would suggest. "The photo of the Maurandya might do things to Munz's pulse, who knows?" writes Dwight a few days later, and, fearing perhaps that Rupert's approach is too diffident, adds: "Bitch him for all you're worth, anyway." After their halcyon spring in Nevada, it was Dwight who corresponded with Howell at the California Academy of Sciences on behalf of Rupert's first publication. What they had proposed to Howell was not the *Cymopterus*, but a longer paper based on their *Astragalus* finds. "I shall love to see your drawings one day," wrote Sandwith to Rupert that June, "& hope you will make your début as an author with the *Astragalus*." But Howell did not have room in his upcoming issue for a paper of that length, and he had suggested the shorter *Cymopterus* piece instead. He and Eastwood paid the publishing costs for *Leaflets of Western Botany* themselves. In England, Dwight subsidized—to what extent we haven't ascertained—the publishing costs of the *New Flora and Silva*. That journal had ceased to publish due to the war; perhaps he now sponsored the *Leaflets* in its place. Years later, Howell would thank Rupert in print for the favors he and Dwight "showered" on the academy's herbarium and on the *Leaflets*. In any event, Rupert's paper on *Astragalus* duly appeared in the January issue of *Leaflets of Western Botany*, 1942. It included the descriptions of five new species and three new subspecies, was illustrated by Rupert himself, and was titled "Pugillus Astragalorum Nevadensium," a handful of Nevadan astragali. Only Rupert could have known what was to come. In the introduction to his paper he wrote: "The author wishes to put on record his appreciation of facilities most courteously extended by Dr. Philip Munz of Pomona College."

At the memorial tribute held at the Botanical Garden in 2001, I heard Stanley Welsh, himself a student of *Astragalus*, explain that Rupert was so astonished by the diversity of the astragali he first collected in Spain that he went immediately, on his return to England, to research them at Kew. There he was even more startled by the North American members of the genus: *A. asclepiadoides* was one, but could there really be an *Astragalus* that resembled *Asclepias*, i.e., a milkweed? It was also at the memorial that I heard Noel Holmgren, an expert on *Penstemon*, describe a similar burst of enthusiasm that he and his wife, the botanist Patricia Kern Holmgren, witnessed on a trip taken with Rupert when he was already sixty-seven years of age. The three plant hunters were setting up camp in a desert north of the Grand Canyon, when Holmgren, busy reparking the truck, looked in his rearview mirror to see Rupert jumping up and down so furiously he thought he had run over Rupert's foot. No, the excitement was that they had parked on a new *Astragalus*. Can you imagine, then, the jumping up and down that must have occurred on the San Rafael Swell, Utah, on June 1, 1942, the day Rupert and Dwight first encountered *A. asclepiadoides*,

looking indeed like a milkweed? Or the excitement four years later
at the mouth of the Green River Gorge, where they found a new
Astragalus that looked just like a grass? Rupert named it *A. chloödes*
(as in the shepherdess Chloë, from the Greek, meaning young
grass). "You really are a wizard at thinking up names," wrote Peter
Davis. "I lay awake at night puzzling & puzzling—& then decide
to name it after a place!" For the benefit of nonbotanists, I should
hazard my own nonbotanist's explanation that the astragali are
legumes, that is, they have pods like a bean, but they have evolved
into so many species, so diversely structured, that they may look as
dissimilar as a milkweed and a grass. At present, there are 2,500
separate species attributed to *Astragalus*, which makes it the largest
genus of flowering plants in the world. But only a few of those
species are widespread. The majority, like the *Maurandya* in Titus
Canyon, are narrow endemics; they are confined to marginal habitats where other flowering plants refuse to grow. They also tend to
be xerophytes, drought-lovers, yet even in hostile soils they still fix
nitrogen, true to their heritage as legumes. The astragali have cen-
ters of diversity in Himalayan Asia, on the Iranian highlands, and in
the North American West—where there are more than 550 species
and subspecies, as if every flat and elevation had evolved its local
Astragalus brand. A common name in North America is milkvetch;
nearly half the American species are poisonous to livestock and are
known also as locoweed. "These loco-weeds," explained Dwight
to his alpine garden readers, "have the reputation of driving cattle
crazy, so that the poor creatures are occasionally seen staggering
about their pastures or lying in the most uncomfortable positions,
their motor nerves at sixes and sevens. Astragali have much the

same effect on the botanist." The botanist Arthur Cronquist recalled *Astragalus* as a "bewildering" genus that was made no easier to understand by the "equally bewildering monograph" of Marcus Jones. Rupert himself noted dryly that "In his day Jones knew more about *Astragalus* than anyone alive, but a volatile impatience with details of presentation tends to obscure that fact." He found the disorder irresistible, perhaps because the task of correcting it would demand Proustian stamina.

Rupert the taxonomist was a creative inventor of Latin names. His object, however, required a further eloquence: a system of classification to express fluently the arrangements already made in nature by his cherished plants. "The imagination is staggered," he wrote, comparing the pod of *Astragalus feensis* to that of *A. tephrodes*, "by the number of coincidences in the course of convergent evolution required to create two organisms so similar in fine structural detail except for the fruit." In an ideal taxonomy, the evolution might be inferred by comparing the evidence in a herbarium: the root and crown; stem, leaf, and flower; and, in the case of *Astragalus*, especially the pod. But if two Englishmen in a Dodge could find six new astragali in just one month, then the evidence in the herbaria of North America was bound to be incomplete. Marcus Jones did bring a rich harvest of specimens out of the desert on his bicycle, but he had shown scant patience for scholarship in the museums, which is probably why his taxonomy proved bewildering. Competing with Jones had been the taxonomist Per Axel Rydberg, whose scholarship in the *North American Flora* was prodigious if not obsessive, but who made only a half-dozen forays into the field at a time of the year, summer, when *Astragalus* was not in bloom, and at altitudes, high and cool, where it seldom grows. The new student of the astragali would have to be scholar and explorer both. "I imagine from Dwight's letter that you went back to get the *Astragalus* fruits," wrote Sandwith, hardly concealing his advice. "The second visit is frightfully important: you can study the size of a population, & varieties within it, and this prevents herbarium 'splitting' on the evidence of secondary characteristics chosen from a single gathering or even a single plant." Taxonomists, according to their own professional lore, could be classed as two kinds. There were "lumpers," who emphasized similarities, and "splitters," who fixed on differences. Rydberg was a splitter. By the time he finished classifying *Astragalus* he had separated its species into twenty-eight distinct genera; he didn't split the genus, complained Rupert, he dismembered it. Sandwith's point was that the gradations in stem, leaf, and pod should not be considered in the abstract, but as part of a plant's natural response to pressures over its geographic range. To the boy who had grown up exploring the hills at Trewyn, this must have seemed the advice he would get from the plants themselves. In that same insight, perhaps, the idea for an *atlas* was born. "So much for the true alpines," concluded Dwight. "Now for the xerophytic species of the plains and plateaus, which is where our heart really lies." In just three years their efforts culminated in a paper that seems to me Rupert's most significant early publication, one that makes clear his intention to take the field from Rydberg and Jones, and revise the genus himself. The two men were in San Francisco together when it was published in June 1944 as "Pugillus Astragalorum Alter," another handful of astragali, in volume twenty-five of the *Proceedings of the California Academy of Sciences*. The ambitions implied in this paper were expressed more emphatically in a letter to Peter Davis. "The exciting point," wrote Rupert to Davis, "is that we have the morphologically primitive forms in greatest abundance, and it may be possible to show that the genus had its origins hereabouts, and NOT, like *Crepis,* and *Homo,* and so many other burdens to the human spirit, on the roof of the world."

Rupert would publish thirty-six taxonomic papers and notes in *Leaflets of Western Botany* (twenty dealt with *Astragalus*), and Tom Howell was justified to insist, as he did in 1974, that "Rupert's relation to the Calif. Acad. of Sciences was the important one that has led to the merited recognition he has today." A nook in Napa, however, was not to be. From Kew, Sandwith had already questioned whether the collections at California were sufficient for the *Astragalus* task, and had suggested, none too subtly, a trip to New York. The citizens of New York, who were accustomed then as now to think of their city as a cultural, financial, and media capital, might have been surprised to learn that they lived in a botanical capital as well. Today there are seven million plant specimens preserved in the William and Lynda Steere Herbarium of the New York Botanical Garden, which makes it equivalent in size to the Royal Herbarium at Kew, and ranks it—after the Muséum National d'Histoire Naturelle in Paris, which holds eight million specimens, and before the Komarov Botanical Institute in St. Petersburg, which holds six million—as the second or third largest herbarium in the world. For Dwight, meanwhile, the prospect of the metropolis was attractive for another reason. Beverly Hills had made him restless. Early in 1942, before the collecting season in the West, the two men headed for New York, the Botanical Garden, and their friend Jean Connolly, who had moved east and could introduce them immediately to the art world that Rupert liked to call "Upper Bohemia." Jean's current lover, only somewhat to the chagrin of her likewise active husband back in England, was Clement Greenberg, the critic who would help make Jackson Pollock famous. Greenberg, writing to his friend Harold Lazarus to describe the new arrivals ("Dwight Ripley, a millionaire and rather masculine . . . and his pal, Rupert Barnaby"), joined a long line of Americans who never could spell Rupert's last name. "They are both botanists and English," reported Greenberg, "and Dwight is in addition a philologist, expert in the Latin languages and Russian. Something new." Together the four toured the art galleries, where Dwight discovered a world as irresistible to him as was *Astragalus* to his pal. Greenberg, however, was drafted, and the two botanists soon were collecting again in the field. That May they embarked on a six-week expedition to retrace the trail of Marcus Jones through the Green River Basin in eastern Utah. Farther south, near Kanab at the Arizona border, they came upon *Astragalus ampullarius,* a species that grew in the hoofprints left by passing cattle, and occurred in but two other locations— a species so narrowly endemic, wrote Rupert, "that each population becomes, in effect, an insular endemic as securely quarantined against its nearest neighbor as if separated by leagues of sea." In August the two men took a one-year lease at 147 South Spalding Drive in Beverly Hills. By the time the lease was ready to expire, they had bought an old farmhouse and its surrounding hundred acres on Noxon Road in the town of LaGrange, Dutchess County, New York. This was twenty miles from Jean Connolly's house in neighboring Connecticut. Dwight arrived first, July 24, 1943. On a shale outcrop behind the farmhouse they started a rock garden. The train to New York, and the postal address they always used, was at nearby Wappingers Falls. Dwight, with a long-distance bow to the Spinney, called their new home the Falls.

Jean Connolly by this time had dropped Greenberg and was involved with Laurence Vail, the Surrealist artist and former husband of Peggy Guggenheim—heiress, angel of expatriate European artists, and owner of Art of This Century Gallery. With bohemian aplomb, however, it was the two women who began living together in Guggenheim's duplex at 155 East Sixty-first Street. Thanks to this arrangement, Rupert and Dwight found themselves frequently in New York at the center of Upper Bohemia. "Jean Connolly, Dwight Ripley, Matta, Duchamp were around a great deal," recalled Lee Krasner, the painter who was Jackson Pollock's

Farmhouse at the Falls

wife. "They were at all the parties." Rupert and Dwight were at the now famous party during which Pollock's *Mural* was first shown and Pollock relieved himself in the fireplace. Rupert did not witness the act of relief itself, but he had other stories to tell. He remembered Marcel Duchamp, the avatar of cool in the art world today, as a "pompous pundit." He recalled Guggenheim herself as "mean"; she "dressed like a hag," her stagy conversational asides were "like a dagger in the heart." He also remembered, in her defense perhaps, "She did preside over the French." This was a heady world, in which Rupert himself was an object of attention. Once, when he came years later to our apartment for dinner, he brought Frank and me a poetry anthology, *The War Poets*, which had been published in 1945 and which I predictably regarded as quaint. Only long afterward did I discover in it the love sonnet "Letter to R," written by an army private at Camp Crowder, Missouri, and intended for Rupert Barneby. The soldier poet, Willard Maas, was to become an influential avant-garde filmmaker after the war, and Dwight would help finance his projects. For his part, Dwight soon was having an affair with Guggenheim, who admired his English accent, his youth (he was ten years younger), and his indifference to her wealth. She liked to introduce him as her fiancé. "She fell abruptly out of love with Dwight," said Rupert. "He was staying at her house at East Sixty-first and she'd gone out to some party, and Dwight came back in a cab with a very handsome driver, and Peggy found them in bed together."

Rupert loathed publicity. Both he and Dwight were educated by class and era to a kind of privileged obscurity that can seem, to an American, downright foreign. Publicity, he observed in a letter to Frank, is for "the sort of people who would sell their grandmother's

dentures to buy a new shade of lipstick." And yet it was Rupert himself who volunteered to a biographer the story, published in *Peggy:
The Wayward Guggenheim,* of Dwight and the cabdriver. Rupert
almost never saved personal letters (while his own seem composed
to be quoted), nearly tossed out his field notebooks (they were rescued at the Botanical Garden by Thomas Zanoni), claimed to side
with Auden against biographies (though he admired Painter's biography of Proust), and despised what he called the "dismal cult of
personality"—a memorable opinion that I have since found quoted
on the Web. I had to think twice, then, before risking his privacy in
a book like this. I wish I might ask his approval. By implication,
however, he previously gave it; he gave it without regard to himself
but for the sake of Dwight. At Harrow, Dwight already liked to
draw (there are two pencil drawings of the young Rupert Barneby),
and in the United States he began to draw with the same kind of
attention he gave to languages and botany. His work was done
almost entirely in colored pencil on paper—at a time that made him
a pioneer in this medium—and his first showing was arranged by
Peggy Guggenheim (the year *after* the cabdriver) at Art of This
Century. Rupert had three of Dwight's early drawings displayed in
his loft, but for years I ignored them. Eventually, when I had seen
Dwight's later drawings, too, I discovered that I wanted to write
about them and the artist who could create them. Of course it
proved no more possible to remove Rupert from Dwight's story
than to separate Dwight from his, and Frank decided we had better
give him my exploratory—and revealing—first outline to read. It
came back in short order (Rupert always was prompt), it was amply
corrected, and it was accompanied by the observation that he had

not thought their story of much interest, and by the instruction that "work should continue." I was glad for his benediction, while at the same time I remembered the recoil in his other expressions of approval. When he read an introduction I had prepared for Emerson's *Essays,* Rupert wrote, "The immortal should not, by definition, require new clothing, but it seems that you contrived just that."

The year before Frank and I met Rupert, he himself had ensured that his collecting life with Dwight would be made public when he arranged, with editor and art dealer John Bernard Myers, to publish his "Botanical Journal" in Myers's obscure but prestigious literary magazine, *Parenthèse.* This, the only example of Rupert's journal that we know to exist, describes the Ripley & Barneby expedition of 1944. (It was misdated in print, though one entry clearly refers to D-Day, as 1942.) As soon as it was published, Rupert brought a copy to our apartment; here was our first intimate look into his past. On the night before D-Day the two men were in Burns, Oregon. "Tonight," records Rupert, "after giving my grandmother's maiden name, a photograph of my teeth and an assurance that I have never slept with Earl Browder, I am allowed to purchase, at an outrageous price, a bottle of poisonous hooch." In the days ahead, he and Dwight would locate three new species. But a species did not have to be new to be memorable, as revealed in his account of an *Astragalus* (he calls it the Loco, for locoweed) that was discovered by Sereno Watson, observed next by Jones, and rediscovered by Rupert and Dwight on June 10, 1944, near Battle Mountain, Nevada.

The great objective in these parts is Astragalus pterocarpus along the Humboldt, and about 10 miles west of Battle I start off across

the alkaline flats. Nothing could be more sterile than this association of Atriplex, Picrothamnus and Salicornia which covers the
valley, but as one approaches the river itself the soil changes,
becoming more sandy and alluvial, and the low shrubs give
way to a thin cover of Iva and Sporobolus mixed with a taller
Spartina-like grass. And here at last, at the third attempt, we
come across the Loco, forming rounded domes of interlacing
stems and spiky glaucescent foliage, the racemes so laden with
translucent fleshy pods that the peduncles are bent to the ground,
breaking at a touch. It is a supreme moment, for only Jones and
Watson have ever beheld the living plant. In the afternoon (while
Dwight trucks) I walk out of Battle for a few hundred yards
along the miserable ditch which is all that is left of the Reese
River at its confluence with the Humboldt, and find a few more
plants of the Loco, perhaps at the very spot where it was first discovered 70 years ago. The evening is clear and still, the mountains north and east, snow-capped and bathed in the oblique rays
of the setting sun, have the true Nevada atmosphere of space and
purity.

Rupert's devotion, so evident in his journal, seemed never to
flag, and the explanation once offered by botanist Melissa Luckow
was surely right: "Rupert loves plants and his enthusiasm is conta-
gious." Dwight, in his letters and articles, left firsthand evidence of
the happy contagion. *From Idaho:* "Leaving the car with strangled
cries of anticipation and with much flapping of paper, we scrambled
down the cobblestone bluff, Rupert on one side of the road, I on the
other." *Oregon:* "Below us a rivulet flashed between moss-grown

Rupert Barneby, Astragalus pterocarpus

boulders, and before I knew it Rupert had performed a sort of swallow-dive into the tangled greenery and was down at the bottom of the ravine, exclaiming in wonder at what he saw." *Nevada:* "As we turned on to the main Las Vegas–Salt Lake highway, my companion let out a yell which would, had we been in overpopulated Europe, have brought every peasant running from miles around. As it was, I merely stepped on the brake and enquired the reason for this sudden display of emotion. He replied tersely, 'The Boerhaavia.' "

The whole West fascinated Rupert, and it refreshed him, but together he and Dwight accorded a special status to Nevada, in particular to Nye County—for there grew the *Cymopterus,* namesake and ally, that had served them in their new country as a kind of protecting spirit. Mars, however, was once more making plans. The war in Korea began at the end of June 1950, and in response to military requests President Truman that December designated a huge area of Nye County, including Yucca and Frenchman flats, as a site for the atmospheric testing of atomic bombs. One month later, on January 27, 1951, the Nevada Test Site was inaugurated by a one-kiloton bomb, Ranger Able, dropped from a plane over Frenchman Flat. Somewhere directly below was the chocolate-flowered *Cymopterus ripleyi.* "Ta-ta, Dwighteen!" wrote Dwight in a long poem, *Spring Catalogue,* which was published the following year as a chapbook, and which commemorates the Ripley & Barneby collecting trips, the plants in their garden, and his ill-fated namesake (together with its associate species *Phacelia parishii*) on Frenchman Flat.

> Ta-ta, Dwighteen! And you, Miss Parish,
> May radioactive daydreams nourish!

Dwight refused ever to go to Nevada again. Rupert tried later to determine if the plants at their collecting station had survived, but he, a resident alien, was denied entry to the site. From 1951 until atmospheric testing was halted in 1962, there were 126 nuclear devices detonated over the Nevada Test Site, a region that Dwight once described for the *Quarterly Bulletin* as "an ecologist's dream." In the halcyon spring of their collecting he had begun a meticulous, handwritten *Record* (225 folio-sized pages) of the species he and Rupert located and identified. According to this *Record,* the two men collected in the western United States the defining specimens, or holotypes, for fifty-three species that had never been named. The fifty-three species were *Aquilegia barnebyi, Asclepias eastwoodiana, Astragalus amblytropis, A. callithrix, A. camptotus, A. chamaemeniscus, A. chloödes, A. consobrinus, A. cremnophylax, A. deterior, A. endopterus, A. eurylobus, A. gypsodes, A. microcymbus, A. micromerius, A. molybdenus, A. musimonum, A. nyensis, A. onciformis, A. ophiogenes, A. proimanthus, A. pseudiodanthus, A. ripleyi, A. sterilis, A. titanophilus, A. toquimanus, A. uncialis, A. xiphoides, Castilleja barnebyana, Cordylanthus uintahensis, Cryptantha semiglabra, Cymopterus ripleyi, Dodecatheon spilantherum, Eriogonum aretioides, E. ripleyi, Gilia ripleyi, Haplopappus microcephalus, Lepidium davisii, L. demissum, Lesquerella barnebyi, L. paysonii, Mimulus brachiatus, Oxytropis jonesii, Parthenium tetraneuris, Penstemon barnebyi, P. clausus, P. meistanthus, P. paysoniorum, P. porphyranthus, Phacelia piersoniana, Psoralea epipsela, Physaria cordiformis,* and *Swertia gypsicola.*

These discoveries, the patience and exaltation—the dust!—they must have entailed, come to mind whenever I see Rupert's photograph of that first innocent *Cymopterus.* Amazed at the botanical wealth just of Nevada, Noel Sandwith wrote: "I *can't* understand how you reached a pocket of such wonderful new plants so easily. I know the size of these states is huge, but even so, Americans in their own country . . . !"

THE YEAR THE BOMBS began to explode over Nevada was also, by a twist of fate, the year Rupert and Dwight had arranged to burn the last bridge back to the world of their youth. It was more than a decade now since Peter Davis had written from Athens, marooned there by the outbreak of the war, to express his anxiety about their separation. "I hope you won't desert the Mediterranean," he all but complained. "I can't bear the thought of you grubbing up all those horrid Yankee pentstemons." Of course it was not *Penstemon* (they spelled it then with an extra *t*) but *Astragalus* that had become the main object of Rupert's attention. Standing in his way, however, was *Oxytropis*, a much smaller genus that includes species in some cases so similar to the astragali that they, too, are commonly known as locoweeds. To a nonbotanist, these two sets of locoweed will look much alike. They must look alike to botanists, as well, for a longstanding disagreement was whether *Oxytropis* was truly a separate genus or just a sub-*Astragalus*. Rupert determined the separation to be valid, but that was not enough. The lookalike species that threatened to overlap the two genera had to be carefully sorted out, a task complicated by the uncertain and, as Rupert thought, reckless number of species attributed over the years to *Oxytropis*. Rydberg had suggested as many as seventy. Rupert, ready to publish his first taxonomic monograph, would allow but twenty-two. Certainly this was an assertive performance for a first monograph. When it appeared in 1952, published in *Proceedings of the California Academy of Sciences* as "A Revision of the North American Species of *Oxytropis*," it suggested both in style and in systematic resolve what lay ahead. Its single new species, discovered by Rupert and Dwight in Utah in 1947, had been named *Oxytropis jonesii*, in honor—but clearly in pursuit—of Marcus Jones, their predecessor among the astragali. "I am burrowing gradually through the New World Astragali," wrote Rupert to Davis, "hoping to live long enough to present a coordinated view of them." Was this no plan? Already Rupert knew it would entail additional collecting in the field, and require the study of specimens beyond the resources of his own herbarium, Pomona College, the California Academy of Sciences, and even the New York Botanical Garden, the collections on which he primarily had relied so far. Eventually he would review *Astragalus* specimens from forty-nine separate institutions, the majority of which, along with all the field collecting, of course, were to be found in North America. The decision to remain had become inevitable, and by November 1951, when Auden and Isherwood arrived to spend a nostalgic weekend with Rupert and Dwight at Wappingers Falls, it was irrevocable too. England, for all four, was the place they had left behind. The rare species cultivated at the Spinney, Waldron, Sussex, were auctioned earlier that spring. The Spinney itself passed to a new owner, the solicitor who all these years had managed Dwight's interests under the terms of his father's will.

Dwight missed the excitement generated by Peggy Guggenheim's art gallery, closed in 1947 when she followed the last of the exiled Surrealists back to Europe. In London, his Oxford contem-

porary Peter Watson had helped found the Institute of Contemporary Arts and was planning shows to feature the painters Francis
Bacon and Lucian Freud. Encouraged, probably goaded by this
example, Dwight turned to his art-critic friend Clement Greenberg for help. On the Monday evening of January 23, 1950—it is
recorded in his pocket diary—he took aspiring art dealer John
Bernard Myers to Greenberg's apartment in Greenwich Village.
"Ripley and John Myers," confirmed Greenberg's biographer forty-
seven years later, "came to Clem's apartment to consult with him
about a noncommercial gallery that Ripley would finance as silent
backer and Myers would run." Greenberg suggested the initial
artists, Dwight wrote the first check, and the result was Tibor de
Nagy Gallery, which opened its doors that December and rapidly
became one of the influential art galleries in New York. In its first
full year Dwight provided the gallery with more than five thousand
dollars, or five times its annual rent. This was a historic contribution. Tibor de Nagy (teebore de NAHZH) sponsored the first solo
shows of Larry Rivers, Grace Hartigan, Helen Frankenthaler, Kenneth Noland, Fairfield Porter—artists whose works would alter
the conventions, then supreme, of Abstract Expressionism. When
the gallery's director John Myers published the first chapbooks of
poets John Ashbery, Frank O'Hara, and Kenneth Koch, Dwight's
support altered the conventions of poetry as well. Rupert, several
years after Frank and I met him, took us to meet Myers at his house
(believe me, *I* drove) in Brewster, New York. Myers was retired
from the gallery then for many years, had published Rupert's
"Botanical Journal" in *Parenthèse,* and was writing his own memoir,
in which he describes visits in the 1950s to the farmhouse at the

Falls. "Rupert," he reveals, "spent most of his day peering through his microscope." During one visit Rupert emerged long enough to take a snapshot he had kept through all the intervening years: Dwight outdoors was seated on a rock—he was holding his drink—while next to him sat Myers and his business partner, Tibor de Nagy (who lent the gallery its name). Flanking them on the lawn and rock were the young painters Hartigan and Frankenthaler. Between de Nagy and Frankenthaler sat a friend of de Nagy's whose name Rupert no longer remembered, while unseen outside the picture stood Alfred Leslie, who was preparing a model airplane for its maiden flight. It amused Rupert that the literary and artistic figures Frank and I knew as unassailable reputations, he knew when they

Grace Hartigan, Dwight, John Bernard Myers, Tibor de Nagy, unidentified friend of de Nagy, and Helen Frankenthaler at the Falls

were youthful aspirants. In his loft he once showed us a copy of O'Hara's *Oranges*, its cover individually painted by Hartigan, who in those days signed herself George. It was inscribed "to darling Dwight and Rupert, oranges and kisses, George."

Rupert, in order to complete his monograph on *Oxytropis*, skipped his annual collecting trip in 1952. When he went west the following year (and discovered *Astragalus gypsodes* at White's Eddy, New Mexico), Dwight for the first time was not along. When in 1954 he visited the Henry Tosten ranch in California to inspect a weed suspected of killing the sheep (it was also a new species and he named it *Astragalus agnicidus*), Dwight again was not along. Dwight had begun more seriously to draw. In the twelve years from 1951 through 1962 he had five solo shows at Tibor de Nagy. Rupert recalled these events as "disagreeable" because he, Rupert, ended up doing the footwork. Dwight would not select the art, frame it, or hang it at the gallery; frequently he contrived not to sign it, and he did not attend his openings. Considering the ebullience of his writing, and the anecdotes that are told about him, it was a surprise to learn from Rupert that Dwight was acutely shy. As a young man he was subject to unexpected, uncontrollable blushing, and he was miserable in gatherings of more than four. Yet his drawings were joyous, uniquely conceived, and even prescient. A reviewer in *Arts* magazine described them as "witty and erudite punning on a facet of art which at bottom the artist must take quite seriously" (a definition ahead of its time, it would seem, for what later was called Postmodernism). The critic at the *New York Times* described them as "essentially indescribable." Neither critic was prepared, perhaps, for the artist's adjunct passion: botany. Rupert's friend and fellow botanist Jacquelyn Kallunki showed one of Dwight's drawings in a slide biography that she presented at the garden's memorial tribute in 2001. Titled *Portrait of Rupert Barneby, Esq. (botanist)*, it featured Rupert in profile, wearing, in place of a hat, a flowerpot. This same drawing caught the attention years earlier of Judith Malina, who, having the usual trouble with Rupert's last name, described it on March 1, 1956, to her diary: "Rupert Barnaby, at Dwight's exhibit, stands in front of a portrait of himself. In the picture an exotic Himalayan plant blossoms from his headgear, accompanied by a botanical description of which every other line is written upside down."

Rupert's colleagues frequently portray him, more solemnly than did Dwight, as the Bentham of our time. By this, they mean not Jeremy Bentham the philosopher of utilitarianism but his nephew George, the nineteenth-century English taxonomist, or "systematic botanist," as they prefer to say. The comparison makes sense. Both Rupert and George Bentham brought systematic order to a broad company of the legumes, both were influential, and both were prolific. William Buck has determined, at last count, that Rupert published 7,676 pages of taxonomic text in 263 separate publications, was the publishing author of 2,562 taxa (a "taxon" is a named unit of any taxonomic category), and named in the process 621 new species, 16 new subspecies, 355 new varieties, and one new form, for a total of 993 taxa never before identified by science. Even so, it was not until I saw the comparison rephrased—Rupert was *our* Bentham, wrote Kancheepuram Gandhi from Harvard—that I understood fully the parallel being drawn. Bentham, like Rupert, was not academically trained to be a botanist. His education was in languages

and law, but when he was near thirty he began to assemble a private
herbarium and to write monographs, much as Rupert wrote *Oxytropis* using his own herbarium at the Falls. When Bentham was fifty-
four, the director of the Royal Botanic Gardens, Joseph Hooker,
had arranged a place for him as a nonsalaried associate at Kew. For
the next thirty years he worked there tirelessly, until he was as thoroughly identified with Kew as anyone before or since. Rupert—our
Bentham—was thirty years old when, in January 1942, he first
walked up the allée of tulip trees to the steps of the Museum Building at the New York Botanical Garden, there to study *Astragalus* as
Sandwith had advised. He was thirty-three when he was joined
there by Bassett Maguire, who was to play a critical role, just as
Hooker did for Bentham, in Rupert's career. Maguire had arrived at
the Botanical Garden to organize a flora of the intermountain West
(Utah and Nevada, with adjacent areas in California, Arizona,
southern Idaho, and southeast Oregon), an area, being the central
locus of *Astragalus*, that Rupert and Dwight knew from their own
expeditions, of course, and loved. Maguire "came up to Dutchess
county to stay over weekends," Rupert recalled to Frank. "That was
in the early fifties, and we had been friends ever since." It was
Maguire, soon named head curator at the garden, who ensured for
the nonsalaried Rupert the working conditions to complete *Oxytropis* and move on to *Astragalus*, and Maguire who in 1959 secured
Rupert's appointment as honorary curator, still nonsalaried, but
with the institutional imprimatur he would need to solicit materials
from other institutions worldwide. Rupert then was forty-eight
years old. By the time Frank and I knew him he seemed so much a
part of the Botanical Garden—he even lived in it—that I never

properly grasped how extraordinary it was for him to be present there at all. Sometimes, when I consider the uncertainties and the diversions that Rupert encountered in his life, I think *Astragalus* was the compass that guided him day to day, and the garden his refuge for observation and intellect—a kind of second Trewyn (where a similar allée, though not of tulip trees, extends from the massive steps on down the hill). Ted Barkley, who was a student at the garden in 1957, remembered Rupert from these *Astragalus* days, when he drove down to the Bronx from Wappingers Falls bringing his Sheltie, whose name was Possum. "Rupert had a little dog that was his close companion," recalled Barkley, "and after lunch he would go to his car and let out the dog, then for a quarter hour or so, the two would run together across the great open lawns in front of the Museum Building. It was interesting, to say the least, to see this very thin and politely reserved man running full tilt across the lawns, with a little dog."

In Rupert's loft there were many curious objects. One that holds my attention in retrospect consisted of a tablet-sized platform, as for a bonsai arrangement, on which sat a porous gray rock that might have been the scale model of a malevolent asteroid. It was a chunk of tufa, the calcareous (as in limestone) deposit from springs and streams which is favored in the rock garden or the alpine house by plants like *Lepidium nanum,* is coveted therefore by the rock gardener, and from which Rupert and Dwight constructed their rock-and-tufa cliff at the Spinney. Tufa was present, though in diminishing quantities (it is scarce and unaffordable), in the gardens the two men built in the United States, the first at Wappingers Falls, the second at their final home, in Greenport, Long Island.

Rupert thought the garden at the Falls had been their best. There, in addition to the outdoor rock garden, he and Dwight built a rock garden on a platform, complete with plumbing, pools, and water-falls, but entirely enclosed within a greenhouse. This was a more intricate version of the Spinney's glass-sheltered cliff. "The rock-ery and greenhouse," recalled John Myers, "contained copper-striped miniature tulips from behind the casino at Monte Carlo; a tiny lilac from Siberia sent by their fellow botanist Justice William O. Douglas; small, exquisite iris from Turkey." Myers, gaga for exotics, had missed what truly was impressive: the garden was com-posed primarily of species from the North American West. Dwight once prepared a list for Alice Eastwood, who, interested always in horticulture, was curious to know what he and Rupert could culti-vate in the Northeast. Growing in their garden were 181 western natives; of these, 36 were "horrid pentstemons." (We do not know if Peter Davis was informed.) Dwight was especially fond of *Pen-stemon desertipicti*, or at least its name; he applied it to the paintings of a friend. But it was Rupert who, as he himself later told us, "moved every rock" with his own hands. "The rockery was so fas-cinating one went back to it over and over again," observed Myers, "often discovering tiny specimens one had missed." Like-wise fascinated was the experimental filmmaker Marie Menken, whose five-minute, 16 mm film *Glimpse of the Garden*—described by Stan Brakhage as "one of the toughest" of her influential works— was shot in Rupert and Dwight's garden in 1957. Menken was the wife of Willard Maas, the soldier poet once enamored of Rupert. She was also a painter (hers were the *desertipicti*), and gradually, but not so satisfactorily, she was to assume a role like Jean Connolly's in the two men's lives. Menken's *Glimpse of the Garden* was screened during the film festival "The Color of Ritual, the Color of Thought: Women Avant-Garde Filmmakers in America 1930–2000" at the Whitney Museum of American Art in September 2000. Her camera was handheld (she would inspire Andy Warhol to reject this technique), and the effect in *Glimpse of the Garden* may be imagined, perhaps, from the homage of Stan Brakhage, who wrote, "Marie's film really works Dwight Ripley's garden of rare and unique flowers."

Rock garden at the Falls

Sixteen years had elapsed since Rupert and Dwight moved into the farmhouse at Wappingers Falls, but they never intended to make it a permanent home. It was meant as a waystation during the war, selected partly because it was near Jean Connolly. She, however, had moved with Laurence Vail to France and died there, aged only thirty-nine, in 1950. Rupert had a focus in the Botanical Garden, but Dwight, who felt isolated in the farmhouse, became increasingly restless as in Beverly Hills before. His unfortunate solution was to drink. The painter Elaine de Kooning remembered 1950 as "the year booze flooded the New York art scene," but in that case Dwight had a good head start. His reports to the *Quarterly Bulletin of the Alpine Garden Society* included lyric impressions not just of *Lepidium nanum* but of his hangovers. (They also suggest the lyric impression that our two botanizing sophisticates themselves may have left on the American West. Reporting his hangover in Mountain Home, Idaho, Dwight explained, "I had spent the previous evening pounding a piano in a bar for the amusement of the local cowboys, and these innocent souls, inflamed no doubt by the novelty of my urban tempo after a lifetime of 'Home on the Range' and similar forthright compositions, had kept me well supplied with refreshments.") For a few years beginning in 1957 the two men sought to remedy Dwight's isolation by renting an apartment at 416 East Fifty-eighth Street, near Sutton Place, in New York. The young Gore Vidal collected the rent. In the city, Dwight seemed only to drink more heavily. When he tried simply to stop, the effects of the withdrawal landed him in Vassar Hospital. Shaken, he resolved on sobriety, and together he and Rupert decided to move to a house they had found for sale in Greenport, Long Island, not far from their painter friends

Theodoros Stamos, Lee Krasner, and Alfonso Ossorio. They arrived in October 1959, eager to renovate the decaying Greek Revival mansion that stood at 3135 North Road on the east edge of town. To Tom Howell, Dwight wrote that he was "now happily ensconced in a divine house which, along with its new owner, has been saved in the nick of time from Crumbling into Ruins."

Rupert was optimistic about their move. He named the mansion after a nearby creek—he called it Stirling House—and went immediately to work with Dwight to build a garden that would rival, once again, the Spinney. This time, however, he needed a radical approach; for here on their Long Island terrain he faced the prob-

Stirling House

lem of how to build a rock garden without shelter or rocks. The
problem of shelter he solved with a wall of concrete blocks, constructed in the form of a box canyon, but laid up in a fantasy of
setbacks, cutouts, crenellations, and protrusions so that the whole
structure when painted white reflected the light in changing and
unexpected patterns. On the floor of the box canyon he laid a carpet
of fine sand. There, to make up for the absent rocks, he positioned
raised beds that he had devised from sewer conduits, septic tanks,
and chimney tiles, all cut to varied lengths, set on end, painted
white, and filled with the proper layering of gravel, sand, and soil to
accommodate the plants he and Dwight most admired. The result
was a garden—remarkable, given the climate—of Mediterranean
clarity. Lincoln Foster, a president of the American Rock Garden
Society, called it "a modern Alhambra." Rupert's own assessment
reflected that sense of comic necessity that we, in later years, came
to recognize and anticipate from him. The raised beds, he wrote
Peter Davis, were "not simply a convenience against the arthritic
years ahead, but more directly a defence against the almost Australian pullulation of coneys and a protection against the cruel
northwesterlies which sweep down from Poluninland in the winter." Dwight remembered the enclosure for its "extreme insola-
tion," so sun-beaten and dry they could not grow rock-garden
heaths, Ericaceae, but only xerophytes—this was, of course, the
intent—from Spain, Algeria, and the American West. The year
before Frank and I met Rupert, and the year after Dwight died, the
American Rock Garden Society awarded the two men, jointly, its
Marcel Le Piniec Award in recognition of the species they had
introduced into cultivation. One of these, cultivated in their own

gardens, was the *Cymopterus ripleyi* var. *saniculoides* that had outlived its unfortunate fellows on Frenchman Flat. Still others were aquilegias (not in the insolated Alhambra perhaps), of which Dwight wrote, "*Barnebyi* and *scopulorum* have done well, but *jonesii* cannot bear our company and always departs with a backward glance or two of loathing."

Dwight was not the only artist in the family and both men knew it. They knew it long before that night in the Death Valley motel when Rupert stayed awake to make his drawing of *Gilia ripleyi.* "I do hope you've shown your drawings to Munz (tho' I'm sure you haven't!)," wrote Dwight. "They'd melt an iceberg, je t'assure." Dwight may be called a colorist, but Rupert was more interested in draftsmanship, in line, than he was in the self-promotional brushstroke of the New York School painters who had become their friends. It was the line in Jackson Pollock, and especially in Miró, that attracted him to the paintings he and Dwight had collected themselves. Rupert and Dwight owned two of Miró's "Constellation" gouaches, numbers one and five, bought immediately when that series of paintings had safely reached New York in 1945. The Mirós were as "precise as Mozart," Rupert said. In art, as in literature, he expressed opinions that could be startling, while they revealed always how acutely his attention had been trained. Of Louis Agassiz Fuertes, whose watercolors of birds are widely celebrated, he observed: "I know he has a great reputation for anatomical accuracy, but I'm not sure he was the artist that he's sometimes proclaimed. Like Redouté in the world of Flora." Such opinions were not gratuitous; his own drawings, indeed, would melt an iceberg. How beautifully Rupert drew is proved by his frontispiece drawing in the "Atlas of North American *Astragalus*," volume one, of *A. asclepiadoides*—the *Astragalus* that looks like a milkweed. It was executed, as was his *Gilia ripleyi*, in a style that today we might call information-rich. Both drawings were densely shaded, intensely detailed, but so attentive to their subjects that the artist seems to have vanished into the evolutionary triumph of the plants themselves. Rupert's *Gilia* was not just correct but free; it is reaching already toward the light. In Greenport he began a set of such drawings to illustrate his atlas. He had completed a third of these by the end of May 1963, when, in the garden where he was moving rocks, he crushed his hand. Joseph Kirkbride, who as a graduate student shared an office with Rupert at the Botanical Garden ten years later, was told that the fateful rock had weighed two tons. The extent of the injury can be gauged by the awkward way that Rupert held, in later years, his pencil: scissor-clamped, straight up and down, between the index and the middle finger. He never told Frank or me about this accident; it was only after his death that we learned of it from Kirkbride and Noel Holmgren. I checked. Yes, Dwight has recorded in his diary, May 28, 1963, Rupert's "ordeal." What prompted Rupert to keep, ever after, that ominous souvenir rock he displayed in his loft? No one knows what he did with the drawings he had already completed, though grimly we can speculate. The "Atlas of North American *Astragalus*" is not, except for each frontispiece, illustrated. Bobbi Angell, the botanical illustrator who, beginning with the Cassiinae, drew the illustrations for Rupert's later works, was likewise never told about his hand. "Rupert said at the time that his hands shook too much to produce his own drawings, and that's all I ever knew as a reason for his hiring me." Rupert

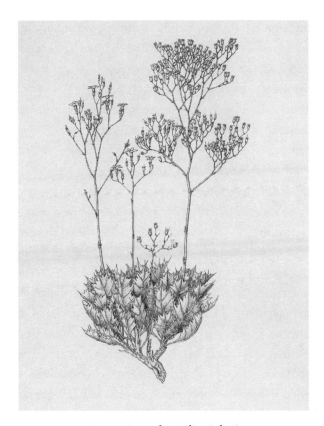

Rupert Barneby, Gilia ripleyi

was stoic, in nineteenth-century British fashion a Roman throw-back. He did not expect sympathy for what he might have done; he expected to perform with what he had available. Once, when I was moping yet again, he asked what was wrong, wasn't I writing? By way of reply I listed all the extenuating circumstances that afflicted me, before I concluded, No, and waited for the bath of sympathy.

"Well," he responded, "I suppose it's the one sin against the gods." In his final apartment, after age had forced him to abandon his loft, Rupert kept only a very few books. Next to the bed were his own publications, the illustrated *Legumes of Bahia* by Gwilym Lewis, a tattered guide to drawing that had been printed in London in 1860, the *Meditations* of Marcus Aurelius, and the essay *On Reading* by Marcel Proust.

Sometimes I think Rupert could have described no discovery more provocative than the combination he made in his own life of Marcus Aurelius and his beloved Proust. The poet Kenneth Rexroth once observed that Marcus Aurelius is Proust without the narrative. Proust, by reverse analogy, is Marcus with a sense of humor. Both are, in an exalted way, self-help, and a lesson the two together teach is the same distinction Rupert always taught, of character versus personality. One way to read Proust is as the triumph of artistic habit over personality, and one way to read Marcus Aurelius is as the triumph of duty over personality. "Remember that here in life every piece of duty is made up of separate items," Marcus writes to himself, "and so ensure the methodical completion of your appointed task." Rupert in his life had seen much spectacle and much personality. He knew the circle around the Connollys in England, around Huxley and Heard in California, around Peggy Guggenheim in New York. He witnessed the same dynamics being played out all over again in the circle around the Tibor de Nagy Gallery, and he had good reason to conclude that personality alone does not get you through. Personality has hopes, deep plans, and defeats. Character has habits. Here was the extended insight behind his now widely quoted comment on the Millennium Botany Award, which was to be presented to him at the International Botanical Congress in 1999. The ceremony was in St. Louis, and Frank and I had been scheming to get him there. But Rupert wouldn't go. "I'm conscious of the prestige of the medallion (gold)," he wrote to explain, "but hideously aware that it's an award for survival rather than merit. It's part of the dismal cult of personality that started in Hollywood and now has infected the entire planet." Certainly the "Atlas of North American *Astragalus,*" when it was published in 1964, represented a triumph of methodical habit over personal oblivion and chaos. The two volumes total 1,188 pages. Dwight called it Rupert's *Monographia monumentalis.* The New York Botanical Garden honored it by presenting Rupert with a Distinguished Service Award and the first of his two Henry Allan Gleason Awards. In his own copy of the "Atlas," Rupert kept one of the very few letters he ever saved, the congratulations that came from Sandwith at Kew. "The sheer labour & courage, confidence & conviction, which has gone into it all!" wrote Sandwith. "In the same way, in another medium, Proust struggled triumphantly in turning his Life into Art."

Then, as apparently Rupert never complained to Sandwith about his hand, no more than he had to Bobbi Angell or to us, the English botanist added, "I always imagined there was an original drawing for every species: it would be an enormous cost to reference them, I know, but could there be a companion volume?"

Although Rupert was unimpressed by empty display, he did not dismiss the professional honors that appeared in the form of plaques and medals late in his life. I know; he asked us to preserve them. He was especially pleased by the Asa Gray Award from the American Society of Plant Taxonomists, because it came from the community of his colleagues. "Pat Holmgren brought my Asa Gray plaque back from the triple A meeting in Canada," he wrote happily in the fall of 1989. "The supposed likeness of the medallion to Asa is not close—looks more like the head of St. John the Baptist on a dish." He made sure we knew of it when the Brazilian genus *Barnebya* was named in his honor. He must have been equally pleased by the three other genera, *Barnebyella, Barnebydendron, Rupertia,* and at least twenty-five species that, thanks to his colleagues, now bear his name. When he himself named plants (on his nightstand were papers in which he had bestowed the epithets *ackermanii, dalyi, ertterae, grimesii, holmgreniorum, isidori, johannis-howellii, kallunkii, marcano-bertii, moriorum, schultziorum, shevockii, sousae, souzana, tiehmii, turneri, yoder-williamsii,* and *zanonii*), the eponymous donors can be sure he meant to honor their earned accomplishments and not to flatter their personalities. At the same time, he privately honored his colleagues with opinions that Frank and I were frequently asked to share. He was saddened by the death in 1991 of Bassett Maguire ("the end of an era, and yes, it has been a big separation"), was perplexed by the earlier death in 1988 of Julian Steyermark ("snapped another link, almost my last, with my early times in the States"), was distressed by the retirement in 1998 of Bill Weber ("the absolute premier student of the Rocky Mt. flora"), and was moved, long before we could have heard him say so, by the death in 1953 of the ninety-four-year-old Alice Eastwood ("clay feet and all she towered over most of us through the dynamism and simplicity and good will of her character"). Rupert also asked us to preserve his honorary doctorate, awarded in 1978 from the City University of New York, that degree he did not have when his career began.

The award I most vividly remember was the Engler Medal, presented by the International Association for Plant Taxonomy in recognition of his "Sensitivae censitae: *Mimosa*" in 1993. Frank and I had come to his loft for lunch; later we were to tour the nearby Peggy Rockefeller rose collection, then recently restored, where Rupert would greet the gaudier hybrids with his emancipating dismay. But we were barely inside the door when he produced the limp fax—"from Berlin!" he announced—that had come from Prof. Dr. Werner Greuter, announcing the Engler Medal in Silver to Dr. Rupert C. Barneby. The titles amused me. Rupert always insisted on addressing his letters to Frank as Dr. Polach, and more than once confounded the doormen in our building by asking for that distinguished personage rather than Frank. Egalitarian to a fault, I commented facetiously on Professor Doctor Greuter's double-barreled title. Rupert, not reciprocally amused, explained to me as deliberately as to a foolish nephew that Dr. Greuter was not only European, he was German, and would consider it a solecism to overlook a title. Weakly, I nodded, and when Frank and I reached home in Chelsea rushed to the dictionary. *Solecism:* a blunder in speech; a breach of etiquette or decorum; an unmannerly act or practice; an impropriety. I never addressed a letter to him without its proper title, *Dr.* Rupert C. Barneby, again.

PEOPLE THOUGHT RUPERT AND DWIGHT were truly rich. The poet Harold Norse, when he discovered at a party how much Dwight fancied him, asked for a Picasso, and never understood that he had been put in his place when Dwight then bought him one. The gallery director John Myers and his business partner, Tibor de Nagy, up for weekends at Wappingers Falls, tried to double their appeal. Myers worked Dwight in the living room and de Nagy cornered Rupert in the kitchen. "Did they think we wouldn't compare notes?" Rupert asked us, aghast after thirty years. But Myers thought he was the one doing the favor. " 'So much the better,' " he claimed others told him, " 'that *you* get a bit of all that money than *some* of the people who gouge poor Dwight.' " Judith Malina noted in 1957 that the Living Theatre had found a permanent space, and with nine thousand dollars could buy it; but, she complained to her diary, "Dwight refused." She never considered that perhaps he did not have the money. Early in 1941, Dwight had been notified by his solicitor that the wartime British government intended to seize all his mortgages and securities in the United Kingdom, which, he was informed, would leave him penniless. "What matter if they *do* 'confiscate' the Spinney?" he protested to Rupert. "All I want is to be left in peace to see the Gilia in flower and resolve certain problems of Bulgarian syntax; that's all." Frank and I never were told if the seizure of assets finally occurred. We do know that the Spinney was requisitioned for wartime use; it was dezoned in February 1945. In the United States, Dwight's accounts were managed by Gleaves, Crawford & Levie, of 70 Pine Street in New York. Their report in 1952 shows $153,000 recently arrived from England. This, together with capital already under their control, brought Dwight's assets in the United States to $491,000. If those assets steadily generated 6 percent (a heady assumption), and if the return was not reinvested, then Dwight had an income of perhaps $29,000 a year. Yet this is the same period in which he undertook to support the fledgling Tibor de Nagy Gallery, providing it, in its first twelve months, with nearly 18 percent of his income. In addition, he assisted the widow of Dylan Thomas, frequently did come to the aid of the Living Theatre, subsidized Thurairajah Tambimuttu's journal *Poetry London–New York*, financed the film projects of Marie Menken and Willard Maas, and supported the field collecting of *Astragalus* and, later, *Dalea*. For years, Dwight and Rupert lived by selling, one by one, the paintings they had collected at modest prices when art was not yet a speculative investment. "Every room is full of paintings," wrote Malina of a weekend that she and her husband, Julian Beck, spent at Wappingers Falls. By the time Frank and I knew Rupert, the paintings mostly were gone. Rupert never said if he missed them, although in reference to the Miró "Constellations" he once remarked, "Their mixture of sunshine and terror are the best medicine there is." At the Cleveland Museum of Art is "Constellation" number five, *Femme à la blonde aisselle coiffant sa chevelure à la lueur des étoiles*, which hung formerly in the library at Stirling House in Greenport. Dwight sold it so that he and Rupert could buy a Jeep and hunt for plants, at last, in Mexico.

The affection Rupert and Dwight felt for Spain, and then Nevada, reemerged in their response to Mexico. Together again in the field, they were where they seemed most to belong. Dwight resumed his *Record*, and the two men devoted one month each year from 1963 through 1967 to collecting, not in May but from mid-October to mid-November, when they were likelier to meet with mature specimens in the genus that had become the new object of Rupert's attention, *Dalea*. Like *Astragalus*, but, at some two hundred species, not so sizable a genus, *Dalea* is among the legumes. (It is pronounced DAYLeea, having been named for English botanist Samuel Dale.) Some Daleas that occur widely in Mexico are known as *escobilla*, little broom, because their flexible stems when tied in bunches make effective whiskbrooms, or little brooms. From New York the two men drove, or sometimes took their Jeep by train, to Texas. All this time, Dwight was afraid to fly. They crossed the border at Laredo, Eagle Pass, or El Paso. They had not lost their touch—in the first autumn alone they discovered three new species of *Dalea*—and they had not lost respect for what they saw. On November 19, 1966, on a mountain road east of Teotitlán del Camino, in Oaxaca, Rupert was taking a good look at a roadside weed that he had seen earlier at the markets in Morelos, where it was brought in by the bale to be tied together and sold as brooms. This common weed, he suddenly realized, had never been named. He would put it in the genus *Marina* and call it *scopa*, for broom. Uncommonly, it blooms at night, and Rupert's homage to it was delivered in uncommon prose.

By day a dowdy weed, [it] is transformed by early morning into a thing of beauty. Shafts of oblique sunlight then illuminate the panicle into a tangle of lustrous red branchlets along which are strung innumerable small but vivid flowers of glowing magenta-purple. With every breath of air the whole mass of thready stems moves and bends, the oddly insectlike flowers seeming to hover rather than hang among them. Shaken, the petals fall readily away and left untouched all flutter earthward as the day brightens. The long androecium, briefly extended at full anthesis of the flower, soon afterward coils back neatly toward the slowly forming pod.

Twenty years had elapsed before I read that passage and exclaimed, Rupert, it is a poem! and then was embarrassed because to him it must have seemed so long ago. But I have known ever since, from the shift of tense in his response, how truly devoted to plants he was. "I tried to describe," he said, "something I feel."

Noel Holmgren, remembering Rupert at the Botanical Garden in 2001, proposed that he was among the great botanical explorers of all time. That would have pleased Dwight and Rupert both. In their youth they admired the same heroes. The flowerpot Rupert wears in *Portrait of Rupert Barneby, Esq. (botanist)* grows not just any plant, of course, but a *Primula* sent back in 1913 from Yunnan to Edinburgh by the intrepid George Forrest, botanizing explorer who, academically untrained, contributed thirty-one thousand herbarium sheets to British botany. Since I had heroes in my own youth, I think I can imagine the mix of excitement and anxiety that Rupert would feel as he mailed his first Ripley & Barneby specimens (they would be pressed on sheets as if they were unsolicited manuscripts) to the leading herbaria of the United States. "We all want you to know

Rupert on the San Rafael Swell

how fully we appreciate your kindness and thought and how beautifully prepared the material is," responded a surprised M. L. Fernald,
director of the Gray Herbarium at Harvard, in 1942. "You doubt-
less know the latter point, but perhaps others have not told you of
it." The first Ripley & Barneby sheets to arrive at the New York
Botanical Garden had been acknowledged December 19 of the year
before. Some of these, including a sheet of *Cymopterus ripleyi*
var. *saniculoides*—Dwight's truffle-flowered reminder of a prewar
confiserie—can now be reviewed online. (Go to www.nybg.org/
bsci/hcol/staf/Barneby.html; from the index of Rupert's specimens, click on *Cymopterus* and follow the menus from there.) The
image that comes to the screen will be labeled "isotype," which is
not a stray term from particle physics but an indication that this

plant was collected at the same time, at the same site, as the holotype, or original, defining specimen to which the published description of a species should always refer. In short, Rupert had sent
his duplicate to New York. The holotype went to the California
Academy of Sciences, where his description, in *Leaflets of Western
Botany*, had appeared. At both herbaria the *Cymopterus* carries the
same collection number, Ripley & Barneby No. 3429, because a collector may press two, three, or several specimens from a single collection made at any one site. By the end of 1967, their last year
of searching for *Dalea* in Mexico, Rupert and Dwight had made
more than seventeen thousand collections in the series they called
"Plantae Occidentales Selectae," or selected western plants. If they
pressed only three sheets on average at each collection, then these
two men contributed some fifty-three thousand specimen sheets to
the herbaria of the United States. They had surpassed Forrest in
quantity and perhaps in quality too. In the meantime, according
to Dwight's *Record*, they collected another seventeen new species
while botanizing in Mexico. The seventeen were *Boerhaavia chrysantha, Dalea bacchantum, D. cinnamomea, D. dipsacea, D. gypsophila,
D. laniceps, D. mixteca, D. piptostegia, D. simulatrix, D. transiens, D.
verna, Lopezia nuevo-leonis, Marina melilotina, M. sarodes, M. scopa,
M. stilligera,* and *Polygala erythrorrhiza.* For Rupert, however, the
work of discovery could not stop at collection. It stretched ahead in
herbaria and at the microscope, because the way in which *Dalea*
most seductively resembled *Astragalus* was not as a legume but as a
taxonomic knot to be untied. Eventually he would reshape this genus
as well, segregating three smaller genera from the original, until,
instead of one, there would be four: *Errazurizia, Psorothamnus,*

Marina, Dalea. Some species that were Daleas when he began, like
the familiar smoketree of the American Southwest, were not when
he finished; and some that were not Daleas when he started, like the
purple prairie clover, would be Daleas when he was done. This was
lumping and splitting, both. Even Dwight was fooled. In his *Record*
he had listed no *Marina* species at all, but called them all *Dalea.*

   Dwight did not tire of Rupert's botanical devotion, which he
had observed by 1970 for forty-five years. In December of that year
he wrote to Rupert's sister, Geraldine, at her home in Wiltshire.
"Rupert, thank God, works with demonic zeal at his various monographs. His collaborator on the Menispermaceae, the formidable
Dr. Krukoff, has finally gone back to Guatemala (again: thank
God), so R. can get on with the Daleas (which is what *I'm* interested
in—)." What Dwight and Geraldine knew was that Rupert slowly,
stubbornly, had been retraining his injured hand to draw. The awkward way we saw him hold his pencil was not, after all, some upper-
class affectation acquired at Harrow (Rupert had preserved the
pronunciations caPITalism and caRICature) but a victorious adaptation to necessity. Thanks to this adaptation, his revision of *Dalea*
could appear at last in 1977 as "Daleae Imagines"—the Daleas illustrated. What a triumph was secretly present in that title. In "Daleae
Imagines" there are 142 plates of illustration, all in Rupert's own
retrained hand. Frank and I knew how gratified he was by the positive reception and reviews. We knew how especially delighted he
was by a review that appeared in *Madroño,* written by botanist
Grady Webster entirely in Augustan couplets, like the verse of
Alexander Pope. We never knew, until now, how moved he must
have been by just four lines.

The many illustrations set this book apart
Through exquisite detail of patient art:
The author's pencil draws each plant's Gestalt
As BAUER might have done, without a fault.

Dwight, who thought Rupert's drawings could melt an iceberg,
never read Webster's tribute. In his life Dwight had reflected the
qualities in his own book of poems. They were "qualities," as
Rupert once described them to me, "of intense romanticism and
immaturity that contrast with sophisticated preciosity in surprising
ways." This must have been a precarious balance, and perhaps it
partly explains why Dwight was prey to public and private events
that never threatened Rupert himself. In ten years at Greenport,
Dwight had created the best drawings of his career; he also began
again to drink. His subsequent decline was precipitous and not
reversed. Dwight Ripley died December 17, 1973, in the Greenport hospital. His drawings meanwhile had become another of the
transformations—his own version of an "Atlas" or "Daleae Imagines"—by which he and Rupert changed their lives from spectacle
into science and art. Dwight's drawings were done in series, each a
set of variations on a theme. One set was of *Travel Posters*, designed
not for tourists but botanists. *¡Visitad el Cabo de Gata!* urges the first
poster, and it features a beckoning *Antirrhinum charidemi*, the plant
Noel Sandwith discovered at that cape and named. Another was a
set of *Language Panels*, for which landscapes were divided into panels like cartoons, while in each panel Dwight put word balloons that
feature plant and animal names in Russian, Polish, Czech, or in one
case a familiar name in Latin, *Cymopterus ripleyi*. In this latter draw-

ing two figures approach a *Cymopterus*, spouting its name in Latin as
if they were botanists. Dwight has drawn them, however, as ants,
in the ironic admission that Ripley & Barneby might seem to his
namesake plant no rescue team, but just another pair of predators. A
third series, his *Botanist UFOs*, recalled the flying saucers that first
were reported in the West while the two men were collecting there
in 1947. In one of these drawings the alien craft has landed, the
abduction is in progress, and loaded into the spaceship are the
species an alien visitor truly would covet: rare desert plants.

Dwight and Rupert had no health insurance. They never thought
of it. By the time Dwight died, the assets that subsidized *Astragalus*,
Tibor de Nagy, and *Dalea* were gone. The two Pollock drawings in
Rupert's loft soon disappeared as well, sold to the art dealer Jeffrey
Loria to satisfy the debts of Dwight's estate. The botanist Howard
Irwin, then recently named president of the New York Botanical
Garden, arranged for Rupert to complete the revision of *Cassia*
which his own duties had forced him to set aside, and secured for
Rupert an appointment, with paycheck at last, as his research assistant. It was Irwin, too, who arranged a place for Rupert to live, first
at the Irwins' own house, and then in that unique loft where I would
complain, theatrically, that my short life was done. Rupert, when
Dwight died, was sixty-two years old. He had published 2,747
pages of taxonomic text, *Astragalus* included, and ahead of him lay
another 4,929 in *Dalea, Cassia, Mimosa, Pithecellobium*, et al., com-
prising in total the achievement for which he was called a Bentham
of the twentieth century. "As the years went by," recalled Irwin, "he
felt the press of time, so worked ten or twelve hours a day, seven
days a week, alone among his beans, making sense out of seeming

Dwight Ripley,
Language Panel: Cymopterus ripleyi, *1968*

chaos." And yet Rupert was not sentimental about his achieve-
ments. His true respect was for the principle, call it scientific observation or loving attention, that lay behind them. He believed in this
principle because it spanned borders, language barriers, personalities, and especially time. It also spanned methodologies. "The Garden has been looking to enter the molecular age, and has been
interviewing prospective candidates," he wrote to Frank on the last
day of December 1994. "This has meant a daily seminar, way over
my head, consisting mostly of cladistic trees and arcane tricks with

enzymes, i.e. methodology and molecular chemistry only remotely related to the plant organisms that have preoccupied me since boyhood." What had happened since boyhood, of course, was that molecular biology made it possible to go directly to DNA—without stopping at stem, leaf, or pod—for a systematic comparison of apparently related groups of plants. Even an outsider can see the promise of this methodology. Given the explicit evidence of a plant's lineage, there would be no need for lumpers and splitters to disagree at all. In practice it has not worked out this way. But Rupert had grafted to his stoicism an Enlightenment faith in science, and we knew him to honor his convictions in respect to work that might seem, to an outsider, even to supersede his own. Proof came, dramatically enough, in the shape of the first new species he had spotted in the field, the *Gilia ripleyi* that he spent all night sketching in the motel. Mark Porter, a molecular systematist at the Rancho Santa Ana Botanic Garden, discovered while comparing selected gene sequences that he could not match *G. ripleyi* and its closest relatives with the other species in the genus *Gilia*. Porter resurrected a name that was no longer in use, and the *Gilia* that Dwight wished once to see in flower became *Aliciella ripleyi* instead. What did Rupert say? His reaction can be extrapolated from an article he wrote for the *Bulletin of the American Rock Garden Society* in response to a reader's question: Was the creeping snowberry really *Gaultheria hispidula,* or could it be called *Chiogenes hispidula* as it was before? Preference is a matter of taxonomic opinion, answered Rupert, and those who prefer to go on using *Chiogenes* are "at liberty" to do so. "Indeed they will be in good company doing so," he continued slyly, "for Ohwi, in *Flora of Japan,* persists in calling the Nippon Snowberry

Chiogenes japonica. But among botanists Ohwi must appear as a lonely holdout, like that marine on Okinawa, in a battle that was decided years ago."

Rupert, though he was pleased to be an autodidact, never thought that made him autonomous. When he was eighty-one he was contacted by EG&G Energy Measurements, a consulting firm that had been engaged by the Department of Energy to update the list of threatened and endangered species at the Nevada Test Site. The question posed was whether *Cymopterus ripleyi* var. *saniculoides* should continue to be regarded as a valid taxon worthy of separate attention. The population on Frenchman Flat no longer existed. The botanists Lincoln Constance, James Reveal, and Mildred Mathias had concluded that the plants being called *saniculoides* at other locations were no more than gradations in the apple-green species. In California, the U.S. Fish and Wildlife Service no longer recognized the variety. ("Ta-ta, Dwighteen!") In Nevada, surveys at the Test Site were discovering plants of both descriptions, the apple green and the chocolate, intermingled as one population at the same locations. Rupert earlier might have gone to see for himself. Each year since we had known him he disappeared westward in the spring, a practice he continued (his driving had not improved) thrillingly late in life. *At age seventy-seven:* "The drought, which Dwight called Ella Cinders, was uninterrupted between Dallas and the Colorado River, not a flower to be seen, even along the roadside ditches." *Again at seventy-seven:* "From Needles I went north through Nevada in the Snake River valley in Oregon. Here there had been rain, and there was still rain. Not only rain but sleet, snow, powerful winds, and rain again, which turned the back roads into slippery lanes of gumbo, difficult and even dangerous to negotiate." *At seventy-nine, a sudden message from Afton, Wyoming:* "I felt compelled to find out whether I could still make it to the West, if only once more, and so here I am on the Idaho border, 7 days out of the Bronx. The high plains and Colorado Rockies are dry as trisquit so I'm not getting anything much for the press—but the scene is enough." *At eighty-one:* "I woke in a sordid motel in Del Rio, TX (on the lower Grande) last Thursday to find myself stricken with Bell's Palsy, i.e., with only half a face. I returned at high speed." The palsy abated, and the query about the *Cymopterus* arrived later that year. But Rupert, who obeyed nature, never drove west again. When the consultant's report was issued it noted that Rupert himself had examined the Test Site collections. These must have been sent to him. He would have been grateful for the chance to inspect the evidence. Even so, it makes me shiver to think of him in his New York Botanical Garden office, fifty-two years after he took the type photograph of *Cymopterus ripleyi* that hung silently on the wall above his desk, now typing intently to his Nevada correspondent the right answer: "It is hardly worthwhile to continue recognizing the two varieties."

I regret, of course, that Rupert and I could not really discuss taxonomy. From Rupert, I did learn the scientific names of quite a few plants. These surfaced so gracefully in even his casual conversation that the vernacular name for a species soon seemed, indeed, to be a solecism. By contrast I could remember having learned, perhaps from my high school biology teacher, that the species was the only unit of taxonomy to be recognized in nature itself. All the rest, including the genus and its scientific name, are the inventions of taxonomists. I suppose I thought this was clever, if not daring, at the time. Now I think it was glib. It belongs with the same sort of wisdom that tells us quarks exist only in the mind of Murray Gell-Mann. Probably I had pictured the genus as a "container" that holds the species, and it's true that no one will see, in nature, a container that corresponds to *Astragalus*. But *Astragalus* was not the name for an entity; it is the name for an event that distinguishes all the species that have occurred from it. Rupert proposed an *Astragalus* to explain his apprehension that the plants he was seeing in North America had diverged from those in Asia, that they had their origins "hereabouts" and not on the roof of the world. Scientist that he was, he and Dwight in the Dodge went looking for the facts. It was therefore a triumph of the "Atlas of North American *Astragalus*" that all the facts he finally assembled there—by discovery in the field, by examination in the herbaria—would not let Rupert prove what he had wished to prove: that there are not 2,500 species of *Astragalus*, after all, because the two hemispheric groups have been separated by an evolutionary event. He could only predict that their *taxonomic* separation would one day be justified, while he was compelled by his science to conclude that "clear morphological evi-dence for such a separation" was lacking. By 1993, three decades after Rupert was forced to state his conclusion, the study of *Astragalus* had been taken up by a new generation of botanists, fluent in molecular systematics, who could supply the new kind of evidence. In a series of publications beginning that same year, these younger botanists (they include Martin Wojciechowski of Arizona State University, Michael Sanderson and Jer-Ming Hu of the University of California at Davis, and Aaron Liston of Oregon State University) were to report DNA comparisons that suggest that the North American astragali are, just as Rupert believed, derived but separate from their Eurasian relatives. If further results agree, then the genus is sure to be split, and the evolutionary event that Rupert and Dwight pursued through the North American West will no longer be called *Astragalus*. Some botanists call it "Neo-Astragalus" instead. I wish we had Rupert's reaction to that term. It might come as a discourse on botanical Latin, but we would not have to fear for his personal feelings or be on guard against professional jealousy. When it was time near the end of his life to distribute favorite possessions, Rupert gave some friends paintings, others furniture, and he sent his lifetime library of books on *Astragalus*—he typed the shipping labels himself—to Aaron Liston, molecular systematist at Oregon State University in Corvallis.

Tea with Rupert in his office at the Botanical Garden was, by every report, an occasion to be remembered. In all the years I knew him, it was a privilege I never shared. Teatime was recalled in reminiscences I have seen from Joseph Kirkbride ("a landmark in my life"), Steven Carpenter ("sincere moments of sanity"), Vicki Funk ("much needed"), Sylvia Stein ("tea and cookies"), John Pipoly ("Earl Grey tea with plain biscuits"), Patricio Mena Vasconez ("in his office, NYBG's warmest"), Sir Ghillean Prance ("teatime seminars"), Stanley Welsh ("highlighted my trips"), Ted Barkley ("drinking tea and eating cookies"). The cookies, to judge from Michael Nee's report at the memorial tribute, were not themselves a reason to go to tea. The Latin lessons, to judge from Douglas Daly's, were. Probably everyone remembered from teatime the fluted (they were also cracked) blue-and-white china teacups. These had been at Trewyn. During the years Frank and I first knew him,

Rupert went several times to England to visit his sister, Geraldine. Clearly devoted, he wrote back, even so, that he was "drowning in amniotic fluid." Later he revealed more about his early life. To Frank he explained his taxonomy of ancestors, cousins, great-aunts, and great-uncles. To Jackie Kallunki he showed photographs of Trewyn, Saltmarshe Castle, and himself as a child. Once I remarked to him that Frank and I had been amused by discoveries in our own humble genealogies and that I, despite my egalitarian leanings, found them sort of interesting. "Of course you do," he exploded instantly. "Otherwise you might as well be a gnat!" His father had died in 1943, his mother in 1967; his brother Tom was killed in an auto accident in Sweden in 1972. Gradually the Barneby properties were dispersed. His grandfather Barneby's castle, Saltmarshe, was torn down for the value of its copper roof; the grounds are occupied today by the Saltmarshe Castle Caravan Park. The estate manager's house survived. It is a bed-and-breakfast (Littlebridge House, Bromyard, Herefordshire, Tel: 01885 482471) from which the tourist may survey former Barneby lands. One of the Saltmarshe farm-houses is also a guest house (Middle Norton Farm, Bromyard, Herefordshire, Tel: 01885 488079). Trewyn was listed by the Knight Frank agency for sale in 1999 at £850,000, and is probably a private residence again. But the tourist may stay close-by in a house that belongs to Bwlch Trewyn estates (Brynhonddu Country House, Pandy, Abergavenny, Monmouthshire, Tel: 01873 980535). Among the few properties left from Rupert's childhood was a parcel one-and-a-half miles uphill from Trewyn—the "mountaintop," he called it—where he, Geraldine, and Tom had played as children, and where he as a boy had liked to observe the flowers: no fit occupation, his father thought, for a man. When Tom's eldest son consigned the mountaintop to auction, Geraldine was alerted by a local magistrate who provided her with an estimate (it was remarkably accurate) of the highest bid. She successfully bid five pounds more, she and Rupert split the purchase, and when next he went to England—he was sixty-seven, she sixty-three—they packed a picnic lunch and hiked to the top of their hill above Trewyn, from which England is seen on one side and Wales on the other. Geraldine died ten years later and Rupert gave the mountaintop to the National Trust. It is now part of Brecon Beacons National Park.

Rupert moved from his unforgettable loft at the Botanical Garden on January 12, 1998. Frank and I had asked him to live with us but knew what his answer would be. He had arranged to live at Kittay House, 2550 Webb Avenue in the Bronx, because it was only minutes from the garden, it was close to Jackie Kallunki, and because this new residence, "Crone Heights," he liked to call it, was "designed to shelter frail organisms that modern medicine creates—clinging to life beyond an allotted span, when they are biologically and socially irrelevant." He was never in life, nor will he be in death, irrelevant. His other friends know acts of kindness, brilliance, alarming stubbornness that I do not, and the disclosures I make here are only representative. But the year after Frank and I visited Trewyn, Rupert repaid the gesture by finding his way to the Oklahoma county where Frank grew up, and the town where he went to school. "I found Wellston suspended between its cinnabar silos," he wrote. "I inspected the sandstone masonry of the school where someone took THE WRONG PATH (bravo, alas)." I myself had grown up on a farm, no Trewyn but dear enough, and when my

Rupert at eighty-five

parents realized that Frank and I were not to be separated they transferred the farm to my sister and brother-in-law, in order to keep it in the family. It was only then, in Rupert's reaction, that we understood the toll his own father took on him. He deliberately made available to us, as a replacement heritage, the whole story and momentum of his and Dwight's life together. It is an important heritage, I think, and it does not belong alone to Frank and me. When we bought a house in the country, Rupert was the first to visit it. And this wise friend, who warned us from the start to have no deep plan, brought as his contribution to the household gods a compass!—as if to say, there are no extenuating circumstances, only time and distance, and how you travel them. Rupert had become an ambassador for character, who, through his own example, brought his friends the motto in his coat of arms to make their own: *by force of character, not by force,* VIRTUE NON VI.

Rupert Barneby died at 5:07 p.m., Tuesday, December 5, 2000, at the Jewish Home and Hospital, adjacent to his last apartment at Kittay House, in the Bronx, New York. Three months earlier he had suffered a stroke, rallied, then steadily, purposefully declined. He was eighty-nine years old (he was sure he was ninety). An obituary published in the *New York Times* contrived somehow to compare him to a reclusive, once glamorous movie star. It was a bizarre comparison, and not just because he so eloquently disdained the Hollywood idea of personality. The Rupert who accepted our first return invitation, who came down to Chelsea to our apartment for dinner, was the Rupert who insisted on being as alive in the present as we ever were. At sixty-three he had been both distinguished and mischievous, and so, until the end of his life, he remained. The cruelties of aging vexed him, but he tried to observe their comedy too. He had constant trouble with his hearing aids and endless negotiations with the hearing aid technician. Once he complained in exasperation, "You would think that a professional audiologist would not insist on communication by telephone with the deaf; but of course *she* can hear and I *ought* to." To botanist Alicia Lourteig in Paris, whom he had met through Noel Sandwith long ago, he wrote, "We have had the impertinence of living too long." But after reading an obituary in the *Times* he sent us an instant happy scrawl: "So I outlived the pretentious Spender!" He was delighted when Eric Brown, director of Tibor de Nagy Gallery, came to the garden to meet him before the gallery's fiftieth anniversary. "I've had a visitor!" he exclaimed with pride. And when Joe Kirkbride returned to see him in August 1999, he expressed his own wonder in search of *temps perdu*; how could this graduate student, with whom he so recently

shared an office, have children in college? "Time is incomprehensibly elastic," he said. Rupert had so many friends, diverse friends, it
was as if they too were all astragali. Of gardening with Dwight he
wrote, "I think we chose a plant for the reasons one chooses a
friend, not for splendor of apparel or purity of profile, but for character and individuality." Botanist to the end, he valued in people
what he valued in plants: the sign of their artful adaptations to
necessity. On June 1, 1944, in the extreme northwest corner of
Nevada on gravel slopes at an elevation of eight thousand feet,
Dwight, reported Rupert in his journal, has made the discovery of
the day—"an annual Composite, flat on the ground and subacaules-
cent, with fat spoon-shaped leaves arranged around a nosegay of
tubular white corollas. The whole thing an inch across or less. And
the capitula (mirabile dictu) have but two or three florets and bracts!
At dinner we can talk of nothing but the Composite. Exquisite,
what *is* it?"

Dwight

WHEN DWIGHT DIED IN 1973, and after the body was cremated, Rupert did something that troubled him off and on for the rest of his life. He never claimed Dwight's ashes. "But they were only ashes!" he protested, while each time he went on to recall how Dillon Ripley had suggested Dwight be buried with the family and this was the last thing, surely, that Dwight would want. From Rupert's description we understood that the final weeks in the Greenport hospital had been an ordeal; the alcoholic destruction of Dwight's liver and kidneys made him unrecognizably bloated, paranoid, and eventually delirious; the end early December 17 before Rupert set out that morning for the hospital came as an intense relief. He did not go to the hospital then or ever again; he never saw Dwight dead. "I expect to be much freer to move now and in the near future," he wrote Tom Howell at the California Academy of Sciences, "& hope to visit you all at the Academy sometime next year." Rupert was not too stoic to wonder aloud on occasion what he might have become apart from Dwight, how much he might have accomplished free of his frequently difficult partner of forty-eight years. "Dwight looked and acted like a handsome international playboy," recalled John Myers in his memoirs; he also had a "Falstaffian" appetite for drink. Was it true, I later asked Harold Norse, that Dwight was bounced from the Plaza Hotel? "Many times," he responded, laughing. "Dwight the Learned," was the name bestowed by Peggy

Guggenheim; "a genius," said Tibor de Nagy. "He's always pinch-
ing or patting my ass," reported Clement Greenberg, who in turn
once autographed a book *for Dwightie, with all my mixed love, Clem.*
He was "a Gidean nightmare this Dwight," observed Judith Malina;
he was "kind & hard & terrible & lovable." So I suppose it was
inevitable that Frank and I, too, would develop mixed feelings
about our friend's departed friend, an ambivalence that was hardly
resolved in our case by Rupert's repeated characterization of Dwight
as a fine draftsman who drew only to please himself and whose most
significant accomplishment had been his unfinished dictionary of
vernacular plant names. I suppose further that our ambivalence
served self-protective interests of my own. The baroque furnishings
of Rupert's loft, the Surrealist paintings, the books in too many languages and especially those in English—not so much Auden and
Isherwood, but Firbank and Corvo, the three Sitwells, the whole
privileged cohort of Harold Acton, Evelyn Waugh, Nancy Mitford,
Henry Green, and Anthony Powell—put me on guard. Prominent
on one shelf was *Memoirs of an Aesthete,* perhaps the best known of
Harold Acton's titles, which in those days stood out to me mainly for
the awkward rhyme it cast from aesthete to effete, and which practi-
cally advertised that here was a library written by and for the frivo-
lous, the highbrow, the undemocratic, and the epicene. When it
turned out that Dwight in England had known all but the elder two
of these suspect authors, the threat came only nearer. I did not want
to know more about Dwight Ripley.

For several years I responded to stories about Dwight with the
panic reserve that in youth I believed might pass for courtesy. Rupert
took no offense. He was, his friends will recall, insightfully gener-

ous, and when Frank and I left his loft after dinner and cigars we were likely to carry away in addition to his stories a rare book, a lithograph, even a rug. Sometimes the objects were of the kind made special by their use: Frank got Dwight's camera, and I received his 1938 Webster's unabridged. Eventually we were asked to take things away in bulk, and in this way we acquired the immense steamer trunk that had accompanied the two men on their trips around the Mediterranean, together with an antique leather suitcase handtooled by one Tom Hill of Sloane Square Station and stamped *H.D.D.R.*, for Harry Dwight Dillon Ripley. These went to our house in the country; they claimed even there an imperial lot of space. Alone one night in the house, vexed by the intrusion and thinking ahead to the recycling center or the auction barn, I opened the trunk and suitcase to see what lay inside. For hours thereafter until the sun rose, I removed one by one from their storage a total of 313 drawings in colored pencil on paper, sometimes on artboard, a few also in colored ink or gouache, ranging in dimension from poster-sized works of twenty by thirty inches down to stationery-sized drawings of eight and a half by eleven, and consisting mostly of landscapes. They were landscapes so greatly stylized, however, and so deftly combined with text and other allusions that even on first sight they presumed an attention more complex and historicized than ordinary landscape, and they were so structurally and keenly colored that each drawing as I retrieved it seemed almost to project an alternative spectrum of its own. I had found the drawings Dwight made in the ten years at Greenport before he died: his botanical *Travel Posters,* his *Language Panels* with their vernacular plant and animal names, his *Botanist UFOs.* The devoted pencil strokes, the obvious devotion

to subject, had combined in these drawings to reveal a vision that
was bright, after all these years, with wit and foreboding, affection,
and, above all, a radiant intelligence. I liked them—the truth is they
had seized my imagination and would not let go—and I wanted to
identify, at least for Frank and myself, the source of their unexpected power.

I was not the first, we soon learned, to react to Dwight's drawings
this way. In Zurich, at a festival for experimental video and multime-
dia held at Cinema Xenix in 1996, the audience viewed also an animated, three-and-one-half-minute, 16 mm film with the peculiar
title of *Dwightiana*. This film, which has been seen since in pro-
grams of early avant-garde cinema at Arsenal 1 in Berlin, Anthology Film Archives in New York, the Art Institute of Chicago, and
the Kommunales Kino in Freiburg, Germany, was made by Marie
Menken in 1959 from stop-motion sequences that she filmed in
Rupert and Dwight's apartment at 416 East Fifty-eighth Street in
New York. Menken was the filmmaker who earlier shot *Glimpse of
the Garden* among the rare plants the two men grew at Wappingers
Falls. Both titles are available today from Filmmakers Cooperative
in New York or from Canyon Cinema Cooperative in San Francisco; I saw them at Anthology Film Archives in New York. For
Dwightiana, Menken assembled a bumpy, colorful animation of
beads, pebbles, shells, and yarns that dance, and in various configu-
rations jitter, mince, and writhe across the face of five drawings in
colored pencil which are all, of course, drawings by Dwight. At one
point the beads and pebbles are replaced momentarily by colored
pencils—Dwight's palette, I realized—that fan out in peacock fash-

ion to fill the screen. The animation is matched throughout with a soundtrack for steel drum, guitar, flute, and voice that was written for the occasion by Maya Deren's youthful husband, Teiji Ito, a composer whose scores, heard today, seem not so much forerunners as contemporaries of styles developed since by Steve Reich or Philip Glass. The soundtrack of *Dwightiana* is startling in this regard. Although Dwight's drawings were employed sequentially as flats, they, the animation, and the music appear to evolve together on the screen. Filmmaker Stan Brakhage called *Dwightiana* a pioneer example of the film portrait, and he praised Menken for having recognized that such a portrait could be abstract, instead of a narrative or a talking head. By itself, *Dwightiana* as a title might foretell a collection of playthings or a Surrealist cabinet of forgettable marvels. In context, it alludes to the botanical nomenclature that was a preoccupation of the household where Menken was a friend and regular visitor, where in fact she was making the film. Botanists frequently will convert the surname, or even the personal name of an individual into a species epithet (Billie Turner did this when he named *Mimosa rupertiana*), both in tribute and to identify a species. Menken transposed the practice to her film, and *Dwightiana* became the epithet by which she too identified a kind of species: a specific creative sensibility. She made portraits of Isamu Noguchi, Kenneth Anger, and Willard Maas in addition to her portrait of Dwight. "Of course I have a feeling about these people," she told an interviewer, "and somehow created, cinematically speaking, what moves them or has moved me, having what I thought was an insight into their creative work."

Rupert would not have cared for Marie Menken's opinion. In twenty-five years he never told us *Dwightiana* existed. But he was pleased by our new interest and he was visibly stirred when Frank showed him photographs of the drawings from the trunk. Seeing Dwight's *Travel Poster* for Tavolara, the island massif off Sardinia that is now a nature preserve, he remembered how he had climbed to the top of that island in search of plants when someone began firing shots at him. He descended empty-handed and "rather in haste." At first he was reluctant to relate his stories to the drawings, as if once he believed that the personal narrative ought not to intrude on art. No theoretical attention, he explained (brushing *Dwightiana* aside), had been accorded to Dwight's art and career. At the library we discovered reviews, however, for each of the shows Dwight had at the Tibor de Nagy Gallery in the 1950s—not extensive reviews, to be sure, but respectable, positive notices that appeared in *Art News*, *Art Digest*, and the *New York Times*. In a separate instance the writer was Larry Rivers, who, in the course of an *Art News* article about Saul Steinberg, had reflected, "Except for Dwight Ripley I can think of no one who is better at being witty with drawings." During its first full year of operation, in 1951, the Tibor de Nagy Gallery sold more work by Dwight than by any other artist. Nine of his drawings were sold that year for a total of $440, while four works by Alfred Leslie sold for $90, two by Rivers for $158, and one by Pennerton West for $50. (Robert Goodnough recalled that a painting of his sold for $300 during this same year, but no sale of that magnitude appears on the gallery's books.) The list of collectors who owned Dwight's work could be read as a network of friends or as a sign of shared tastes within an avant-garde; included were Grace Hartigan, Helen Frankenthaler, John Latouche, Betty Parsons, Peggy Guggenheim, Alfonso Ossorio, Joe LeSueur, Marie Menken, and Willard Maas. "Dwight," Menken advised a correspondent in 1955, "is truly a great artist in his own right." Unfortunately, she continued, he was also "truly modest," and few realized he was an artist at all. Dwight never wrote about his work, and he was never interviewed. A clue to his motives might be found, I hoped, in his reports to the rock-garden bulletins or in the copy of his *Poems* that Rupert sent. Other sources might be his unpublished poems, short stories, and a satirical roman à clef that was titled, in his hand, *A Sunlit Scene*. One inspired night I searched on the Internet and located his chapbook, *Spring Catalogue;* it was Peggy Guggenheim's copy, at a bookshop in Lyme Regis, Dorset. In an abandoned bureau, Frank found Dwight's pocket appointment diaries. And, in response to our interest, Rupert offered to our surprise the letters Dwight wrote when the two were on opposite coasts, separated by errands, during their early years in the United States. Illustrative as these sources were, they yielded no immediate theme. Rupert's life was guided by a series of taxonomic problems. Dwight's by contrast seemed a mix of friendship, travel, enthusiasm, and incident. What were the problems of *his* creative life? Stan Brakhage, who as a Menken protégé knew Dwight only through her gossip, implied that the answer was obvious. "Dwight," he wrote, "was an alcoholic who was forever having rich people's troubles—which are absolutely incurable."

D WIGHT WAS BORN OCTOBER 23, 1908, at his father's London residence of 22 Sussex Place, in the most elaborate of the John Nash terraces (today it is the London Business School) bordering Regent's Park. His father, also Harry Dwight Dillon Ripley but called Harry, had moved in exalted society. He is buried in the old St Marylebone, now East Finchley, Cemetery beneath a bronze monument by William Reid Dick, the socially prominent sculptor whose later subjects would include Queen Mary, the Duke of Windsor, and King George VI. When he died in 1913, Harry Ripley was only forty-eight; when Dwight was born, which is more to the point, he was already forty-four. His fortune, an inheritance from his railroad-building grandfather, was locked tight in two American trust funds. He had an allowance but not the principal. In fact, the only way Harry could affect the principal was to die having willed it to his child, if he had a child—a stipulation in which his relatives saw reason, presumably, to feel secure. At thirty-five he married the actress Alice Louise Reddy. Time passed, while Louise, as she was called, perhaps considered her prospects. Clearly she surprised and alarmed her American in-laws when, after nine years instead of nine months, she produced the requisite condition of her future financial ease and named him, boldly, with the full complement of her husband's names. The in-laws looked for a way out. They found it, they hoped, in the language of Harry's will, and refused to release the funds. Louise took Dwight to press her case in New York. She settled in the Waldorf-Astoria, then still at Thirty-fourth Street and Fifth Avenue on the site of the present Empire State Building, where she was warned of a series of recent hotel-room burglaries. Each evening, before she embarked on the long night out, Louise hid her jewelry beneath Dwight's bed. Five years old, he was certain he would be murdered or carried off and never found. His fears were not entirely misplaced; this was the trip during which police searched three days for him because his mother left him with friends but forgot which ones. Louise had attracted notice in New York. The results of her litigation were announced soberly in the *New York Times* and sensationally in the *Herald:* COURT MAKES BABY A MILLIONAIRE. Even then it was not quite true. Mother and son returned to England having been awarded $848,866—the equal, granted, of $14 million today. Rupert implied, by dismissing her taste (the Spode dinnerware once was hers; he thought it showy), that Mrs. Ripley was not the better sort. At the Spinney she entertained a succession of suitors who found, as apparently did she, that her son was not just annoying but an obstacle to adult designs. Dwight was to receive a quarter of his inheritance at twenty-one, a quarter at twenty-five, the balance on his mother's death. He did not have to wait for twenty-one. Sometime following his tenth birthday but before he arrived at Harrow, aged fourteen, Louise Ripley died. He remembered her chiefly for her boyfriends and appetites, or, as he put it in a scathing limerick, her "carousing and feasting / And brain like a bee-sting." In photo albums he kept pictures of the Spinney's gardens and its moody interiors, but the only picture that comes close to an ancestral portrait was taken in the

American West of a locomotive in a freight yard. On its tender appears the name Union Pacific Railroad.

Frank and I had not seen the drawings from the trunk the year we visited Trewyn, or we would have gone bravely to East Sussex to find the village of Little London, behind which the Spinney still stands: an ersatz Tudor hall to which Harry Ripley added the porch—"an American *veranda*!" sniffed Rupert—that ruined it. In America, when Dwight first visited his cousins near Litchfield, Connecticut, he reported gleefully, "They have an enormous, ugly house (built by our great-grandpère & almost as hideous as the Spinney)." Spinney means woods or thicket, and, while there are many places with this name in England, the Spinney's seclusion was

Dwight at the Spinney

an advantage Dwight would elaborate, until, behind its hedges, he built a boyhood preserve that was very much his own. Of course he did not have the control of his fortune when he still was a boy. At Harrow he received an allowance and had to budget his pencils and art supplies. From his father's death forward, his accounts were managed by B. W. Horne, of Horne & Birkett at 10 Little College Street in Westminster. "Had a letter from B. W. H. yesterday," he complained to Rupert, "telling me absolutely nothing, as usual, in an incredibly circuitous way." Dwight's boyhood companion at the Spinney was his dog, an Aberdeen terrier called Blackie that was a gift from Rudyard Kipling. The famous author, a year younger than Dwight's father, lived once in the United States and had an American wife; his household at Bateman's, eight miles to the east of the Spinney near Burwash, was as imperfectly English as the Ripley one. Kipling was fifty-three when Dwight was ten, and Rupert stressed without irony that he was thus an *old man* when Dwight knew him. Even so, and while he was becoming a joke to the smart set whose books one day lined Dwight and Rupert's shelves, Kipling provided the example of an adult friend whose life had been realized both in the imagination and in the country-house ideal. As the young Rupert prowled the west country in search of mosses, fungi, and flowering plants, Dwight set about creating the first gardens of his Sussex sanctuary. He poured his affection into plants and their attendant insects, snakes, and birds. Later he reflected on the influence of his boyhood devotion. "I am not mean with my admiration," he wrote. "It is simply that I am still dazzled by the incredible diversity of natural forms, whether of plants or animals, of climate or atmosphere, of everything, in fact, which may be experienced by the physical senses." He liked the fugitive color of flowers, the glint of beetles, the kinetic brilliance of butterflies, peacocks, and lyrebirds. For their shyer colors he admired stones, pebbles, and shells of the kind that Menken would animate across his drawings in *Dwightiana*. Looking back, it is easy to believe he loved the grounds, plants, and animals of the Spinney because they expected nothing, did not regard him as an obstacle, and because like Blackie they were secret allies against his mother and Horne. He explained his affection for the Umbelliferae (*Cymopterus ripleyi* is an umbellifer) to readers of the *Quarterly Bulletin of the Alpine Garden Society*. "To the author there has always been something special about the Umbelliferae, or Parsleys, and a patch devoted to their culture was begun at the tender age of nine. Coriander, chervil, sweet cicely and fennel were at that time accorded the lavish care I would probably bestow today on *Kelseya uniflora*, and a week-end guest of my mother's was known to have packed his bags precipitately after tasting one of my terrifying salads."

If Dwight's parsleys could discourage his mother's suitors, his increasingly esoteric gardens might isolate him from his own prospective friends as well. Among his unpublished poems we found:

> *Je veux que tout le monde regarde*
> *Mes fleurs,* it's really rather hard
> When one finds something specially rare
> To think there's no one there to care . . .

The lament was satirical, no doubt. But the crosslingual rhyme was not gratuitous or unusual; truly, the friends with whom Dwight first shared his plants, even before Rupert, were other languages. A second language is an anodyne for loneliness (it makes, after all, the sound of company), and this was a reason Dwight would learn so many, why the chorus of names he entered in his multilingual dictionary kept his attention, why his *Language Panels* bloom with the reflex affection of naming the world in different tongues. "For years *zanahoria* has struck me as the loveliest word in the Spanish language," he wrote, "but one can scarcely moon around repeating 'carrot . . . carrot . . . carrot' to oneself, at least, not if there's anybody within earshot, and in Spain there usually is." He was nowhere near Spain at the time. Of the thirty-one poems he included in *Poems,* thirteen were in Spanish, six in Portuguese. Each has a dateline, but the dates and some of the places too are fictitious. "Dwight was always doing things like that," said Rupert, as if he regarded as willfully perverse a practice that was impeccably Modernist instead. The two schoolboy botanists, once they were introduced at Harrow, set off immediately to herborize (Dwight's word for it) in the English countryside. Cecil Beaton, whose last year at Harrow coincided with Dwight's first, remembered of the school that "any signs of intelligence were seen only out of class." Indeed the most meticulous, as well as prophetic entry in Dwight's school notebooks is his record of plants, from the Ranunculaceae through Naiadaceae, together with the places where he and Rupert first encountered them (places, to my American ear, that surely they found in the land of the elves: *Crumbles, Bagshot, Wicken, Tring*). But after Harrow, certainly after university, England was not botanical world enough. Auden and Isherwood liked Germany, "for social reasons," Rupert said. He and Dwight were drawn to Portugal and Spain. Friendship,

youth, discovery—these nearly erupt from Dwight's stories, especially the one in which Rupert (whose sister was Geraldine) has been
renamed Gerald. "After some weeks of wandering in the Algarve,"
writes Dwight, "we had crossed by ferry to Ayamonte, and, faintly
disgusted with the squalor of the hotel at Huelva, taken up almost
permanent quarters in Puerto de Santa María. From this refuge we
herborized, not always with the gravity of scientific research. Gerald
had discovered that the popular label, in Catalonia, of a weed which
is not uncommon in the south, is 'The Little Salad of the Mother of
God': And I remember that we got a good deal of amusement out
of the name, greeting every appearance of the plant with cries of
'Behold the B. V. M.'s Broccoli!' or 'Lo! The Immaculate Cos!' "

Today it should seem ironic, if not unfair, that Dwight was
thought insufficiently English to be Rupert's friend at Harrow when
later in the United States he was *too* English (he had a "campy
Oxford accent," said Harold Norse) to be a real American. At
Oxford he attended Oriel College, which was not one of the more
prestigious; these were said to be Christ Church, New College, Bal-
liol, and Magdalen. Auden attended Christ Church. Spender, at
University College, recalled feeling that he was thereby on the
fringe of Oxford life. Dwight was four months older than Spender,
a year younger than Auden, and the same age as Peter Watson, the
heir to the Maypole Dairy fortune, who attended St John's but left
after just one year. All were at Oxford in the brief interval between
the Firbankian subtleties of the generation that included Acton and
Waugh and the Marxist pieties that came later. Anglophilic Americans might be surprised to learn the extent of anti-American sentiment among the upper-class English during these years. Not a few

university students emerged convinced that their role was to save European virtue from American capitalism, of which Dwight's family was naturally an example. The grace bestowed by the British empire, as in India, was held out as the counter-ideal. Robert Byron, a friend of Waugh at Oxford, was widely admired in this regard for his book *An Essay on India,* which was published the year Dwight graduated. Wrote Byron: "The hard Hebroid scum of racially indeterminate, machine-worshipping, truthless little men who have laid hands on half the world since the War, stencilling the American pattern where they touch, have found no place in India." As late as 1938, Auden could produce a poem in which it pleased him to write that the Sphinx was "Turning / a vast behind on shrill America." At Oxford, Dwight's "chum" (he used this Britishism all his life) was Harold Chown, whose father was French and whose girlfriend, soon to be wife, Hope Manchester, was American. (It is the Chowns who, with Rupert and Dwight in Baja California, will be forced to sleep overnight in the disabled Packard.) Among Dwight's chums from the Waugh generation were Cyril Connolly, distantly Irish and married to an American, and Brian Howard, who was raised British but whose parents were American and whose father, moreover, had changed the family name. Rupert, by contrast, was the born aristocrat, never smug, but no matter how diminished his state never unsure of his privilege. At the old-age home, where he was impatient one day to exit the elevator but blocked by a fellow resident slowly tapping her way out with her walker, he embarrassed us by commanding loudly, too loudly because he was deaf, "Out of my way you old crone!" This inborn noblesse was irresistible to Dwight. When Rupert was still at Cambridge, Dwight sent photos

of himself—he is posed in swim trunks at Antibes—designed perhaps to make Rupert jealous, or at the least to make him wish he too
might be on the Côte d'Azur. On another occasion he warned
Rupert that he had let his hair grow, the result being that "ton p'tit
copain looks like a little bit of all right." And of course from Oxford
to Cambridge he once sent *Poems,* dedicated to Rupert for all their
world to see. Its single poem in English was a madrigal that proposed, from behind prison bars, a paradise where "polyhymnia lov-
ingly dilutes / the richer alchemy of cambridge flutes."

The place Dwight would have liked to call his home was Spain.
"I absolutely ADORE *all* Spaniards," he enthused, "& the feeling
seems (tho one never really knows) to be mutual." But while Spain
was the country where Rupert discovered *Astragalus,* for Dwight it
was the country that confirmed his love of color. Rupert's descriptions of color could sometimes be technical. Dwight responded to
color as though it was not the metaphor but the body of all that was
potent, fertile, and promising in the world. There is no other way to
explain his paean to the Cazorla violet, *Viola cazorlensis,* which is
found in the Cazorla (caTHORla) mountains in Jaén. Granted, it
does not look like the violets in the backyard. It is a twiggy mound
from which rises a long stem topped by a flower of intense pink—a
description that would not go far enough for Dwight.

> Yet "pink," inadequate word, quite fails to describe the brilliance
> and anguish and venomous perfection of this violet, at sight of
> which the hardened botanist has been known to fall sobbing to
> his knees, as deeply moved as was the schoolgirl Bernadette
> when first confronted with the image of Our Lady. It is the color

of flags, of tragedy at mid-day, and of the bullfighter's satin thighs. It is at once delicate and garish, hopelessly sophisticated and the despair of aunts with taste.

Art critics use the term "colorist" to characterize certain artists, and the term, it appears, might be applied to certain botanists as well. Gertrude Jekyll, to cite the famous example, designed her gardens for both simultaneous and successive color contrast. She planted for the afterimage by which orange flowers, say, will appear more intensely colored if the brain adds to them the orange afterimage it has retained from nearby flowers of grayish blue. Dwight liked for this reason to plant *Tulipa hageri* 'Splendens,' a squat copper-centered tulip, beside the taller milk-blue *Iris pumila* 'Bride.' The effect, looking down from the pale-blue flag to the copper cup, was "ravishing," he said. A garden provides interactive color training, too; it corrects misperceptions. From the Spinney, Dwight reported to an absent Rupert that their *Dipcadi serotinum*, a relative of the grape hyacinth, was at last in flower. "The *Dipcadi* is an almost invisible shade of chamois, really quite extraordinary," he wrote. "I had imagined it to be a dull orange-brown. In fact, they're grey with an 'int of *fawn*." And beyond the garden, for both Rupert and Dwight, came the intensive practice of color perception in the field. From the triumphs, but more notably from the disappointments of collecting, the two young botanists learned how inaccurate the previous reports can be, and how fugitive color is—especially when measured by the exact days of the year, even exact hours, that the plants they sought would be in flower. Color had to be apprehended, to such a degree and with such consistent attention that Dwight

seemed sometimes to think and feel, if not to speak, in color. Surely
he came to associate color and language. Already in his Harrow
School notebooks he had listed twenty-four terms in French for
shades of red, seventeen for blue, eighteen for brown. The flowers of
Ramonda myconi, a fussy gesneriad from the Pyrenees, he thought

Flower walk at the Spinney

"mauve as a Firbank metaphor," while those of *Omphalodes luciliae,* an uncommon cousin of the blue-eyed Mary, were "milk-blue-and-pink and rather vacant, like the eyes of the rich." When the two men encountered *Delphinium armeniacum* in northern California, etymologist Dwight criticized its name by noting that the species had never been nearer to Armenia than he had. It was named by an earlier botanist for the color of its flowers, "which," observed Dwight, "he compares with that of the apricot *(Prunus armeniaca),* though to my eye they are plain orange. Perhaps he had the tinned variety in mind."

Dwight had chosen his British over American citizenship by the time he met Jean Connolly, or he might have decided otherwise. Jean, unfretfully American, was born Jean Bakewell to a wealthy family (Bakewell glass) in Pittsburgh in 1910, arrived in Paris when she was eighteen, and met Cyril Connolly there the next year. On their honeymoon in Mallorca in 1930 the Connollys became friends with Tony Bower. He too was American; his mother was a friend of Dwight's grandmother in Connecticut, but he had lived in England since he was six, and Dwight knew him from childhood. Bower also attended Oxford, and it was he who introduced Jean to Rupert and Dwight. Connolly said of Jean that she had dark hair, green eyes, a "lovely boy's body," and an independent income. He loved her for all these attributes, if not, he freely confessed, in that order. Her income financed their flat in London and their travels abroad. Isherwood's description of Jean—the one in *Down There on a Visit* that offended Dwight—was that "she might just have emerged from a warm burrow under a hill." In his diary, Isherwood more successfully wrote, "She has a way of suddenly looking up at you, smiling in a wistful, shame-faced way, and exclaiming hoarsely, 'Hi-de-ho!' " Dwight put the Connollys into his own unpublished novel, *A Sunlit Scene* (it takes place partly at Antibes), where he portrayed Jean as having trouble with her weight, making her own clothes from patterns she took on faith from Firbank, and spoiling her husband with a misplaced maternal devotion. The reader may wonder how this portrait is kinder than Isherwood's; it has the fond custodial dismay that signals the people, and things, Dwight cared for most. He took a dismayed delight in Jean's dress, which, "whether in castle or café, never failed to be spectacularly unsuited to the occasion"; her habits, "dancing & so on till 3.0 a.m., with Jean at the end as lively as a cricket and me feeling like death"; and her sense of humor, "in whose retorts the tu quoque was apt to run hand-in-hand with the non sequitur." Her non sequiturs revealed laconic wit. In England after her honeymoon, Jean was asked what she thought of her new country. "I don't dislike England quite as much as my husband," she replied. "I haven't seen so much of it." She called Auden her "Uncle Wiz." Her approval was coveted; Constant Lambert played a new piece for her, and when she failed immediately to react he rose from the piano and rushed from the room in tears.

Jean moved in an entourage of young male couples that included Dwight and Rupert, Tony Bower and Cuthbert Worsley, Peter Watson and Denham Fouts, Brian Howard and Toni Altmann. "Drink, night life, tarts and Tonys," complained Connolly, who referred to the whole entourage as "Pansyhalla." Jean and her circle did not use the expression *avant-garde* (they were still the Bright Young People or, as Rupert said, Upper Bohemia), but they were inextricably part of the avant-garde in their day. They liked Picasso, Proust, and

Poulenc, favored in architecture the Baroque, admired Josephine Baker and jazz. Someone took a copy of Dwight's *Poems* to Cocteau, who responded *"Quel néuropathe!"*—a diagnosis that Rupert relayed to us with wicked relish (if not linguistic accuracy). In retrospect, Jean and her friends may seem driven, even credulous in their enthusiasm for whatever was newest in culture and the arts. When Gerald Heard published two books in 1931 to propose that evolution demanded an evolved human consciousness, Brian Howard called them "the most important that have ever been written since the Ice Age." Connolly mocked such enthusiasm, but he personified it. He simply inverted it, as an anxiety, in his conversation, his life, and finally in his book *The Unquiet Grave*, which offered the unforgiving formulation that "the true function of a writer is to produce a masterpiece and that no other task is of any consequence." Artists could extrapolate this expectation to their studios. Others turned to patronage. In Pansyhalla, a compelling example was set by Peter Watson, who joined with Connolly in 1939 to found *Horizon* and then financed that influential journal throughout its career. Until the war, Watson lived mostly in Paris; a portrait of Jean, by Man Ray, was in his apartment. In 1938 he subsidized the publication of a first book of poems by Charles Henri Ford, the young poet who was painter Pavel Tchelitchew's lover, and who, back in New York by 1940, would found a counterpart to *Horizon*, the trendier but likewise influential magazine *View*. I am getting ahead of the story. But it was *View* that brought John Bernard Myers from Buffalo to be its managing editor, and Myers who, as director of the Tibor de Nagy Gallery that Dwight himself sponsored, acted as impresario for a cast of painters and poets that seems to us, now, to typify the postwar New York scene. It adds perspective (it restores potential, too, I think) to discover how that scene was contingent on a trajectory that began in London and Paris, and to meet at critical points along the way the hi-de-ho of Jean Connolly. Said Dwight: "She knows absolutely everyone, it's amazing."

The annals of Upper Bohemia imply a world of sophistication and allure, but Dwight's blushing—"my famous gardenia-peony-gardenia trick," he called it—interfered with his presence in high society. Beginning with his mother and Horne, Dwight learned to consider himself a focus for the frustrated hopes of other people. In public he felt exposed, sometimes that he was being observed. In America, when he was required to visit Washington, D.C., to meet the United States senator whose influence would be needed to restore his citizenship, he was overwhelmed by the advance anxiety. "Meeting the Lord High Muckamuck of something or other, will be loads of fun," he wrote Rupert, "especially as I'm going thru one of my periods of agonizing self-consciousness when if I meet a squirrel's eye in the park I get all hot under the collar. I haven't ceased to blush since I arrived here, & the first 2 days were given over to suicidal melancholia." From this and similar accounts, it seems certain that Dwight was complaining of no ordinary moment's blush, but of a syndrome that is medically recognized today as severe facial blushing, or simply FB, in which an otherwise normal response of the sympathetic nervous system habitually cycles out of control so that embarrassment causes blushing, which causes embarrassment, which causes et cetera. People who have endured such episodes report a treasonous self-consciousness, disorientation, and panic—an experience so humiliating that fear of repeating it causes some to

devise strategies for remaining at home as much as possible throughout their lives. Severe blushing can be corrected today by an out-
patient surgery, endoscopic thoracic sympathectomy, that involves
severing or, more recently, blocking the overactive nerves in the
chest. Some doctors prescribe anti-anxiety agents or antidepres-
sants. Dwight in the fashion of his day tried psychoanalysis, but he
got better results with alcohol. After a reception at the home of his
uncle in Oyster Bay, he wrote, "Altemuses & Stuyvesants were two
a penny, so I helped myself to a fair number of rum cocktails to keep
my psychoses at arm's length— However it was all right, & no sudden crimsoning disgraced the Sussex branch of the family." Eventually his self-medication made him an alcoholic. At parties he could
be explosive. "Sat. night was quite fun," he reported to Rupert on
one occasion. "I got silly & covered myself in lipstick (*you* know
how I get) & wore Jean's earrings while dancing." He could also be
reckless. In New York he registered at the Plaza or at the Prince
George Hotel, in later years the Chelsea, and in behavior eerily reminiscent of his mother at the Waldorf he sometimes disappeared for
days at a time. Rupert believed he should have foreseen these events
from an incident that occurred while the two men were students
together in Grenoble. They had been out drinking ("experimen-
tally," said Rupert, as if to suggest oenological research), when
walking home late they came to a bridge that spans the Isère. They
were midway across when Dwight, weaving, disappeared suddenly
over the side. Horrified, Rupert rushed to the edge, only to find that
Dwight—he was athletic then, his notebooks contain schedules for
skiing and luge—was hanging by his fingertips, and had begun
already to hoist himself, laughing, back to the surface of the bridge.

Home at the Spinney, Dwight meant to create for Rupert and himself a securer venue for enjoying the avant-garde. Rupert remembered keenly the day in 1932—he was still twenty, Dwight was twenty-three—when they went to the Alex Reid & Lefevre Gallery, on King Street in London, to buy their first painting. Dwight had picked *Parrots in a Cage,* painted in 1927 by Christopher Wood, an artist who is not well known in the United States, but who, along with Paul Nash, is sometimes credited with bringing the flat forms and bold colors of modern European art to English painting. Certainly the Ballets Russes colors of *Parrots in a Cage*—pink, yellow, and blue, with accents of scarlet and green—would have brought sudden glamour to the dim interior of the Spinney. Surrealism, too, was appearing in England. Edward James, another Oxford contemporary with rich American forebears, supported Dalí for more than a year. Dwight's response was more prudent. He buried a boat in the garden, installed a tree painted gold in the drawing room, and kept as a pet that favorite Surrealist totem, the anteater, sensibly stuffed. But the way in which he most profoundly brought the avant-garde home was in the plants of the greenhouses, cliff house, and garden. If Rupert described their botanical preferences in terms that were characterological, or even moral, Dwight described them with barely concealed erotic glee. Central to his novel, *A Sunlit Scene,* is a botanist he called by Rupert's middle name, which of course was Charles.

Charles had noticed, ever since he entered their little world at the age of fourteen, how the more muscular and extroverted the gardener, the more fragile the bloom that took his fancy. On the other hand a few friends and he, who constituted a small but shrill minority in horticultural circles and could never be classified as anything but hopeless *finocchi,* definitely preferred the thorny and the ligneous, not to mention the dome, the cushion and the coat of fur. Ephemeral petals gave him, as he put it, "the creeps."

It must verge on paradox to propose bringing the avant-garde home. But Dwight's experience with Rupert at the advance edge of botany and horticulture was indisputable, and it endured for him as the inmost standard of artistic response throughout his career. When he turned from the garden to art, Dwight opened himself to a contradiction between the avant-garde in *botany,* which demands attention to the detailed and local, and the avant-garde in *art,* which, first as Surrealism and later as Abstract Expressionism, largely rejected the observed detail in favor of the spontaneous and marvelous, the accidental, and the gestural. When he turned from the garden to his friends who were preoccupied by the latest in politics or economics, he encountered systems of discourse and self-regard that disdained to notice the natural world at all. In *A Sunlit Scene* he related a confrontation that had developed with the Connollys while he and Rupert were discussing a question of horticulture, namely, whether *Vella pseudocytisus* might be grown in loam as well as radiolarian chert. Connolly cut the discussion short, reminding Dwight haughtily that in polite society one does not talk shop. Dwight tried to sound haughty in turn—but mostly he sounds to me hurt—when he responded, "I fail to see why the natural sciences as a subject of conversation should be any more out of place than, say, the subject of pragmatism. The *New Statesman* (to which you contribute so

Greenhouse at the Spinney

brilliantly) is perhaps more lucid than the average nurseryman's cat-alogue, and better printed on the whole, but the substance of its pages is every whit as specialized." Connolly, in Mallorca on honeymoon with Jean, gathered material for *The Rock Pool*, his novel of a receding, doomed society. Dwight, in Mallorca with Rupert, made maps to show where they had found *Centaurea balearica* (Mallorca is one of the Balearic Isles). When *A List of Plants Cultivated or Native at The Spinney* was published in 1939, Dwight was afraid their plants would not seem rare enough. But after Noel Sandwith spent a weekend alone at the Spinney, he was reassured by a report of the older botanist's reaction. "The cliff-house almost sent Noel out of his mind," he wrote to Rupert happily. "It is from all accounts the biggest thing ever in English horticulture."

By the time they learned of Sandwith's visit to the Spinney, Rupert and Dwight were in the United States. The list of émigrés who left Europe for America during these years is long and distinguished, and reflecting on those who failed to make that list we sometimes wonder why they didn't get out in time. It is odd if we wonder of others, how dare they leave. In 1940, during the autumn height of the Blitz, Stephen Spender published an open letter to Christopher Isherwood in the *New Statesman*. "You can't escape," wrote Spender. "If you try to do so, you are simply putting the clock back for yourself: using your freedom of movement to enable yourself to live still in pre-Munich England." Isherwood, who left long before the Blitz, was annoyed. So was Dwight. "It takes in all of us refugees," he complained to Rupert, while implying that there was more than politics at issue. "I shall always think of the Spenders henceforth as Delight and Inez— How bitter they are, and no wonder." Earlier, Spender in fact urged Isherwood to emigrate to America in search of refuge for his German lover, Heinz Neddermeyer. In Dwight's circle of friends, Brian Howard likewise had a German lover, Toni Altmann. After Hitler was named chancellor, Isherwood spent the next four years, Howard the next seven, each contending with a succession of revoked visas, expired passports, and sudden deportations in their continuing efforts to find asylum or new citizenship for Neddermeyer and Altmann, respectively, and so prevent their eventual repatriation and arrest in Germany. Both Englishmen tried to get their lovers into England, and both were refused on moral grounds. Erika Mann married Auden and became a British subject overnight. When Neddermeyer was arrested in Paris, it was Tony Bower who went to rescue him. Isherwood joined them in Luxembourg, but from there Neddermeyer was expelled into Germany, where he was arrested, charged with reciprocal onanism ("in fourteen foreign countries and in the German Reich," remembered Isherwood), found guilty, and sentenced to successive terms in prison, at hard labor, and in the army. Brian Howard's efforts on behalf of Toni Altmann were likewise frustrated at the end. Howard was an early and outspoken antifascist—the first Englishman to understand the Nazi threat, claimed Erika Mann—who, when asked to describe his plans for returning to serve England, had responded in language of persuasive spontaneity: "So—really, I have no plans, except to do my best for Toni." Altmann was interned by the French at Toulon in September 1939, then moved to Le Mans, where Howard lost track of him. Howard remained in France trying to locate his lover until, in June the following year, he escaped on a coal freighter that departed Cannes the day before the Germans arrived in Marseilles.

The stories of forced separation in fascist Europe are grimly familiar. I recount these of Neddermeyer and Altmann because they were the ones known at the time to Dwight, and because Dwight, too, had no plans, except to do his best for Rupert. Although Dwight may have felt in England that he did not truly belong, it was Rupert who had drawn the punishing attention of the state. At Cambridge, while Dwight was sending him photos from Antibes, Rupert was having an affair with a German journalist, twenty-two years his senior, whose name was Jakob Altmaier. A prominent social democrat, Altmaier had been editor of the *Frankfurter Zeitung*, Berlin correspondent for the Manchester *Guardian*, and foreign correspon-

Altmaier in Paris

dent for an association of social democratic presses. He worked out
of Belgrade, then Paris, where he met Dwight, and finally London,
where he fell in love with Rupert. It would appear that his journal-
ism was effective, because he incurred the displeasure of the British
government, which wanted him out of England, or of the German
government, which wanted him discredited, or maybe both. Whatever the motives, they were sufficient in 1932 for British police to
enter Rupert's rooms and locate, without much difficulty, the letters
from Altmaier that Rupert had never imagined he had to hide.
Rupert was sent down (briefly, it must have been, since he took his
degree that same year), but Altmaier was deported to Germany and
Rupert never heard from him again. Altmaier was Jewish, a social-
ist, and caught having an affair with a younger man; he was not
likely to survive the National Socialist regime. Rupert believed, for
the rest of his life, that he had been used by his own country to murder someone he loved. Isherwood wrote that when England rejected
Neddermeyer it became for him, in that instant, "the land of the
Others." Rupert's response was private but quite as intense. He
never saved letters again. This is why Frank and I were surprised
(we were astonished, really) to see his letters from Dwight, whose
ashes he could not claim, whose letters he could not throw away.
During the years leading up to the war it was possible to conceive of
a Britain that might be fascist or communist, in neither of which
Rupert and Dwight as a couple should expect to be welcome for
very long. Dwight's comments, made during the Phony War that
preceded the fall of France, do not seem politic, and surely were not
meant to be, but they are typically mocking and center typically
on his garden refuge. "My boring jeremiads regarding the fate of

that tight little, bright little jewel set in a silver sea seem to be confirmed by to-day's papers. If only the Huns would walk in & con-
quer the goddam country, we might be able to go back soon & settle
down again, even if it meant saluting the gardener or drinking beer
for breakfast."

A FTER FRANK AND I GOT A CAR we sometimes brought Rupert from the Botanical Garden to our apartment in Chelsea, which meant traveling down the Henry Hudson Parkway and the West Side Highway. On these excursions, especially during the return trip at night with the lights of Manhattan on one side and the dark width of the Hudson below us on the other, Rupert liked to recall the excitement he and Dwight felt in 1939, when, accustomed instead to the deep lanes of Sussex, they first burst free of cross-traffic and ascended the elevated highway (it had been completed to West Seventy-second Street only three years before) to soar at high speed between the city and the river. Rupert continued west to hunt for plants, but Dwight stayed behind for remedial American dentistry. Trapped in a dentist's chair two hours every other morning for six weeks, he realized, even so, that he too was on one of life's adventures. "I sweep through New York like a prophylactic typhoon," he wrote to Rupert. He treated his enforced sojourn, together with the presence in the city of many refugees recently arrived from Poland, as the occasion to learn Polish—a feat he accomplished, according to Rupert, in the same six weeks he was seeing the dentist. Some credit for this achievement was due perhaps to his tutor, Stephanie Wanatowicz. "She's without any exception," reported Dwight, "the most *frightful* woman I've ever met." Meanwhile he had rented an apartment at 206 West Thirteenth Street, in

Greenwich Village, and set out to master the customs of the country. In short order he discovered the notorious instant familiarity, and corresponding expectations, of the Americans. "I'm setting my—er—cap at one of the waiters in the Troc, but no progress so far," he complained. "They're all venal in that joint, from the manager downward, but the *approach* is so difficult in God's country. I long to say just '$20,' but that's impossible for some extraordinary reason." One had to pretend, he continued in exasperation, to be "doing it all for 'love'—My God, Americans don't know what that word means—." In Hollywood, where the two men were reunited a few weeks later, he encountered the peculiarities of the country in what seemed yet higher relief. At first he reacted with disdain. "Our opinion of America," he observed to Rupert, "seems to coincide with that of a prejudiced Russian Communist." Soon their circle of expatriate friends had expanded to include several who found work, as did Isherwood, in the motion-picture industry. Especially close to Dwight were Keith Winter, a novelist, playwright, and Oxford classmate who worked as a screenwriter on Joan Crawford movies (he wrote the screenplay for *Above Suspicion*), and Richard Kitchin, a set artist who painted the Surrealist portrait of Dwight that hung in Rupert's bedroom. Thanks in part to these contacts, Dwight developed, as Rupert demonstrably did not, a fascination with the movies that began to seem almost American in outline. From a house they rented in 1940, he discovered they could look down with binoculars on neighbor Cary Grant. "Noel Coward's staying with our Cary, a ce qu'il paraît, so that's one question settled," he announced. He quickly showed promise as a critic, whether of the stars (Garbo's secret was her "sepulchritude"), the studios (*Fantasia*

Rupert near Malibu

was "the Hollywood Blvd. gift shop en apothéose"), or the directors ("Capra *stinks,* really"). When Rupert by chance shared a train ride with Gary Cooper, and found him talkative, it was Dwight who was the most delighted. "Contacting the Cooper must have been quite a thrill," he ventured. "Wouldn't the over-wrought little pansies back in Blighty be jealous if they knew?"

But before all other attractions in America came the plants. Botanists who look back with admiration on Rupert's career should be interested to know it was Dwight, of the two men, who first appeared at the New York Botanical Garden. There, during the weeks of his dental overhaul and Polish lessons, he searched through the specimens in the herbarium to determine which locations to visit when he too was able to travel west. "Honey, your letter was heaven," he wrote to Rupert, who was then still in New Mexico. "And am I jealous. The thought of canyons blazing with canary entonnoirs, bignoniaceous megaphones & citron acousticons, etc. is almost too much, & the temptation is to fly out there before they fade." Clearly this was no moment's impulse. Given the pitch of Dwight's impatience, it seems obvious that a botanical project had been foreseen, and likely that an expedition from England had long been planned. "I am wondering what you are doing," wrote Sandwith to Rupert in the tone of a somewhat bossy mentor, "and shall be dismayed if you turn to ecology." The nurseryman Walter Ingwersen at the same time was writing to Dwight: "I hope you will have good herbarium hunting & discover many new plants to bear your name." By relating his research in the herbarium to the season (it was late in November), Dwight determined to stop on his way west at Alpine, Texas, where he might find an orange-flowered Buddleia, *Buddleia marrubiifolia,* and its white relative, *B. scordioides.* His first day there he traveled 140 miles south of Alpine in search of the orange species, only to conclude he was going in the wrong direction because he was descending in altitude and finding mainly ocotillos. Besides, he had discovered the white Buddleia almost the moment he stepped off the train, and it, growing in the dumps and

back alleys of the town, was "a little horror." The town had character of its own.

Alpine is really a hellish little burg, when all is said and done.
Everyone gets up at 6 a.m., trains shunt and scream all night like
honeymoon couples, & altogether there is more fracas than on
28th Street. The men don't seem to have heard of sex, & their
facial expression is so bottomlessly dumb that they cease even to
be attractive— (Tho I must say . . . the way these huge creatures
mince about on high-heels is v. exciting, & they all have hair up
to their throats, every single one, & forearms like gorillas.)

Disappointed, in the Buddleia at least, Dwight contacted botanist
Omar Sperry at Sul Ross State Teachers College, and on Sperry's
recommendation he spent the next day in the Chisos Mountains.
The advice was well timed. "Bergdorf Goodman had been to the
Chisos a few weeks ago," he reported to Rupert, "putting finishing
touches on the various ensembles, & decreeing, in a tiny but powerful voice, that pillar-box and violet were the only colors you could
reasonably be seen in." The pillar-box, or scarlet, was provided by a
Salvia, a *Gilia,* a startling *Houstonia,* and a *Drymaria.* The violet
was courtesy of *Salazaria* and *Leucophyllum violaceum.* As in Spain,
Dwight was being seduced by a climate of allusive sex and color,
and, as with the Cazorla violet, he associated his surrender with a
contravention of good color taste. Breaking the lines of a letter into
free verse, he celebrated his arrival in the American Southwest,
where "the lilac evening / Touches, regardless of the laws of taste,
/ The coffee-colored grass, the crimson rocks." That day in the

Chisos he collected five hundred seeds of the *Houstonia*. He sent them the next morning to Player, his head gardener at the Spinney.

When Dwight and Rupert left the Spinney they had expected the Connollys to arrive there behind them. Jean at that time was living in Paris, while her husband in England pursued his affair with a

Dwight in the desert

younger woman. Connolly blamed his marital difficulties on Jean's friends in Pansyhalla. "*WE* have still done nothing," he complained, "we have talked, quarrelled, drunk and laughed a great deal, and made love—but constructed nothing and not even really helped our friends—our only creations, Tony Bower and Nigel Richards." Bower believed, as did Dwight, that the separation (they called it "the parturition") had more to do with Connolly's being the child to Jean. When she returned to England because of the war, it appeared that the marriage might be salvaged after all. Dwight had offered the Spinney, but Jean thought better of it. "The Connollys *haven't* showed up," he reported to Rupert. Instead she went biking near Trewyn with Peter Watson's lover, Denham Fouts, proceeded with him to Ireland, and from there the two departed for New York. Fouts was to be entrusted in America with Watson's five-by-four-foot Picasso, *Girl Reading at a Table*, which had been on view in the Picasso retrospective at the Museum of Modern Art. (Dwight saw this show and exclaimed, "*Mój Boże*, can he paint!") Fouts continued south to visit his family in Florida, where Jean planned to join him for a drive cross-country to California. She first had an errand to accomplish on behalf of Connolly, who had asked her to contact a prospective contributor to *Horizon* and encourage him to submit material. This was Clement Greenberg, an employee then of the U.S. Customs Service, whose now famous essay "Avant-Garde and Kitsch" had impressed Connolly when it appeared the previous year in *Partisan Review*. Jean didn't telephone; she simply knocked at Greenberg's door. In his letters to Harold Lazarus, Greenberg described the resulting affair. "What pushing & pulling," he wrote, "what flipping & flamming, what jumbling & tumbling, rummying

& tummying, fricking & fracking, whipping & whacking." To all this activity, a bonus was Jean's independent income of four hundred dollars a month. Plus, as Dwight had pointed out, she knew absolutely everyone. "She knows all the English writers," Greenberg told Lazarus, "not to speak of lords & ladies, high ministers of state and so forth—from all of which I receive a thrill." Best of all, "better than the copulation," he could talk to her about anything; she read French poetry and had "inevitable taste in literature & in pictures, especially in pictures." Fouts, looing patience, started for California by himself. Jean caught up with him in Dallas, and in Los Angeles they joined their refugee friends, who included, by this time, Tony Bower. The interlude that followed was to inspire the "Paul" chapter in *Down There on a Visit*. Jean became "Ruthie," Fouts is "Paul," Bower is "Ronnie," and Gerald Heard is "Augustus Parr." Dwight, so far as I can tell, does not appear in the book. He shows up briefly on January 1, 1941, in Isherwood's *Diaries*. That spring, when he traveled to New York to meet his American relatives, Jean had returned there already. "She has a sealskin coat now & doesn't look too bad," he reported to Rupert, "although her hair is *just* the same." She had settled in with a friend at 140 East Seventy-second Street. "Denham came up from Pennsylvania for a coupla nights," wrote Dwight, "looking heavier & more attractive, to spread sweetness and blight at a party at Jean's. You simply trip up over authors at 72nd St, most of them tearing poor little Carson McCullers to bits with faultless English accents."

The excitement of life in the new world might seem to confirm that Rupert and Dwight were right to continue their exile. The Blitz, however, had stunned them both; no one thought England would be destroyed. The London residence of Rupert's maternal grandfather was at 40 Gloucester Square, just north of Hyde Park in Paddington. While Dwight's great-grandfather was busy being a robber baron, Rupert's great-grandfather Sir James Ingham was the chief magistrate, sitting at Bow Street, in London. The house on Gloucester Square was his, and the chandelier in its stairway was Rupert's earliest memory of urban splendor. This house was oblit-erated. Noel Sandwith wrote to say that his consignment of rare plants from then British Guiana was destroyed by the raids on the London docks, and his oldest friend killed in a flat near Sloane Square. Even the gardens at the Spinney were bombed. Early in 1941 the two men considered a return to England. Sandwith, in his role as bossy mentor, responded at once. "Meanwhile, the idea of an arrival at Kew this fall! If you did, Jingling in Uniform or not, it would have the effect of the Four Feathers: I should have to rush off for sure to 'do something.' I said five years, didn't I? And the new Phacelias, etc., are *much* more important, and a sound investment for the future." Dwight, moreover, was beginning to like America: a change of heart that becomes complex when considered in con-text. Most of his friends, unlike Waugh and the other acquaintances on the bookshelf, were socialist or communist in politics. Brian Howard, writing in the *New Statesman* (Dwight called it "the parish magazine"), had praised the arguments made by Spender in *Forward from Liberalism* and by John Strachey in *Why You Should Be a Social-ist;* the latter was a best-seller in Britain the year it appeared. In France, the Surrealists André Breton and Paul Éluard had issued a manifesto that called on revolutionary intellectuals to join in "a vast composition of forces, disciplined, fanatical, capable of expressing, when the time comes, a pitiless authority." In Spain, of course, a pitiless authority soon controlled. When Dwight described himself in an article for the *Quarterly Bulletin* as "one who has been exiled far too long from the least understood and most arrogantly beautiful country in Europe," the country he had in mind was Spain. At the same time he and Rupert expressed contempt for the contemporaries they suspected of passing intelligence to the Soviet Union. When Anthony Blunt was exposed years later by Margaret Thatcher, Rupert wondered how anyone could be surprised. In the month following Jean's literary party on Seventy-second Street, Dwight wrote to Rupert that he was sure he loathed himself, his friends, and all Americans. But he went on to express an attitude very much the opposite of the nostalgia that became a recourse, say, of *Brideshead Revisited,* and he expressed it not in political terms but in color. "Yet in spite of going round hating everybody, I *am* very glad to be in America. Europe appears more & more impossible, & any new dawn that's hanging around is, as far as I'm concerned, hued in the exquisite Technicolor horizons of America. Nostalgia's coffin, as you call it, has left the morgue & is now buried deep in the prim & curious soil, the sexy glebe, of this gobby, gooey, heart-warming, nauseous, new & unspeakable A-M-E-R-I-C-A——."

There was a decided, inspirational glamour to the story of Rupert taking Jim Grimes in Paris to see where Proust had lived. In New York, he took Frank to see where Clement Greenberg lived. This was at 248 West Eleventh Street, the apartment where Greenberg resided just after the war. Earlier he lived at 50 Greenwich

Avenue, later 90 Bank Street, all in the same section of the Village not far from Dwight's own first address. It was Jean, in the autumn of 1941, who found the Greenwich Avenue apartment, furnished it, cooked there, and sometimes paid the rent. Greenberg, who died in 1994, was once widely attacked for his influence as an art critic, especially as exercised in the period after 1960 when he moved uptown and became identified with the abstract style known as Color Field painting. Yet his essay "Avant-Garde and Kitsch" makes lively reading even now. In its historical moment it must have been compelling. Most exciting was the implication, unmistakable beyond the details of the essay's argument, that if you can define the avant-garde then you must *be* the avant-garde. Greenberg, in other words, offered in America the same sense of cultural quest that Connolly represented in England. Jean loved and tended to them both, each at the instant he was emerging but before he had achieved success—a parallel that lends substance to Dwight's opinion that she mothered her boyfriends. Another parallel was that Greenberg, too, found Jean's male friends to be an inconvenience. "I want to Blitzkrieg the cities of the plain," he confided to Lazarus. Apparently he made an exception for Rupert and Dwight. The four of them—Dwight was the oldest at thirty-three, Clem thirty-two, Jean thirty-one, and Rupert thirty—met for the first time on the Saturday evening of January 31, 1942, for dinner at Voisin, a restaurant that had various addresses in the East Sixties near Park Avenue, and where, thought Dwight, "the food and décor are the best in town." It was the winter following the discovery of *Cymopterus ripleyi*. At the Museum of Modern Art, the attraction, just closed, had been the dual exhibit of Dalí and Miró. Coming up in March at the Pierre Matisse Gallery was a look at "Artists in Exile": Surrealists, Cubists, and neo-Romantics. The Valentine Gallery was to show Max Ernst that month, while the magazine *View* devoted its spring issue entirely to Ernst as well. Dwight saved his copies of *View*, and it is something of a surprise to be looking through them now and suddenly realize that this magazine's enthusiasms are still—after more than fifty years—enthusiasms today: Duchamp, *Hebdomeros*, Raymond Roussel, Florine Stettheimer, John Cage, Henri Michaux. This is not what we might call a "Greenbergian" list. Greenberg in fact was critical of *View;* it represented for him a certain established taste, against which a true avant-garde would have to rebel. He was to begin his column at the *Nation* only that spring, but in conversation he was testing ideas of great interest to Dwight. Color should be structural, Greenberg thought. Klee's color was atmospheric, while Miró used pure hue to build the picture. "Klee, at least, and Picasso too, need a little deflating," he insisted. "Miró needs to be praised." These were heady opinions to trade over dinner at Voisin. On other evenings the foursome ate and argued at Chambord, a famous restaurant located on Third Avenue under the El, and "even more expensive than Chasen's," according to Dwight, who, needless to say, picked up the tab. Greenberg, writing to Lazarus, had a happy explanation for his new friend's generosity: "He goes for heterosexual middle-aged men and thinks I'm the most attractive thing on earth." Dwight, being called on regularly to console the young critic during the turbulent affair with Jean, recorded meanwhile an impression of his own. He put Greenberg, too, into *A Sunlit Scene.*

His "absurd hair" was like a "tonsure," wrote Dwight. "Even in a normal state he bore a marked resemblance to a Wyandotte; grief merely accentuated the resemblance."

A decade later Dwight offered in his poem, *Spring Catalogue,* a confession that deserves also to be remembered. He and Rupert were fond of *Centaurea clementei,* a species that grows on the cliffs at Grazalema in Spain and at Beni Hosmar in Morocco. A vernacular name for this plant is sweet sultan, while its Latin epithet (still capitalized in those days as *Clementei*) contains obviously the name *Clem.* Wrote Dwight: "At Clem, sweet sultan, I can gaze / For hours when in the mood."

Resident aliens in the United States could be drafted, of course, and both Dwight and Rupert were registered with Local Board No. 244 in Santa Monica. Rupert's notice came first, and at eight-thirty on the Wednesday morning of March 31, 1943, he presented himself at Induction Station No. 2, 406 South Main Street in Los Angeles, to be inducted into the United States Army. Denham Fouts was by this time a conscientious objector at San Dimas Civilian Public Service Camp in Glendale, California. Tony Bower had completed his military service, but because of the new draft laws passed after Pearl Harbor he was summoned back to the army and actually forced to serve twice. Greenberg, who regarded Bower's departure as a clearing of the air, was himself drafted into the Army Air Force. "Of course it's awful," he informed Lazarus. "Words cannot say the miseries of the first week." Dwight's plan was to rely on his facility in eastern European languages to secure a position that would prevent his being sent overseas. "I braved the terrors & Gestapo-like officials of the Public Library twice last week," he reported to

Rupert, "as they have my beloved Adamescu Rumanian dictionary." He wrote an article, "Some Observations on the Polish Language," that was published, just prior to Rupert's own induction
date, in the Polish-American newspaper *Gwiazda Polarna*. Eventually he decided to concentrate on Russian. "If you know Russian,
I've been told it's a cinch getting a soft job," he observed, "so I've
dropped Magyar as superfluous." Many men were deferred from
service altogether. Some deferments seem inevitable, as when Jackson Pollock was classified unfit for psychological reasons. Others
seem a matter of privilege and timing. John Cage was deferred not
by chance but by favor of an assignment as a Manhattan library
assistant to his father, who was employed in nearby New Jersey
on military research. If Rupert had a strategy, Frank and I never
learned of it. At the induction center in Los Angeles he replied hon-
estly during the examination that he was attracted to other men, and
he was rejected. Auden had a similar experience, which he regarded
apparently as a criticism of himself and of society. Rupert, in this as
in other intersections with the state, seemed never to draw a moral;
he continued, as soon as possible, his lifetime objective of studying
plants. That spring he and Dwight explored in a wide arc through
the Southwest, collecting three new species along the way. In the
summer they moved to Wappingers Falls. Dwight, like Isherwood,
was never drafted. By the end of that year he was thirty-five, Isherwood thirty-nine. Greenberg, meanwhile, was assigned to a squadron that was soon to be sent overseas to repair recently captured
enemy airfields. It does seem a little incongruous, given this critic's eventual demonization as dictator of the art world, to find
in Dwight's diary the prosaic and humanizing address, T. F. C.

Clement Greenberg, 321st Squadron, Kellogg Field, Battle Creek, Mich. Greenberg found it a *de*humanizing address. "Battle Creek is a hell hole of G.I. misery," he wrote to Lazarus. "There's nothing within 200 miles that can induce me to go on living." Jean, who went there to visit him, didn't like it either. (Because I was born in Battle Creek, but only after Jean and Clem had left, I am in no position to disagree with them.) Shortly after the visit, Greenberg was discharged from the army on the recommendation of the camp psychiatrist. When he returned to New York that September he discovered that Jean was involved already with Guggenheim's ex-husband Laurence Vail. To Lazarus he maintained that he didn't miss her at all, but he did miss "her milieu." In Dwight's diary the next month it says, "Call Clem."

Jean Connolly was the first critic to earn Jackson Pollock's gratitude. While Greenberg was in the army she had taken his column at the *Nation* to protect his position until he returned. She was perhaps in more danger than he was. On one occasion she was insulted at a party by another critic who resented her role and would have liked to have the column for himself. "He called Jeanie a cunt, whore, etc.," related Greenberg, "and Jeanie threatened to kick him in the balls if he didn't shut up. The next day he claimed that she actually had done so." If Jean's responses at parties were blunt and strategic, her reviews were brief and likewise to the point. They are also historic; she mentioned the unknown Jackson Pollock—and spelled it Pollack—twice. First she commended the collage he made for a group show at Art of This Century in April 1943. Next she remarked on the painting (it was *Stenographic Figure;* she didn't name it) which he entered in that gallery's juried show the following month. This

Jean Connolly at the Falls

painting, she wrote, "made the jury starry-eyed." Rupert thought
Jean was the first ever to mention Pollock's name in print, but there
is a passing reference by James Lane one year earlier in *Art News*.
Jean was indeed the first to earn the painter's gratitude. "Things
really broke with the showing of that painting," Pollock wrote to his
brother. "I had a pretty good mention in the *Nation*——." As a result,
it was Jean who introduced Dwight to Pollock's work, and then to
Pollock and Krasner themselves. Likewise it was Jean who brought
Rupert and Dwight to Peggy Guggenheim's duplex apartment for
dinner, at seven-thirty on Tuesday, September 21, in that same busy
1943. Guggenheim, in her once-scandalous memoir, *Out of This
Century*, portrayed Jean as "Joan Flarity." On the subject of Jean's
alcoholic habits, she was blunt in the book. She could be blunt in
person too. "Our relationship," Dwight wrote to the biographer
Virginia Dortch, "was perhaps initiated by the fact that Peggy
always adored anyone with a British accent, and marred by the fact
that she has an unnerving habit (which I'm sure you're aware of) of
blurting out home truths about one to one's face. I found her
Bohemianism endearing, and vice versa—on the whole." Guggenheim gave Dwight a Max Ernst; she persuaded him to buy a Dalí, a
Tanguy, three Cornell boxes, and five of Laurence Vail's collage-
covered bottles, but she did not approve of the Gottlieb pictograph
gouache that he got from dealer Howard Putzel in time for the first
Christmas with Rupert at Wappingers Falls. There can be no question of her influence. And yet the painters whose work soon domi-
nated on the farmhouse walls were the two Dwight came to know
through Greenberg and Jean Connolly: Miró and Pollock. By the
spring of 1945, Greenberg was calling Pollock the greatest painter

since Miró, and he remarked in the *Nation* that "Those who find his oils overpowering are advised to approach him through his gouaches." Dwight promptly bought four gouaches, the first of which, *Drawing, c. 1943–45,* became the most widely reproduced artwork that he owned. The best reproduction is at page 83 of Bryan Robertson, *Jackson Pollock.* Another is at page 60 of Bernice Rose, *Jackson Pollock: Works on Paper,* where it is called *Untitled (1946),* having been mysteriously renamed by the Museum of Modern Art. The poet Richard Howard, who was a close friend of Lee Krasner in the years following Pollock's death, recalled for me once that Dwight was mentioned frequently in her conversation and added, "He was a figure of a certain kind of glamour and resource for her." By January 1950, Dwight owned seven Pollocks and seven Mirós. The cost of his art collection was exaggerated, however, by his friends. The two Miró "Constellations" were seven hundred dollars each from Pierre Matisse. When Miró made his first visit to the United States, in 1947, he invited Dwight and Rupert to meet him in New York. Dwight greeted him with a poem, "En regardant 'Le lever du soleil' de Joan Miró," which he wrote for the occasion in Catalan. While Rupert compared Miró to Mozart, Dwight had a more visual appreciation. "His art, I suppose, represents the triumph of the potato over the apple—."

The affair between Dwight and Peggy Guggenheim was an "opera booth" romance, according to John Myers in his memoirs. Dwight remembered it differently. Queried by biographer Dortch, he responded, "We were even 'engaged' at one time, if memory serves me correctly." He put Guggenheim into *A Sunlit Scene* as the unmistakably named "Cora Shadequarter," and the sting in his por-

trayal of her there suggests that more than an opera booth had been
involved. "Fleetingly," he writes, "I brushed with my lips the tan-
gerine network of her forehead." Rupert observed carefully of
Peggy and Dwight that "their friendship was based on a shared
delight in being Shocking and Unconventional, to the point of cru-
elty, which was fashionable in Upper Bohemia of that era." Dwight
clearly had reason to believe that the affair was Unconventional,
and just as clearly he was surprised when the unconventional did not
extend to the cabdriver he brought home one evening to Guggenheim's apartment on East Sixty-first Street. He had been helping to
prepare the Christmas show of gouaches—Guggenheim thought
gouaches were more marketable at the holidays than oils—and he
was staying with her downstairs in the duplex. Dwight frequently
helped to hang shows at Art of This Century, which partly explains
why Rupert was annoyed when later he would not help to hang his
own. He even transported paintings between the gallery, at 30 West
Fifty-seventh Street above a grocery store, and the framers, fashionable Braxton's on East Fifty-eighth Street. Conceivably he did
escort Guggenheim to the opera, although private events would
seem more likely. On the Friday evening of December 14, 1945, he
took Guggenheim to a party, fled early by himself, and on his return
to the duplex hailed a cab whose driver proved so worthy of attention that his name is recorded in Dwight's pocket diary: "Henry
Lessner, *chauffeur de taxi.*" Considering the string of private symbols that follows directly after this name, I can only conclude that
Dwight and Henry, when Miss Guggenheim found them, could not
possibly have been asleep. The next morning Dwight was a registered guest at the Prince George Hotel. On Sunday he attended a

party at Guggenheim's apartment, on Tuesday he sent her caviar, and on Wednesday he went home to Wappingers Falls. His infraction, he claimed later, was not getting caught in bed with a man, it was getting caught in bed with a *chauffeur*. The plot of *A Sunlit Scene*—to the extent this Firbankian exercise has a plot—is to trick Cora Shade-quarter into sleeping with someone she believes to be a handsome poet, but who in truth is a handsome chauffeur. "Can't you just *see* Cora's face when he tells her?" remarks the character Charles. "My God, she hasn't slept with anything but a guaranteed Grade-A intellectual in her whole life." He admits to harboring resentment, and yet he wonders why. " 'No one at any rate can accuse me of being jealous!' he thought, remembering the long line of rotund and skinny quill-pushers, daubers and just plain phonies who at one time or another had sheepishly accepted the hospitality of her bed."

Dwight was indeed jealous, however, when Rupert two years earlier had begun a new romance of his own. In Manhattan one autumn midnight in 1943, Rupert met Willard Maas, the poet and filmmaker who had recently completed a film that has since become a classic of early avant-garde cinema. This was *Geography of the Body*, a ten-minute, 16 mm close-up exploration of nude topographies which was unprecedented for its day. Maas made the film with the considerable help of his wife, Marie Menken (theirs are the bodies), and he matched it to the words of a poem by their friend George Barker. Maas's own first book of poems, *The Fire Testament*, was published by the Alcestis Press when he was only twenty-four. By the time Rupert met him, Maas, now thirty-two, had been drafted; he was home on leave from Camp Crowder, Missouri. Rupert was innocent in those days of literary personalities, and perhaps he was hard of hearing already as well, because he believed for a week that he was having an affair with a writer named *Ngaio Marsh*. Both members of the household at Wappingers Falls were confused by the Western Union telegram that arrived, care of H. D. Ripley, signed I L U WILLARD. Maas called Rupert "the boy prince," and from Camp Crowder he sent weepy letters and neo-Romantic poems in the manner of Barker. "Dwight seems surely to have overcome his objections to Pvt. Willard Maas," wrote Sandwith more than a year after the surprise telegram. Dwight had not. Among his own unpublished poems I found an acrostic sonnet, PVT WILLARD MAAS, which chronicles the progress of a spiro-

Willard Maas and Rupert at the Falls

chete. Maas had brought syphilis back from Camp Crowder, and it made its way to Wappingers Falls. The treatment, as penicillin was not yet widely available, required a series of inconvenient and painful injections with an arsenic compound that had to be administered with precision over a period of six months. Dwight's friend Francis Turville-Petre, an archaeologist who was "The Fronny" of Auden's lost play by that name, as well as the character "Ambrose" in Isherwood's *Down There on a Visit,* also contracted syphilis, but his case was not properly treated because he was unwilling to stay in one place for the injections. Rupert was not willing to stay in one place either; it was soon spring in the West and there were plants to collect. He and Dwight departed in February 1944 by train for California. Dwight noted his preparations in the pocket diary: dinner with Guggenheim, dinner at the Crémaillère with Jean, and "bottle for train!" In San Francisco, Rupert delivered "Pugillus Astragalorum Alter" (this was the paper that announced his intention to revise *Astragalus*) at the California Academy of Sciences. Moving north into Oregon and Idaho, then south through Nevada, the two men discovered in each state a new species *(Astragalus sterilis, Physaria conformis, Lesquerella barnebyi),* while all along the way they kept an eye out for the local doctors before whom Rupert would appear, unannounced, to request his injections. "They regarded me as a depraved creature!" he told us merrily. He himself regarded his condition as an inconvenience to be managed—if it rains you take a raincoat, if you contract syphilis you inject arsenic—in the best interest of a life's objectives. When he was diagnosed at seventy-seven with the adult-onset diabetes that began to age him, Rupert adapted to this necessity too. "You may feel the world is unjust," he once wrote to Frank and me, "but that is a fact of life, guilt is masochism."

Only the twin energies of youth and devotion can explain how Rupert and Dwight were able to balance the demands of Upper Bohemia and botany while they explored across the immense distance of desert and mountain in search of plants. In fact, they were aware of their transitory opportunity. To his readers in the *Quarterly Bulletin,* Dwight admitted how difficult it was for most botanists to reach botanically unexplored territory. "Yet in central Nevada," he continued, "less than 250 miles from the pious gloom of Salt Lake City to the east, and only 190 miles from the impious glitter of Reno to the west, there exists to-day the paradox of a tarred road—broad, straight, and incredibly smooth—traversing an entire region never explored by botanists." Thanks to Dwight, Rupert could accumulate from such regions the evidence he needed for his monographia monumentalis. Dwight sympathized with the project from the beginning. He also sympathized with the plants. After a successful search in New Mexico for *Astragalus feensis,* the Santa Fe milkvetch not seen since it was first collected in 1847, he lamented, "So ended a hundred years of privacy for *A. feensis.*" And from Nevada, Dwight registered for the *Quarterly Bulletin* his unguarded sympathy for the country he now called it a privilege to explore.

In the evening, between the ritual of the press and supper, we climbed by a narrow dirt road to Castle Jackpot, quaint relic of Austin's boom days, a crenellated donjon perched on the steep western flank of the Toyabes and overlooking the Reese. From

here the view was as Nevadan as you could wish: a thousand feet
below you, the uninhabited valley with the river's cold white,
beautiful serpent, coiling in bright anfractuosities toward its
junction with the Humboldt, and above and beyond it the virgin
massifs of the Shoshones and Desatoyas, serenely secret, waiting
in silence for their date of inevitable deflowering, for the rattle
of the first audacious vasculum, the first sharp cry uttered on
the unbreathed air. This single emptiness, this single heavenly
vista of rose and tortoiseshell, of verdigris and dark blue—who
knows how full of undiscovered species—was all Nevada.

Among the books and papers that Rupert one day asked us to
remove from his loft, Frank and I found a heavy black photograph
album that had been labeled, in Dwight's hand, "A Family Portrait." We examined it together, turning the cover with a kind of
illicit excitement, as though we had dared to trespass on parental
secrets. Before us there were fifty pages of mounted photographs,
all black-and-white, each in excellent focus, and every photograph
was of a plant—plants growing in sand, plants growing in scree,
plants on rock. Unfortunately for us, not one was identified. "It
seemed that wherever Ripley and Barneby went," observed Peter
Raven, director of the Missouri Botanical Garden, "they found critical novelties that had been neglected by others or not collected for
many years." But this was the 1940s, and the way was not so
smooth, nor conditions so hospitable, as the paradox of a road
straight from Salt Lake City to Reno might suggest. "Do take care
of yourself & watch out for snakes," wrote Dwight from Santa
Monica when Rupert had gone to Nevada one mid-July. "Your first

letter, sent airmail from Tonopah Sat., didn't get here till Tues. afternoon, by which time I was working myself into a *state!*" The following spring, when the two men went together to photograph *Astragalus uncialis* near Currant, Nevada, they were caught unprepared by a sudden blizzard, which, Dwight later complained, caused his hands to turn actually *blue.* "Dwight had contempt for atmospherics, or claimed to have," remembered Rupert, "but this was an attitude, for he was in reality intimidated by their power." A frequent adversary was the dust storm, one of which overtook the two herborizers when they stopped to explore the Monte Neva Hot Springs, an isolated patch of malodorous alkali in northeastern Nevada. The storm was to last five hours: "a non-stop typhoon," exclaimed Dwight, "charged with a million particles of noxious ore blown northward from the slagheaps of McGill, leaving us dazed and groggy, our bloodshot eyes and raucous voices bearing testimony for a week after to the folly of our enterprise." British understatement had been left apparently to Rupert, who noted dryly in his own "Botanical Journal" that the grit came from the smelters at McGill, where ore from the copper mines was milled "to supply Peggy with lovers and caviar." At a second remote location the two men discovered a corpse in an abandoned car, drove miles to the nearest town where Dwight could inform the sheriff in his implausible accent, and were jailed at once as the most obvious murderers. Kept busy by the snakes, the weather, and the unexpected events, they did not always find the plants that they were looking for. In all their years of collecting, they never managed to locate the phoenix locoweed, *Astragalus phoenix,* which grows only in the Ash Meadows of southern Nye County, Nevada. To botanist Janice Beatley,

Rupert described their last attempt, made at the Ash Meadows in the middle of May 1945.

We drove in on a mule track from the highway, and at the first boggy place found an itinerant preacher with wife, children, and a dilapidated tin lizzie bedded deeply in the ooze. The car was painted all over with encouraging slogans of the Time to Repent, Down with Whore of Babylon sort, and one would have hoped that a Higher Power would have helped them in their distress. The Higher Power turned out to be Dwight and Myself, who in the process of towing them out got royally bogged down ourselves. As soon as they were on dry land, delivered by the im-

Loading the Dodge

probable angels of wickedness, the Holy Family made tracks for the highway, not without leaving us blessed, but without waiting to see how we would get ourselves back in business. This is why, I think, I never saw the phoenix loco.

The improbable angels had not been bashful about their enterprise. "The following species are among those observed by Rupert Barneby and myself," began Dwight in the first sentence of his second article for the *Quarterly Bulletin of the Alpine Garden Society*, published in June 1942. "The following notes are based on collections made by Mr. H. D. Ripley and myself," began Rupert in *his* second article for *Leaflets of Western Botany*, also published in 1942. In the archives at the LuEsther T. Mertz Library of the New York Botanical Garden, Frank found four letters to Dwight from the nursery owner Walter Ingwersen, all written from Sussex between the autumn of 1940 and the spring of 1941, and in each of the four letters Ingwersen closes with the polite acknowledgment, as a letter writer might do today, of his correspondent's family. "All my best regards and respects to you and Mr. Barneby," wrote Ingwersen. When the two men started to have their troubles with the Dodge (it was overheating) they responded with the inevitable, if gentle, domestic bickering. "Find out exactly how much the Ford will cost after the discount," writes Dwight, "and let me know in your next letter. But if you want to keep the coffee-pot for extra-curricular or urban use, I'll make out a check for $915. If it's going to boil on *any* gradient, maybe it's best to get rid of it." Two days later, Dwight had decided to take control. "Enclosed is a teeny cheque to pay for the new Ford," he directed. "Just fill in the name of the firm yourself

(or they can stamp it), & tell them to give you the balance in cash."
But his determination clearly encountered resistance. "Angel," he
wrote diplomatically after three days more, "I gather you hadn't
gotten my check when you sent off your letter, so I hasten to write
back & say, Keep the kettle, tear up the check I sent, & maybe some
day soon take it along to the hardware store to be repaired." Fortu-
nately, the issue of transportation was resolved, and the names Ripley & Barneby, both, appear on those thousands of collection labels
in the herbaria of the United States. The botanist and writer James
Reveal explained to me once that Ripley & Barneby may be written
that way, yes, but it was "pronounced RipleyandBarneby (for it was
one word)." Reveal specialized in the genus *Eriogonum,* the buck-
wheats, and the Marcus E. Jones of buckwheat was Susan Gabriella
Stokes. Rupert, who had known Miss Stokes, had stories about her
that he was easily prompted to share. "She did not approve of
Dwight and Rupert," remembered Reveal. When Frank and I met
Rupert, we had been together for not one year. RipleyandBarneby
were together for forty-eight. Rupert always said it was fifty, but
the two years one way or the other made no difference to me. It
still seemed inconceivable. Even in 1977, when Rupert published
"Daleae Imagines," I could read his dedication without much emotion, as though it had come from another world. "The joyous
adventure of field-work, in the western United States and Mexico,"
he wrote, "was shared and supported by the late Dwight Ripley, to
whom this book, to which he contributed so much, is dedicated."
The last time I would see Rupert on the grounds of the Botanical
Garden turned out to be a day in the autumn of 1999, when Frank
had joined him there for lunch. I was to meet them in the adjoining

gardens afterward. Frank and I had been together, by then, for twenty-five years. The day was windy; Rupert was wearing a red scarf that kept lifting in the wind, as did his now wispy hair. His blue eyes were milky, and it was the wind, I am sure, that made them watery too. People I didn't recognize had begun already to greet him as he left the two of us behind and started slowly up the long walk between the tulip trees toward the Museum Building— returning, at least momentarily, to the professional world that sustained him after Dwight had died—when suddenly he stopped, looked directly back at me, and said, not "Take care," not even "Take care of each other," but "Take care of both."

It was Peggy Guggenheim, Dwight told one of her biographers, who started him on his career as an artist. Not true! protested Rupert, when I mentioned this to him. "Dwight *always* drew." At Harrow he made pencil drawings of insects and flowers that were superior, Rupert believed, to those in the literature or the antique floras the two men went on to collect. In Beverly Hills he made pen-and-ink abstractions the equal, Rupert maintained, of Abstract Expressionist works then still to come. Frank once was corrected in this manner too. When he remarked that Dwight's *Portrait of Rupert Barneby, Esq. (botanist)* was "fun" (a reasonable observation, since the subject wears a flowerpot on his head), Rupert retorted that it was *not*, it was an example of "fine draftsmanship." But Dwight wasn't content to be a fine draftsman, and it is true, despite Rupert's protests, that when he turned from graphite and pen-and-ink toward drawing continuously with the colored pencil he did so during his affair with Guggenheim. Perhaps she does not get the credit directly. More likely it was a time for Dwight of artistic insight, a

time when his personal inclinations toward drawing were validated
by the colored pencil he saw in certain works of the Surrealists and
younger artists who circulated around Guggenheim and her gallery.
Matta used colored pencil because it was inexpensive. Pollock used
it for early drawings and still was using it, brushed with water,
when Jean Connolly introduced Dwight to his work. There was no
colored pencil in *Drawing, c. 1943–1945,* but two other drawings
Dwight bought from Guggenheim at the same time—a smoky
gray-and-orange work by Alice Rahon Paalen and a more tightly
structured one by the young Charles Seliger—were demonstra-
tions, each to different effect, of the potential this medium seemed
to hold for a personal art. Dwight's results with the colored pencil
soon were impressive on their own, and Guggenheim included six
of his drawings in a group show she scheduled at Art of This Century for December 3 to December 21 (more holiday marketing),
1946. The other artists were Seliger, John Goodwin, David Hill, and
Kenneth Scott. Both Dwight and Seliger had responded in their
work to the style known as Biomorphism, a fashionable Surrealist
outgrowth that was suggestive of organic forms under stress, or of
alien morphologies. Seliger's version was earnest and visceral.
Dwight's functioned as a commentary on the style itself. His drawings for this show could be described as Surrealist landscapes—they
were reminiscent of Tanguys or of some Mirós—that had been
invaded by a Biomorphist frolic of fungi and insects, snakes, bracts,
petals, and pods. The commentary arose because these were not
fancifully proportioned invaders, but the taxonomically and chro-
matically correct biomorphs that Dwight had admired all his life.
Their presence seemed virtually to confess that the old argument

with Connolly regarding the place of the natural sciences still rankled, and that a suitable comeback had here been rehearsed in art. Shortly before the show opened, Connolly arrived with Peter Watson in New York. Tony Bower took Auden to meet them at the dock. Dwight contacted Connolly the next day, but I have no record to suggest he saw the show. All six of Dwight's drawings were sold. In the *New York Times,* Edward Alden Jewell commented briefly on the five artists and wrote, "Dwight Ripley— linguist, poet, botanist, artist—has a group of expert, delicate color drawings." The ambiguous identification of linguist, poet, botanist, et cetera, was supplied to Jewell by Peggy Guggenheim.

Dwight was not surprised when Guggenheim returned to Europe in 1947. "Long ago," he explained, "she had determined (while walking one day in Central Park and comparing it unkindly with the Bois de Boulogne) to pretend that America wasn't there." Denham Fouts hoped likewise to resume his life in Europe; he had sold Watson's Picasso and with the proceeds returned to Paris the year before. It was never clear that Watson intended he should *have* the Picasso, rather than hold it safely in America through the war, and the story of this painting and its fate became a lasting legend among their friends. (The painting, *Girl Reading at a Table,* was acquired in 1995 by the Metropolitan Museum of Art.) Toni Altmann, the lover of Brian Howard, had crossed the ocean meanwhile in the opposite direction. He escaped his internment in France and reached the United States, where, in 1942, he married in order to become an American citizen. Howard, who was informed of the marriage by postcard, applied soon after to the Royal Air Force; he spent much of the war in uniform, though his unit never left England. Heinz

Neddermeyer completed his prison sentence, married, and survived the war while serving in the German army. But the most remarkable of these accounts, at least for those who remember Dwight and Rupert, was identified by Frank and Jackie Kallunki only after Rupert's death. Jakob Altmaier, the journalist who was deported from England because of the letters seized in Rupert's room, was not killed by the Nazis after all. Stripped of his German citizenship, he fled to France, where he worked as a resistance journalist and broadcast briefly on German Freedom Party radio from the English Channel. After the fall of France he served as an advisor on Balkan affairs to the now grateful British in their war office at Cairo. When the war was over Altmaier returned to Germany, where twenty-nine members of his family did die in the camps, to become one of two Jewish members in the first Bundestag. He has been called the father of the German-Israeli reparations agreement; he arranged the first meeting between Konrad Adenauer and Israeli representatives, and he was present with Adenauer when the agreement itself was signed. Never married, Altmaier remained a member of the Bundestag until he died in his office, aged seventy-four, in 1963. How Rupert failed to learn this story, when parts of it surely were reported in the press, we do not know. He destroyed letters, even in his last month in the hospital, as though lives were at stake.

The end of the war meant that Jean Connolly, too, could go back to Europe, though not to her estranged husband in England. She had continued to provide Connolly with money (in fact she sent an allowance), but early in 1946 she obtained a divorce in Reno and was married, later the same day, to Laurence Vail. Dwight last saw her at lunch in her apartment, March 19, 1946. He and Rupert were botanizing in the West when she returned with Vail to live in France. Dwight did not want to see her go. Tony Bower, derided by Greenberg as "Jeanie's Tony," was upset enough to intervene. Jean had been a mainstay of Bower's morale; after he was drafted the second time she made regular trips to visit him at Camp Upton, Long Island, taking food, books, and writing supplies in a devoted attempt to lift his gloom. Before the war, Bower had encouraged her separation from Connolly. Now he assured Connolly that she didn't love Vail and might be persuaded to return. That was not likely. Although Vail was nineteen years older than Jean, with five children from his previous marriages to Guggenheim and Kay Boyle, she seemed clearly to love him and her new family as well. "I took to her on the spot," recalled Sindbad Vail. Her health, however, was already failing, and it was a stroke that killed her four years later in Paris. She had been muse to the avant-garde on both sides of the Atlantic. David Pryce-Jones observed insightfully in his edition of Connolly's journals that when Jean met Cyril Connolly she was the younger, but her experience was the greater, "and her emancipation led to his." She performed the same office for Clement Greenberg. Both critics eventually lamented her influence; they even commiserated in this regard. So let us give Jean the last word. To Connolly, who had complained of her socializing, she wrote: "The very quality which made me go off unhesitatingly with you once I decided I wanted to, annoyed you in me. Be logical darling, though I love you so much now, in the beginning you weren't an enormous exception."

Friends in England, who expected that Dwight and Rupert would likewise return across the Atlantic, were eager to catch up on the

Tony Bower and Rupert at the Falls

gossip and news. "How are Dwight's paintings, poems & translations?" asked Sandwith by mail. "Do you often see Tony Bower, and is the cliff at the Spinney kept as it should be?" The Spinney had been spared from further bombs, although Tester, the gardener who took over when Player was called into service, once wrote manfully

to Dwight that he was prepared for such trouble, "as far as can be."
The severest damage was done by the record winters of 1939, 1940,
and 1941, the last made worse by the bombed-out glass of the greenhouses. Tester set out smudge pots to ward off the cold. In America,
Dwight was visited by nightmares: "the awful vision of clouds of
inky smoke," as he described them to Rupert, "billowing all night
(with the temperature at 15° below) over the etiolated cotyledons of
a hideous Ebenus and the corpses of Maurandyas and Phacelias." It
was not just the cold that troubled *Maurandya,* however. Unable to
collect the plant itself in Titus Canyon, Dwight and Rupert had
managed to gather seed, and this was sent to the baffled Tester. "I
had two young Maurandya's Petriphylla, rather close together, in
the seed pan," he reported in 1942, "but had to carefully move them,
when they began to touch one another, which they resent." One
died from the insult, and in the following year Tester had more bad
news. The *Maurandya* had collapsed again. It was, he explained, "a
mortal tricky plant." In Dwight's absence, B. W. Horne and his
family had moved into the Spinney, in part to protect it while it
served as a requisitioned property during the war. Faced with a
dwindling staff, a lack of funds, and the scarcity of supplies, Horne
chose to place a large number of plants elsewhere, mainly at Kew.
More than five hundred plants departed the Spinney this way, according to Tester's report. "Some of our most recondite treasures
have been given to Kew (at whose instigation I know not)," complained Dwight to Rupert. In fact Sandwith himself had transported
fifty rare plants to Kew. Dwight learned of this only later, but
his opinion of Sandwith's missions to the Spinney were already
formed. "He and the Hornes apparently got on like a house on fire,

naturally," sniffed Dwight. "They share the same political & social views, so why not?" The supervision that had meant the most to Dwight and Rupert was provided, all this time, by Ingwersen, who described his wartime watch to readers of the *Quarterly Bulletin of the Alpine Garden Society* in 1945. "The Cliff House is a success, it has proved itself in spite of all war-time difficulties," reported Ingwersen, before he went on to inventory the pleasures that only a gardener, perhaps, could understand. The *Dicentra chrysantha* "needs severe cutting back," he wrote. The rare *Ononis* and beautiful Salvias "need the knife from time to time." Even graceful *Statice asparagoides* required tying back. Ingwersen was proud of the cliff house, but he should have been, for many of the species growing there were those he had collected and brought back to England himself. "Perhaps," he ventured in the *Quarterly Bulletin,* "when at length the owner returns to his Sussex home and when the war is behind us, and the gardens of The Spinney back at full peacetime glory, Mr. Ripley will allow our Society to visit his garden— that would indeed be a Red Letter Day."

By the end of the war Dwight's blushing had grown worse. This was an unwelcome development that neither of the two men could understand, but with current knowledge it might have been predicted. Although normal blushing subsides after adolescence, the effects of the severe blushing syndrome are apt to intensify with age. They may lead also to persistent reddening and rosacea. "Dwight was charming and witty, but horrible to look at, with a red face and runny nose," remembered Harold Norse. "His face was purple, like a purple-assed baboon I always said." Jesse and Lee Effron recalled that Dwight's face sometimes was florid, as might be expected from too much alcohol. In 1946 the Effrons opened the Three Arts, a combined bookstore, record shop, and art gallery at 77 Cannon Street in downtown Poughkeepsie, a modest distance from the farmhouse at the Falls. Jesse Effron organized the bookstore and record shop, while his wife, Lee (she had worked at the ACA Gallery in New York), managed the gallery. One day soon after they opened, Dwight appeared at the door, surveyed the books, the records, the pictures, and announced, "My dears, it's a veritable oasis!" Rupert followed behind. The Effrons were pleased, while suspecting Dwight found them in the first place because they were adjacent to the liquor store—"which," recalled Lee, "was an oasis for us all." The following spring, Lee Effron gave Dwight the first solo show of his career. His drawings, in the style of the six that were in Guggenheim's group show, were exhibited at the Three Arts through the month of April 1947. Despite the show, and despite Lee Effron's continuing support, Dwight grew increasingly depressed. As a home remedy he bought two more Mirós, oils this time, having come to regard his "Constellations" as a kind of sustaining moral force. "Miró," he wrote, "is at present the soundest argument against suicide that I can think of." The tensions of the cold war did not help his spirits, and he reacted anxiously to reports that unidentified flying objects, or UFOs, had appeared over the United States in the summer of 1947. He and Rupert were botanizing north of Bozeman, Montana, when the first of these were reported flying like "skipping saucers" near Mt. Rainier in the state of Washington. Further reports, including the now famous instance near Roswell, New Mexico, frightened the country. A popular speculation was that the objects were secret weapons being tested by the Soviet Union. The commentator Walter Winchell believed they were gyroscopic in design, and he claimed to be vindicated when the *New York World Telegram* reported in 1949 that the air force had photographed three unidentified disks over Newfoundland. Fear seemed only more reasonable in August when the Soviet Union tested an atomic bomb. A civilian Ground Observer Corps was created by the Department of Defense that following January, and volunteers with binoculars were encouraged to warn the air force in case Soviet bombers attempted a surprise attack. During its peak years the GOC included more than 350,000 volunteers, organized into air defense teams that operated from 15,000 observation posts throughout the United States. One volunteer was Rupert, who remained a member of the Dutchess County team until the GOC was disbanded, nine years later, in 1959. While his post never sighted a Soviet bomber, it did report an unidentified object over Poughkeepsie. Jet fighters were scrambled in pursuit, but the object changed color and disappeared into the stratosphere at high speed. Critics today look back on the anxieties of the cold war with condescension, although intelligent people at the time were expected to take the threats seriously. Dwight confessed to an analyst during the war that he had "premonitions of cosmic doom." Now he described them with his customary style. "Here we go through space," he wrote, "our mad little planet spinning like a tennis ball through black, black, black, black, black Eternity, and with it spin the seas and the volcanoes, the temples and hotels, the maharajahs, the icebergs, Walter Winchell and me . . . especially me!"

In the hard-drinking world of New York School painters, poets, and patrons, Dwight was among the first to have the requisite auto accident. Alone, driving home drunk from a bar at eight o'clock one spring evening in 1949, he lost control of his Ford convertible on a narrow dirt road a half mile from the farmhouse and crashed it into a tree. Two neighbors removed him from the wreck before it caught fire. He had a concussion, fractured ribs, a punctured lung, and at Vassar Hospital he was not expected to live. The accident seems

Dwight after the accident

hardly to have restrained him. Harold Norse met him later that year, and the Dwight he portrays in his memoirs as the millionaire "Cyril Reed" is not a chastened individual. Norse was known later for his poems and his collage novel, *Beat Hotel* (the title refers to the small hotel at 9 rue Gît-le-Coeur where he, William Burroughs, and other Beat poets and writers once lived in Paris). But in 1949 his most intimate brush with fame had come ten years earlier when he and Chester Kallman, both recently graduated from Brooklyn College, attended a reading given by Auden and Isherwood in their first joint appearance in New York. The two graduates seated themselves in the front row with the admitted intent of seducing Auden. Kallman, who succeeded, became Auden's lifetime companion. Norse subsequently took an apartment at 573 Third Avenue, where he lived one floor above an Australian painter, Glyn Collins, who was commissioned by Dwight to paint a portrait of Tony Bower. When Collins gave a party he invited his upstairs neighbor Norse. Other guests that evening included the painter-and-poet couple Theodoros Stamos and Robert Price; the Abstract Expressionist painter William Baziotes and his wife, Ethel; the Living Theatre's founders-to-be Julian Beck and Judith Malina; the social philosopher Paul Goodman and his wife, Sally; John Bernard Myers and his roommate, Waldemar Hansen; the poet Ruthven Todd; and Dwight and Rupert. Dwight, reports Norse in his memoirs, was drunk, fell for him with a "thud heard round the room," and before passing out inquired what he most wanted. Norse had no way of knowing that Dwight a decade earlier had complained, "I long to say just '$20.' " No doubt he did know, by way of Kallman and Auden, the story of Denham Fouts and the liquidated Picasso. "Taking it as a big joke," writes Norse, "I blurted out with drunken laughter, 'How about a Picasso?' 'Is that *all?*' he screamed. *'Daahling,* it's yours!' "

A few days after the party a limousine arrived on Third Avenue, and the surprised Norse opened his door to find a chauffeur, in uniform, who had come to deliver a 1923 Picasso gouache, a ten-by-sixteen-inch study for *The Dancers,* certified by Pierre Matisse. Dwight was forty-one. Norse was thirty-three, and, in the words of John Myers, he was also "short, hefty and remarkably hirsute"—an image that calls inevitably to mind Dwight's taste in horticulture for "the dome, the cushion and the coat of fur." In his memoirs, Norse gives a vivid account of the ensuing affair (dinners at Le Pavillon and Chambord, trips to the galleries, visits to the New York Public Library, where Dwight read *War and Peace* in Arabic), and he reveals also that his new admirer never touched him. He credits the forbearance to his own virtue and not to Dwight's. It all came to an end on a winter evening outside the Chelsea Hotel, four days after Ranger Able had exploded over Frenchman Flat. "He had told me earlier," recalled Norse, "because he was a masochist, if you ever want to get rid of me, and you'll never see me again, just say 'I love you' and you'll never see me again. So outside this hotel he said, 'Harold, do you love me?' and I said, 'Yeah,' and I never saw him again." Dwight had not changed his opinion, perhaps, that Americans don't know what love means. The previous autumn he recorded in his diary that Norse and Norse's lover during the whole affair, Dick Stryker, were coming to Wappingers Falls to spend the weekend. He made a note to get his drawings down from upstairs. Fifty years later, when I asked Norse by telephone what he thought of Dwight's drawings, he replied, "I never knew Dwight could draw or would even bother to do something artistic. Dwight an artist, no, I had no idea. I can't believe it."

The shared, and conceivably the convenient assumption among those who benefited from Dwight's patronage was that he could not handle his money. Norse called him "the mad Maecenas." John Myers said he was "madly generous," and further reports seem generally to agree that the sums Dwight spent on art and artists were spent either on impulse, or to relieve the indecisions he otherwise could not resolve. In their later biography of Jackson Pollock, the writers Steven Naifeh and Gregory White Smith would include Dwight in a list of collector "big shots," the wealthy buyers whose presence during Pollock's opening at the Betty Parsons Gallery in November 1949 marked a public breakthrough for Abstract Expressionism. Wrote Naifeh and Smith: "Dwight Ripley, a wealthy painter-poet-botanist-linguist, hovered around two paintings for a long time, unable to decide between them. (He eventually bought both.)" Dwight, having learned at Oxford, perhaps, that it was bad form to get caught being earnest, did nothing to discourage the prevailing opinion. In *A Sunlit Scene* he even made sport of a character, Madge (she is said in the novel to be the sister of Dwight Ripley), who recovers from a sexual misadventure by traveling to Barcelona, where, "after considerable thought, she purchased three Mirós." The trouble with this diverting pose is that it hides from history, of course, the intellectual motivations that Dwight, Jean Connolly, and others transferred to American art from their youth in England. The bright young folk in Pansyhalla, and in the wider circle around Cyril Connolly, were pointedly conscious of their cultural hopes for the future, and conscious, as well, of the odds that were arrayed against them. During the first year of the war, when Dwight and Rupert were already in the United States, the journal *Horizon* printed a widely discussed "Letter from a Soldier" (the soldier was Goronwy Rees) that criticized British intellectuals who were not in uniform, ready to defend Western civilization. Connolly identified the dilemma when he responded in the same issue: "The fact remains that war *is* the enemy of creative activity. The point which *Horizon* has made is that though this war is being fought for culture, the fighting of it will not create that culture." The founding of *Horizon* by Connolly and Peter Watson was itself an attempt to create that culture. Early in the war, Watson had arranged a studio for the Scottish painters Robert Colquhoun and Robert MacBryde (they were known as "the two Roberts" because they were a couple). Later he provided support to John Craxton, Michael Wishart, and Lucian Freud. Dwight joined in this project, if marginally, when he bought an oil by MacBryde and lent it to the Pennsylvania Academy of the Fine Arts. A more intimate example was set by Peggy Guggenheim, who not only encouraged Dwight to become a patron but, like Connolly, supplied a reason. "Samuel Beckett told me to buy modern art," she explained. "He said, 'It's your duty.' " Guggenheim's original gallery, Guggenheim Jeune, had been located in London (it was on Cork Street), and her memoir, *Out of This Century*, was ghosted in part by yet another of Dwight's Oxford friends, James Stern. Even the affair with Harold Norse implied motives that can be traced to Dwight's generation in England. Edward James financed the first book of John Betjeman, the future poet laureate, and Watson was called on frequently to subsidize Dylan Thomas. Norse's first book of poems, *The Undersea*

Mountain, was not published until his affair with Dwight was over, and he never sent a copy to his former Maecenas. Among Dwight's books, I found Marie Menken's copy instead. Next to it was Norse's translation of the sonnets of Giuseppe Gioachino Belli. He would begin this translation in Rome, when, reminding Dwight surely of Denham Fouts, he sold his Picasso and moved to Italy.

D WIGHT AND RUPERT were of two minds about John Bernard Myers, director of the new Tibor de Nagy Gallery that opened December 14, 1950, on the first floor of a converted tenement at 206 East Fifty-third Street near the elevated railway, the El, which then darkened Third Avenue. Or maybe I should say Dwight was of two minds, because Rupert, as Frank and I finally would hear all the way to Myers's house in Brewster and back, was in no doubt on the subject. The two men had known Myers for some time, not from the exact moment in 1944 when he arrived in New York, not yet thirty, to be managing editor of *View*, but certainly since 1947, when Peter Watson paid a visit to Charles Henri Ford at that magazine's office and was invited home to dinner by young editor Myers. At dinner Watson met Myers's roommate, Waldemar Hansen, and recognized in him a replacement for Denham Fouts, who was by then in declining health (Fouts died in Rome the following year) due to a drug addiction that had been funded by the Picasso. Watson returned to London, where Hansen soon joined him, and where he was instrumental in founding the Institute of Contemporary Arts. It was this connection to Watson that secured for Myers his first invitation to visit Dwight and Rupert, the weekend before Christmas, 1947, at Wappingers Falls. Myers was described unforgettably in the autobiography of Larry Rivers, written with Arnold Weinstein: "His eyes were green and changed size with every idea that crossed behind them." He was described likewise in an unpublished poem by Dwight.

> Alert, progressive, not too tart,
> She can discourse on Life and Art,
> And tellingly invoke the names
> Of Goodman, Kierkegaard and James.

That stanza (yes, Dwight re gendered the pronoun) came from a satirical eclogue that was left untitled, but I have named it from its designation of scene as *Beach at Amagansett*. The poem itself was of two minds, as befits an eclogue, and it proceeds antiphonally as if quoting first Dwight, then Rupert, on the merits of John (they never used the "Bernard") Myers.

> But in the sun her wisdom's callow,
> Her "dish" as cold as it is shallow,
> Tasteless at once and over-seasoned,
> As loud as it is under-reasoned.

When the magazine *View* published its final issue, in March 1947, Myers was suddenly out of a job. He was rescued by the wealthy collector Robert Altman, who took over the lease at *View* and hired Myers to market a portfolio of prints to be made by Miró, Tanguy, Matta, and others at William Hayter's studio, Atelier 17, on East Eighth Street. Sales of the portfolio were disappointing. Altman moved his family to France, and Myers turned with the proposal of a joint venture to his new friend Tibor de Nagy. An officer once in

the National Bank of Hungary, de Nagy had been arrested by German authorities late in the war. He was shipped to a prison camp,
escaped, was arrested again by Soviet secret police, imprisoned,
and harshly treated for two years before his release. He arrived in
New York in 1948, "penniless," remembered his daughter, Marianne
Buchenhorner, "with only a few pieces of jewelry that he hoped to
sell." Early the next year he met Myers, who responded with a tender interest in his welfare—or so it appears from Dwight's telling.

> Such tenderness! She weeps at Views,
> At Goya and the Daily News,
> At darling Tibor's daily plights . . .
> She hardly *sleeps* for weeping, nights.

Myers persuaded de Nagy to sell some of the jewelry to finance a
traveling puppet theater, the Tibor Nagy Marionette Company.
(The "de" would be added later for the sake of the art gallery.) This
theater was at first a success; its most popular play featured kachina-
doll puppets and music by Ned Rorem. Attendance declined rapidly,
however, during the polio outbreak of 1950, when parents insisted
on keeping their children at home. That summer, as de Nagy later
recalled, Lee Krasner and Jackson Pollock advised him to start an
art gallery instead. With Guggenheim gone, they explained, there
was no ready outlet for the young artists whose work needed to be
seen. Myers remembered that it was Krasner and Pollock who encouraged him, too, to create a space where fresh talent might flour-
ish and evolve. Clearly, the new gallery would be an idea whose
time had come. Like other ideas whose time has come, it also had a

prior history, and Myers perhaps foreshortened the narrative when he wrote in his memoirs, "I shall never know whether he was drunk or sober, when, one day at lunch at the Chambord, Dwight suggested I go ahead with my plan to open a gallery."

The lunch (Dwight's diary doesn't say if it was the Chambord) occurred not that summer but six months earlier, on January 15, 1950, and it fit into a pattern of determination that, for Dwight, was sober indeed. At Gleaves, Crawford & Levie the same week, he signed a new will. This was the only will he would make in the United States, and it was notable in two respects: it named Rupert his sole heir and it did not mention the Spinney. Dwight once predicted that New York would cure him of being homesick. "I haven't seen a green thing," he wrote to Rupert, "either in the parks or on my plate, since I arrived. One advantage is, it's a cure for idle brooding (in which I used occasionally to indulge in Sta Monica) over the fate of our own serres. I never give the Spinney a thought." Now he was about to relinquish the Spinney and its *serres* for good (the word *serre* is French for greenhouse), and, no matter how many brave resolutions the two men made to avoid "nostalgia's coffin," this ultimate loss was still disheartening. B. W. Horne, who had continued to manage Dwight's affairs in England, arrived later that spring on the S.S. *America*. He brought the Christopher Wood, *Parrots in a Cage*. On his return he arranged the auction of remaining plants from the cliff house and greenhouses, and he managed also the transaction by which the Spinney would pass to its new owner, B. W. Horne. Rupert regarded this transfer with deep suspicion. But the world is unjust, to quote his own advice, and "that is a fact of life." What mattered was how Dwight would adapt to it. Before him he had the examples of Guggenheim's bohemia, Lee Effron's oasis, and Watson's generosity. He recently had seen John Myers at the party where Norse was promised a Picasso. If the question was whether Myers could run an art gallery, then the answer undoubtedly came from Myers himself. "I realized I didn't have the necessary money," confessed Myers, "but I knew I had the gall."

Dwight, considering his experience at Art of This Century, must have suspected that money and gall were not enough. Guggenheim's success had been inseparable from the insight of her advisors (in particular Howard Putzel and Marcel Duchamp), and though her historical moment could not be repeated, the access to insight was an advantage that Dwight, in 1950, was uniquely positioned to emulate. Because of Jean, he could turn to Clement Greenberg. The timing was as good as that day in the Chisos when the mountains were adorned with pillar-box and violet. Robert Motherwell had canceled an upcoming spring show at the Sam Kootz Gallery, and Greenberg was asked to select a group show, "New Talent 1950," to replace it. In preparation he compiled a list that included the painters Friedel Dzubas, Robert Goodnough, Grace Hartigan, Harry Jackson, Elaine de Kooning, Alfred Leslie, and Larry Rivers. On Friday, January 12, Dwight met Greenberg in the Plaza Lounge at six. When he met Myers three days later for lunch—drunk or sober, at the Chambord or not—he knew exactly what he intended to suggest. He had cleared it with Greenberg first. It was the next Monday that he took Myers to the critic's apartment in the Village. This bare sequence of events can be determined from Dwight's pocket diaries, but his *Beach at Amagansett* provides a livelier record. Myers was not the only character in that poem. He is followed, according to the stage directions, by "Larry the Horse, Grace, Clement, Helen, and lesser fry" (Greenberg met Helen Frankenthaler in May), who have assembled on the beach to inaugurate a new era in art by painting their dealer's portrait. To this end, Myers climbs a convenient pedestal, the artists smear him with ordinary black house paint, and Greenberg stands aside to explain ("with total finality," say the directions) the significance of what is taking place.

> Painting was just a bunch of shit
> Until the *scuola* Myers hit
> Upon the ultimate technique . . .
> Art has this morning reached a Peak.

Rupert with Possum, Dwight, and Clement Greenberg at the Falls

Myers, writing his memoirs in Brewster, maintained that Green-berg's list had been helpful but it was a "coincidence" when nearly everyone on that list was asked to join the gallery. Sam Kootz, mean-while, shared Dwight's regard for his old friend's judgment. After he closed his own gallery in 1966, Kootz observed that all the "New Talent" shows had been worthwhile. "Clem Greenberg picked the first, then collaborated with Meyer Schapiro on the second," he told Jay Jacobs of *Art in America*. "It's curious how intelligent Green-berg was. Every painter of the time who later came through was in those two groups he selected for the shows in '50 and '51."

Dwight's eclogue was not dated, but its cast of characters places it early in the gallery's history. The reciprocal respect between Greenberg and the painters soon wore thin. Eventually the three painters in the poem would leave for other dealers. Finally in 1970 the partnership of Myers and de Nagy itself dissolved. Myers at-tempted a gallery on his own, and de Nagy retained the institution to which he had given his name. Rupert took Frank once to meet de Nagy, or Tibor, as naturally he called him. This was another pil-grimage that puzzled us. It must have puzzled Tibor, too, who reached what seems a sensitive conclusion when he got Frank aside and indicated that if Rupert had come to sell the remainder of Dwight's art collection he would be happy, of course, to help. Only later did we realize what Rupert was doing when he took the two of us to meet Myers, took Frank to meet Tibor, took him to stand before the apartment of Clement Greenberg! He knew we could retrieve the "Atlas of North American *Astragalus*" at any time from the shelves, but where on the shelves was *The Art and Life of Dwight Ripley*? Rupert always liked de Nagy, who had been educated at

Cambridge, and whose cultivated, somewhat distant bearing came without pretense, as did Rupert's own. It pleased him further that de Nagy made a point of acknowledging Dwight's role. On the gallery's twenty-fifth anniversary, de Nagy issued a statement that included the observation "Had it not been for the late Dwight Ripley, who paid our rent for the first six years, we would not have been able to survive." It appears from the gallery's initial ledger, now at the Archives of American Art in New York, that Dwight paid the rent for the apartments of Myers and de Nagy, as well. Myers's rent was ten dollars a month and de Nagy's was thirty-two. Dwight's pocket diaries suggest that he also subsidized the poetry chapbooks that launched Tibor de Nagy Editions in 1951. Following a visit by Myers and de Nagy he has entered the memo "Write John re 2 books." Myers brought Chester Kallman to visit the Falls in March, and the gallery published Kallman's *Elegy*, with drawings by René Bouché, later that month. He brought Larry Rivers in August, and the gallery published *A City Winter* by Frank O'Hara, with drawings by Rivers, in the spring of 1952. The chapbooks of Kenneth Koch and John Ashbery followed in 1953. When Myers later characterized the poets published by Tibor de Nagy as "poets of the New York School," he imposed an identity that has become a defining tradition in American poetry.

Because Dwight seldom was seen at the gallery, some of the painters and poets never met him, and others never knew he was their sponsor. In the bedroom he kept a small oil-and-plaster painting, signed HELEN upside-down, that was a gift from Frankenthaler on his birthday. At the head of the stairs he hung his Hartigan, *Southampton Fields*. When Hartigan was included with

Pollock and ten others in a show of American painters at the Tate
Gallery in London, then singled out for praise by a reviewer (it was
Patrick Heron) there, Dwight at home reacted in triumph. His sense
of involvement was stoked cleverly by Myers, who made himself
the conduit of favors and gossip. Alfred Leslie was quizzed continu-
ally at the gallery for news of his romantic life and escapades. "John
loved to hear about these madcap outings which he immediately
retailed to Dwight on the phone," recalled Leslie. "He always liked
my being there when he made these reports to Dwight so he could
ask me to shout details to questions Dwight asked." It was Myers
who orchestrated the field trip to the Falls during which Rupert
snapped the picture of Hartigan and Frankenthaler on the lawn.
The painters had planned to entertain Dwight by flying kites they
made for the occasion, but Myers persuaded a photographer from
Life to record a trial flight in Central Park, where the kites (they
were "gorgeous but impractical," remembered Hartigan) failed to
survive. Leslie built a model airplane to fly instead. "Those days
were fruitful," Frankenthaler once remarked, "and we were all living in the young, lively active nucleus of an 'art family.' I think the
luckiest thing for me was to be in my early twenties with a group
that I could really talk and argue pictures about." Barbara Guest,
another of the poets included by Myers in his original New York
School, offered a summary of his role that was concise and reso-
nant. "In the end they deserted him, I think—his painters left him,
his poets laughed at him. But he was an essential figure of our time,
absolutely essential to our cultural inheritance." The poet James
Merrill, who was Myers's final and by far his wealthiest patron,

called him "a passionate impresario." In Dwight's *Beach at Ama-gansett*, it was Myers the impresario who brought the poem and its portrait session to an end.

> I feel convinced that NO ONE knows
> The effort that it is to pose.
> Waldemar, dear, it's time to snack,
> Helen will pour, while you unpack.

John Myers said he had to "cajole" Dwight into the first show of his drawings at Tibor de Nagy Gallery, and it appears from the drawings themselves that this was true. They are drawn on the back of the farmhouse stationery. Frank and I have seen ten of these early drawings, and it was some time before either of us realized that the smudge faintly visible in each case is the letterhead showing through, backward and sometimes upside-down. (Haughtily minimal, it reads, "Wappingers Falls, New York.") After Lee Effron gave Dwight his original solo show at the Three Arts, he had made no attempt to pursue a career as an artist. He retreated to the Falls as to the Spinney before, a retreat punctuated by the urban forays he conducted from the Plaza for as long as he was welcome there. Staying home was never an aesthetic deprivation. The garden was filled with rare plants, and the farmhouse with Pollocks, Mirós, and other objects unusual for the day. "I remember that the house was filled with strange and wonderful birdcages," recalled Hartigan, "but no birds." The Christopher Wood, *Parrots in a Cage*, had been missed by both men when it was out of sight in England throughout the war. Although they might have replaced it with another painting of a cage, they began to collect cages instead. Nine of these elaborate Victorian and Edwardian constructions made the eventual transition to Rupert's loft at the Botanical Garden. In a position of honor on the highest window ledge was the combination fishbowl-

and-birdcage that had been Dwight's favorite. The fishbowl, a great glass onion shaped like one of the domes of St. Basil's Cathedral on Red Square, was supported by an octagonal tower of Alhambresque columns that constituted the birdcage. Having the fish above the bird in this manner would have been novelty enough. But the onion-shaped bowl was deceptive; its base was deeply vaulted to form an interior air-filled globe that was open to the bird in the cage below. When the bird flew or hopped into this inner globe, it appeared to be in the fishbowl with the fish. Dwight so admired this object (he called it "a bowl of bird, a cage of fish") that he could not resist drawing it. His initial sketch was in the tradition of a captioned nonsense drawing by Edward Lear, and it portrayed a finch named Pinty, and a goldfish, Ponty, at home in their respective parts of the cage. The names were a tribute to de Nagy; *pinty* is finch in Hungarian, as *ponty* is carp. Soon there was a series of birdcage drawings, all done on the back of the stationery. Some were intended obviously to be sent to friends (one is inscribed "to Waldemar"), but Myers must have intervened before they were mailed. The result was Dwight's first solo exhibit in New York, which opened after the first Rivers show and continued until the first Frankenthaler show—clearly it was squeezed in, running only from October 30 to November 10, 1951. The show was titled *Birds, Fish and Cages*, and Dwight's inspired preparation suggests that not much cajoling was finally required. He had the cage itself placed in the gallery window. The note in his diary says, "Call Tibor re cage," BUtterfield 8-9202. Ponty the goldfish was alive, and so was Pinty, at first. "Each day I had to feed and water this elaborate *fin de siècle* construction," reported Myers. "But one day the bird escaped, dashed wildly around the gallery, headed straight toward the window and broke its little neck on the glass. Dwight felt badly and so did I."

It is not clear whether Myers understood just why the gallery had a cage in its window. The whole show, inspired by the cage and

Dwight Ripley,
Miró Mirror No. 1, *1951*

refracted through it, was nearly a Conceptualist installation. Dwight had associated his art collection with his birdcages, and he perceived one collection through the other. His Miró "Constellation" number one, *Le lever du soleil,* featured one of the keenest of Miró's birds, with triangular head, scissor beak, propeller-sharp wings, and a flaring tail. Dwight redrew *Le lever du soleil* to portray it captive, bird and all, inside the cage. Then for good measure he put his other "Constellation" in there too. His Miró oils, both called *Femme et oiseaux dans la nuit* (numbers one and two, 1946), he portrayed as mirrors. Number one became the tilt mirror on a chest of drawers, with the birds and fish in the drawers below. Number two became a wall mirror, in a giddily rococo frame, with the birds and fish in a stern Modernist cage to

Dwight Ripley, Miró Mirror No. 2, *1951*

the side. The mirrors were puns. Each was a pun on *miró,* the third person past of *mirar*—to look at, to contemplate—which is what one does to a reflection in a mirror. And the "reflections" in these mirrors were puns themselves, on the many self-portraits in a mirror. Dwight had put his Mirós where the artist's face should be, which is not a bad place for them if Miró is the soundest argument against suicide you can think of. To compound the irony, these were images that the artist had been instructed to prefer. I don't mean this academically. Rupert and Dwight had lunch with Greenberg at a restaurant called the Auberge on the day, February 10, 1947, that they visited Pierre Matisse to buy the two oils in question. It was a Monday; they took the critic along and had the gallery to themselves. In his imagination, Dwight took Greenberg likewise along when he began to draw. One of the ideas in "Avant-Garde and Kitsch" was that avant-garde art had continued to be an imitation, but not of reality. It was an "imitation of imitating," a meditation on paint itself, color itself, the stroke of the brush, and the flatness of the picture plane. Today this seems an unexceptional way of looking at pictures; then it was an adventure. Dwight pushed the adventure further. He imitated the imitating, but he did it in another medium. He imitated with colored pencil what normally was done with a brush. Even more troublesome at the time, he imitated the avant-garde paintings themselves. When he put a Miró in the place of a mirror, he changed that Miró's context; in the vocabulary of a later era we might have said he recontextualized the work of art. Of course the later recontextualizations were meant to be subversive. Dwight's were possessive instead. He treated his Mirós with the same fond dismay that he extended to Jean and Clem, or to his namesake ("Ta-ta, Dwighteen!") *Cymopterus ripleyi.* His "Constellations," which had been praised by Greenberg for their allover reach toward infinity, he held captive for care and feeding in a cage. The jest was similar to the liberties he took with Surrealist ideology in his Art of This Century show, and it demonstrated again the long reach of his old argument with Connolly about talking shop in horticulture versus talking shop in the pages of the *New Statesman.* Now he equated the shop talks of horticulture and of art criticism. "Parody of gardening article," he reminded himself in a spiral notebook, "(wee, elf, dainty, fairy, jolly, chalice, creamy, etc.). Ditto of art criticism (spatial, integrity, planes, *kitsch,* etc.)."

Nine drawings from *Birds, Fish and Cages* were sold, but critical attention was elsewhere. "Wit and nonsense," explained Stuart Preston in the *New York Times,* "are more or less displaced persons in an age of anxiety." The Korean War had begun June 29, 1950, and after the unexpected entry of China it seemed possible that the United States might be defeated. Rumors, widely believed, were that Washington intended to use atomic weapons against Peking. Isherwood wrote in his diary that the Metropolitan Museum was ready to evacuate paintings from New York, while Judith Malina wrote in hers that Harold Norse was buying a car to deliver them from the city when it was time to flee. "I don't want to leave New York," she protested. "I don't want to consider the destruction of New York as a possibility." The Nevada Test Site was designated at the end of that year, Ranger Able was detonated in January, and the booklet *Survival Under Atomic Attack*—the "duck-and-cover" manual that explained how to survive a nuclear war by hiding under your desk—was published in twenty million copies in 1951. Meanwhile the Spinney was gone, the gallery was open on Dwight's promise to support it, and Rupert's *Astragalus* was well under way. Auden and Isherwood had become citizens in 1946, and it seemed inevitable that Rupert should become a citizen too. He filed his naturalization papers on May 22, 1951. This was exquisitely bad timing. Three days later the double agents Guy Burgess and Donald Maclean disappeared from England, having fled, as it finally turned out, to Moscow. The future spies had been students at Cambridge when Rupert was there. Burgess was queer (this is the word Rupert always used), and the extraordinary significance that attached to this fact in the wake of his defection amounted soon to transatlantic panic. In Britain, an aroused vigilance led to the arrests in the following year of more than fifteen hundred men, not all of whom could have been double agents. One of the arrested was Alan Turing. In France, Brian Howard and his second partner, Sam Langford, were detained, then deported on grounds of *moralité douteuse*. In Italy, they were presumed actually to *be* Burgess and Maclean and eventually had to leave the village, Asolo, where they had hoped to make their permanent home. In New York, an immigration official (Rupert recalled her as "a kindly judge") warned Rupert that if he persisted in his application for citizenship she would have to open his draft record, this would reveal the reason he had been rejected by the army, and she would be obliged to deport him. She advised him to withdraw his application, which he immediately did. Rupert never became a citizen of the United States. For ten years he didn't dare leave the country for fear he would not be allowed to return, not to Dwight or to *Astragalus*. In 1989, when he received the Asa Gray Award from the American Society of Plant Taxonomists, the botanists William and

Christiane Anderson wrote, "Plant taxonomy has profited enor-
mously from the circumstance that led Rupert Barneby to grace our
shore with his presence and our plants with his study." One circumstance was that he could not leave. Dwight had his own premonitions
of cosmic doom, and after the bomb at the Spinney and the fate of
Cymopterus ripleyi he seemed to believe his terrors would soon be
confirmed. "Friends think I'm talking through my hat / When I refer
to Frenchman Flat," he wrote in *Spring Catalogue*. It must attest to his
character, as well as his art, that he responded with wit to the political
anxieties that, for Rupert and himself, were not abstract but personal.
Among the fish he depicted in *Birds, Fish and Cages* one was part
bomb, a sort of merbomb. But Preston in the *Times* was right. Seri-
ous intellectuals believed that frivolity was impermissible, as if pleasure rather than economic and ideological rigidity had been the cause
of the world's disasters, as if intelligent pleasure was not an orna-
ment of civilization that people should desire for others and deserve
for themselves. Even Tony Bower responded to the moment by publishing a translation of *The Rebel*, by Albert Camus. Wrote Preston
of Dwight's drawings: "There is no point in trying to puzzle out
what they mean or even to describe them, for they scoff at the judgment of reason." In *Art Digest*, James Fitzsimmons agreed. "At the
end of a year," he wrote, "Ripley found that he had produced 57
drawings. He made one more in which he baked the fish and roasted
the birds."

Dwight missed Jean Connolly and he looked for a substitute in
Marie Menken. Born in Brooklyn in 1910, which made her the same
age as Jean, Menken was Dwight's consolation prize in the affair
between Rupert and her husband, Willard Maas. That affair cooled

and continued as a friendship; in all the years we knew Rupert we
never heard him criticize Maas. Menken and Maas had been married
six years when the I L U WILLARD telegram arrived for Rupert at
Wappingers Falls, and they maintained the devoted, if unusual marriage that would accommodate Maas's boyfriends throughout their
lives. "Willard was small and rotund," remembered the playwright
Paul Zindel, "of varied sexual appetites, very nice, sweet, provocative, knew everybody in show business. His wife was huge, six foot
if she was an inch—she was built like a football player." Dwight
called Menken and Maas the Big One and the Little One, although
Menken must have been a Big One next to him as well. Maas, in
turn, referred to the relationship between Dwight and his wife as
"that strange *folie à deux*," while Stan Brakhage described it, later
and secondhand, as an unnatural dependency on Dwight's part.
"There is love and it is everywhere," Menken herself once told an
interviewer. "There is no loss, except for those who do not love—
and it is their own loss." In Menken, Dwight had spotted a compan-
ionable eccentric who shared his love of color and expressed it, as
did he, in unusual ways and with unorthodox media. Menken was
known initially not for her films but for the paintings she made from
sand and other nontraditional materials. Her first show opened
at the Betty Parsons Gallery in November 1949 (the show that
followed hers was Jackson Pollock's), and her paintings were described before the opening by *F.Y.I.*, the employee newsletter of
Time, Inc., where she worked as a night clerk on the overseas cable
desk. According to *F.Y.I.*, her paintings were made from "stone
chips, stone powders, marble chips, marble dust, ground silicate,
sand, cement dust, luminous paints, glass particles, glues and lac-

quers, occasionally string and fiber." So Dwight was perhaps right
to call these paintings *desertipicti;* the species epithet means "of the
Painted Desert." Menken had a second show at Betty Parsons in
February 1951, and her third, held at Tibor de Nagy the following
month, featured Pollock-like swirls of phosphorescent paint that
glowed in the dark. John Myers portrayed Menken and Maas as
grotesques when he came to write his memoirs, but for many years
they contributed both energy and focus to the postwar avant-garde.
"The Maases were warm and demonstrative," wrote Andy Warhol

Marie Menken at the Falls

in his own memoir, "and everybody loved to visit them." The parties they hosted in their penthouse at 62 Montague Street in Brooklyn Heights ("a shack on the roof," corrected Menken) brought artists, groupies, patrons, and intellectuals together before a spectacular backdrop of Manhattan across the East River, and were popular, even defining events in the art scene of their time. "It was back in the days of *Narcissus*," remembered Maas, referring to a film he released in 1956, "when we could give big parties, for Dwight Ripley always gave us a hundred or two for our parties, and usually we added the same, so we could really put on the dog." A committed biographer might wince at the thought of Dwight, miserable in groups of more than four, sponsoring parties he could enjoy only through gossip later on. Brakhage recalled the parties organized by Menken and Maas as the most lavish he had attended. "They would include everybody," he reported, "Marilyn Monroe and her then husband Arthur Miller, Charles Addams, Reinhold Niebuhr, Truman Capote and Andy Warhol, to name only a few." He listed also a "blowzy, rich old lady" identified as the Medea of the Twentieth Century. As the guest list of a single party this account is implausible (it conflates decades), but the hosts did know everyone named, including the Medea of the century, Hazel McKinley, who was a sister of Peggy Guggenheim.

Although Dwight claimed never to give the Spinney a thought, a major event at the Falls was the construction, in 1952, of a greenhouse to take the place of the ones Horne was dismantling back in England. The new structure was designed by Lord & Burnham, a prestigious firm that built the conservatory at the New York Botanical Garden, and whose first private greenhouse had been constructed in 1881 for Jay Gould, the notorious business associate of Dwight's great-grandfather Sidney Dillon. (The two robber barons continued their association in adjoining family plots at Woodlawn Cemetery; no wonder Dwight wouldn't want to be buried with the family.) Unfortunately, the greenhouse at the Falls has not survived. The plans are in the Lord & Burnham collection at the library of the New York Botanical Garden, but I had no clear idea of the structure's actual appearance until I saw Menken's film *Glimpse of the Garden* projected at Anthology Film Archives. Menken bracketed her film with long shots of this very greenhouse, sited serenely beside the pond, just east of the farmhouse at the Falls. When the first view of it came unexpectedly to the screen, the recognition— what it was, what it must have meant to the two men—momentarily took my breath away. Anyone who sees *Glimpse of the Garden* without a proper initiation may be excused for wondering, however, if this truly was an art film or just a weekend lark made by someone who did not, and never would have a professional acquaintance with her camera. At Anthology Film Archives, I supposed from the opening frames that the print was degraded. In fact, as I learned later from a book by the film historian Scott MacDonald, Menken's camera gate had not been cleaned. This could be taken as the proof she was incompetent, if it did not so exactly mimic what was being done in vanguard painting at the time. The drip, the luckless housefly, all the accidental elements that prevented a commercial finish and provided an existential moment instead, were being made part of the painting. Directly, but more likely from Dwight, Menken had picked up the idea from "Avant-Garde and Kitsch," and she too was ready to imitate in another medium the imitating of avant-garde art.

Dwight, by this time, had moved on from his Mirós to imitate with colored pencil the drama of Abstract Expressionist paintings. He parodied their energetic gestures by treating them as the depiction of nuclear explosions. The United States detonated the first hydrogen bomb at Eniwetok in 1952, the Soviet Union countered with a similar device the following year, and the U.S. secretary of state, John Foster Dulles, announced a policy of massive retaliation in 1954. At least three of the drawings Dwight made in that latter year featured exploding skyscrapers. I used to think these verged on trite. They since have become painful as well, which does not redeem them. One hurtling tower bears the name TIBOR DE. . . . The whole series, called *The Bomb,* was exhibited at Tibor de Nagy Gallery in January, and at the Three Arts in February, 1955. Menken, who bought one of the *Bomb* drawings from the Three Arts, could not fail to observe that Dwight was using his pencil as she might use her camera, in the place of a brush. She may not have needed the insight, but the encouragement was welcome, because by 1956 she had not made a film since her portrait of Noguchi ten years before. In the spring she fractured an ankle, and, while it healed, she came to stay with the two men at Wappingers Falls. Clearly she brought the camera along. The following year she released two new titles; one was stock footage, newly edited, and the other was *Glimpse of the Garden,* her five-minute action painting in film of Dwight and Rupert's garden at the Falls.

Stan Brakhage, who frequently expressed admiration for *Glimpse of the Garden,* remarked suggestively once that Menken's technique in that film was "like, you know, a bomb has been dropped." He also maintained that "Dwight Ripley's flowers" were merely the occasion for her artistry in the film—which means, I suppose, that she might have seized on flowers anywhere else. This would not be an unusual view of creative independence. Most visitors to the Falls reported that a tour of the greenhouse ("a greenhouse of which Dwight is very proud," wrote Judith Malina) in fact was inescapable. Dwight was so proud of the greenhouse that he described it for the *Bulletin of the American Rock Garden Society* within months of its construction. The truly impressive sight, he informed his readers, was afforded by the deep-green hummocks of *Pyxidanthera barbulata,* a difficult species that could be shipped and replanted only in wads of its native sand. Even then it could not be weeded in a traditional manner. "The roots," he explained, "are inextricably entwined with those of a Lobelia *(L. nuttallii),* whose basal leaves are oval and purplish and not displeasing but the flowering stems are hideous and have to be regularly snipped." With daily scrutiny, it was a simple matter to keep the hummocks looking neat and trim. "I am not ashamed of being caught with nail-scissors," admitted Dwight. Apparently the scissors did their work. When Grace Hartigan arrived for a visit at the Falls she naturally expected to see the exotic plants. "They asked me if I'd like to see them in their greenhouse," she recalled, "and when I walked in I just saw rocks and *fuzz.*" Menken made her report in film. From its first view of the greenhouse, *Glimpse of the Garden* pans to the rock garden, focuses there on some individual blooms, and proceeds by rapid, smearing pans back to the greenhouse where it surveys the potted specimens being nursed to survival under glass. The film virtually collects the plants and pots them, just as Rupert and Dwight collected their species in the West and proceeded home to pot them in

Astragalus coccineus *in the greenhouse*

the greenhouse. "Quite a few seeds were harvested this July in Colorado and New Mexico," reported Dwight to the *Bulletin*, "and sixty-five species brought back alive (or half-alive) in the back of our station wagon." Menken's reenactment of this lifetime project—she had witnessed it in her two friends by then for thirteen years—seems undeniably to identify *Glimpse of the Garden* as the next after Noguchi in her line of film portraits, a double portrait, this time, of Rupert and Dwight. The dirt in her camera gate made perfect sense. Gardening *is* dirty, and all its bloom and color issue from the right kind of soil, whether loam or radiolarian chert. When a retrospective of Menken's work was presented in the Charles Theater at Twelfth Street and Avenue B in December 1961, Jonas Mekas observed in the *Village Voice* that certain of her films, including

Glimpse of the Garden, marked a new stage in film poetry. The young Joe LeSueur, then a drama critic writing in *Scenario,* agreed, and he further proposed that "there should be another retrospective show—at the Museum of Modern Art, we hope." Dwight, in a blurb that has been attributed to him by the online catalog of Canyon Cinema Cooperative, wrote, "She deserves the order of the square halo, first class, with harps in diamonds."

Between painting and film, Menken believed, the practical difference was money. Having painted, she remarked in an interview, "the camera was a natural for me to try—but how expensive!" Her solution was Gryphon Productions, sometimes called the Gryphon Film Group, a pioneer filmmaking and distribution cooperative that she organized in 1946 using her Christmas bonus from *Time.* More reliable funding came from Dwight. "Oh yes," volunteered Maas, "we have an avant-guardian angel in Dwight Ripley, in whose green pastures the Gryphon has been known to graze." In its concept, but also as a center of film culture, the Gryphon prefigured the network of societies and cooperatives that would come to characterize independent film in the United States. The studio occupied a loft at 117 Greene Street, in what is now SoHo but was then a forbidding district of half-vacant buildings and abandoned industrial lofts. Eventually it was relocated to the Ovington Building at 252 Fulton Street in Brooklyn. Descriptions of the communal excitement, jealousies, and even physical violence that occurred at the Gryphon make it sound like an alcoholic prototype for the druggier Factory in the decade that followed. (Andy Warhol met Menken and Maas in 1962—he called them "the last of the great Bohemians"—and began making films of his own later the next year.) Dwight, meanwhile, sponsored projects that went beyond the studio, including filmmaking trips to Europe for both Menken and Maas. They traveled separately. In 1958 he paid Menken's way to the International Experimental Film Festival, at the Brussels World's Fair, where *Glimpse of the Garden* was screened. After the festival Menken took her camera to Spain, and Dwight reported to Jesse and Lee Effron what happened next.

Marie dashed off to Spain the other day to make a movie of some Andalusian monks. Since the dear girl doesn't sling the lingo, she picked up an expatriate American in Paris called Kenneth Anger to 'chaperone' her. They had a gorgeous time, & apparently the film was a success. The first rumor to reach me from Guadix (tiny Spanish village where they were staying, & which I've known for years) was that the mayor had thrown them out because ever since they arrived, the death rate of the population had risen alarmingly & people were dropping dead right & *left*. She was accused of casting a spell over the village & of being a witch. (*As* they boarded the train, a man was run over by a car & killed.) Naively, I believed all this gibberish; then I thought, she was probably ejected for public drunkenness. *Now* the Truth is Out, my dears. Kenneth's interest in one of the acolytes (the ones that wear lace skirts & hang around the monastery) had gone beyond the merely avuncular, & the child, bemused, had begun to Look Back at Anger. They weren't actually *stoned*, Andalusia not being as far south as Peru, but I'll bet there were some nasty remarks.

Dwight observed of himself in *A Sunlit Scene* that he was always "bemused by eccentricity," but in this regard was "rather like an *enfant terrible* staring pop-eyed at a cookie jar that is out of reach." The cookie jar, it seems, was staring pop-eyed back. Julian Beck, the husband of Judith Malina and cofounder with her of the Living Theatre, approached Dwight on several occasions for money. In the course of one such request he actually wrote, "I must say that people with money have always made the best friends." John Myers confessed in his memoirs that he and Waldemar Hansen had attended the party where Dwight met Harold Norse specifically to win Dwight's favors. Hansen, who was by then replaced in Peter Watson's affections with yet another young American, reflected that it was strange how the rich "always turn us on." Myers added an elevating distinction. "Not quite true, of course. The brilliant, the beautiful, the talented rich, turn *all* of us on." Rupert told us Dwight had concluded, even as a boy, that he would have to perform in order to outshine his wealth as he saw it reflected in everyone's eyes. "Dwight paces the floor and talks a rapid barrage of deviltry," reported Malina. "He punctuates his speech with schizophrenic patterns, spelling out words, abbreviating all three-syllable words to their first syllable, using puns, allusions, vulgarities, obscenities, foreign phrases; and all this at a horribly fast clip, with very strong emphasis on '*thee* most meaningless ph*ra*ses.' " At the same time he deployed his wit to keep people at a distance, and he enjoyed shocking them. On Malina's first visit to the Falls, he placed a billy club in the guest room, and when she inquired he responded, "It is put to *use*, honey!" She believed this, even as she believed it when told he could be sexually aroused only in a dentist's chair. Dwight and his friends in Upper Bohemia had a Surrealist faith in the value of creative mischief. Rupert said of Tony Bower that he was "like others in that set, always trying to do something malicious to each other." Sometimes Dwight set people up (having a Picasso delivered by limousine was not exactly innocent) to see how foolish they might be. When Malina was arrested for civil disobedience in 1955, Menken appealed to Dwight to send her some financial help. Malina had been jailed, along with Bayard Rustin, Dorothy Day, Jackson Mac Low, and nineteen others, for refusing to descend to a bomb shelter during a civil defense drill. She was free on bail, but a trial was imminent. Dwight responded as soon as asked—which is attractive in him, and provides a clue to his political reflexes if not to his politics—but he proceeded in a manner that perhaps was needlessly cruel. Surely Menken knew how to contact Malina. Dwight nonetheless telephoned John Myers at Tibor de Nagy Gallery to obtain Malina's number. To her diary (the unedited version, now in the New York Public Library for the Performing Arts), Malina reported the jealous advice that Dwight promptly received. "Johnny tells Dwight 'Judith is going to jail for a year & the Living Theatre is folding. Besides you can't run a theater in a dungeon.' & only two days ago at John Ashbery's bon voyage party I had talked to Johnny for an hour & he knows our play opens on the fifth & that I will not go to jail for a year & that even if I did The Living Theatre would not fold! I cannot understand downright treachery."

Dwight sent Malina a check, as he must have intended all along, for $150. Apparently this was a welcome sum, being the equivalent of about a thousand dollars today, and yet it hardly seems adequate to excite the plot that followed. Malina and Beck encouraged the third member of their ménage à trois to seduce Dwight. "This horrible scheme may not work after all," confided Malina to her diary. "But it will not be Lester's fault, who plays his role like a Venetian courtesan, advancing & retreating like a sensual dancer." The unlikely foursome had attended a matinee (it was *The Chalk Garden* at the Ethel Barrymore Theatre; Cecil Beaton designed the sets), and Malina failed to understand why, after all the sensual advancing and retreating, Dwight went to a nearby bar and burst into tears. "Wept because of Lester," she recorded, "& then wanted to be alone & wanted above all that Lester leave him." The rich may be different, or not; but perhaps the moral to be drawn from Fitzgerald's famous observation is that *we* become different around the rich. Years earlier Dwight had written from Santa Monica to Rupert, who was then on tour from one herbarium to another, to describe a new boyfriend he had found for himself in the interval. "He's terribly nice to talk to, dumb as hell but not in the least irritating, & since he's broke and doesn't in the *least* mind accepting 'pecuniary recompense' (which he earns, ¡y cómo!), the affair should last till you get back. There's the usual chit-chat about his becoming my chauffeur & so on, but that's all routine stuff. Sometimes they think they're going to New York with me, the poor poops."

Friends who knew Rupert only in his later years seemed to form an image of Dwight that was diminished by regret. There was a reason for the regret. "He was so vitally alive," wrote Rupert one December to explain why he could not celebrate during this month— it "casts a long shadow"—in which Dwight had died. But friends who knew the two men together, as a couple, formed meanwhile an image that does not match perfectly the one that Rupert then passed on to us. This seems to me predictable. I am confident that if I learned how a visitor described Doug and Frank after two hours, or even a weekend, I would hardly recognize the pair in question, let alone want to visit them myself. Stanley Welsh, whose name was given to the Stanley L. Welsh Herbarium at Brigham Young University as these pages were being written, had a sane observation to make in this regard: "I do not attempt to understand the relationship between Rupert and Dwight." Rupert, while he was tending gently to our educations, insisted of course that Frank read Proust, but (this was consistent) also Montaigne. He sent his own copy, just to make sure. When it arrived we discovered that it was enhanced by discreet check marks, including one that had been placed in the essay "Of Friendship" next to the following sentence: "But knowing how remote a thing such a friendship is from the common practice, and how rare it is, I do not expect to find any good judge of it." Malina, staying at Wappingers Falls in 1956, confided to her diary that "Dwight pretends to rule here as in a palace. Rupert cooks & keeps house & serves him & 'takes care of him.' Well, I want to say this sounds like an excellent arrangement! If only Dwight can get it to last once the visitors leave." Writing about the woeful state of their garden, particularly the *Astragalus,* the *Oxytropis,* and *Xylorrhiza coloradensis,* all of which were exasperating to cultivate, Dwight interrupted his narrative to inform readers of the *Bulletin of the American Rock Garden Society* that "Mr. Barneby has just peered over my shoulder and pointed out that as far as *he*'s concerned, *Xylorrhiza coloradensis* is perfectly O.K. and I'm grossly exaggerating its state of health." Did the two of them pursue separate adventures? The record speaks for itself. "I would be so worried about him," said Rupert, "certain he would endanger himself or worse." We can't ask Dwight if the concern was reciprocal, but it is satisfying to note that his eloquent and sassy letters contain also the recognizably banal anxieties of dumb affection. "I do hope you're having a wonderful time, darling," he wrote. "But don't get over-tired or try to do too much, will you. Do keep on writing me. I must know where you are all the time." When the *New York Times* interviewed Rupert for his profile in 1992 he told the writer that his relationship with Dwight had been a "lifetime partnership." At Rupert's loft in the stable, *this*, we learned, was Dwight's favorite cup and *that* his favorite rug. We heard that Dwight admired Lee Krasner, that he liked his Hartigan better than his Dubuffets, that he took down the Tunnard and replaced it with a Leslie, and, because he thought they looked dowdy, one day he varnished the Cornells. In particular we learned what he thought of flowers. He *hated* gladioli and the paintings of Georgia O'Keeffe. Lincoln Foster, of the American Rock Garden Society, raised a Saxifrage that he named *S.* 'Dwight Ripley,' but the bloom was so kitsch Dwight wouldn't have it in the garden and he told poor Foster exactly that. At the same time, Dwight recognized Rupert's interests and he regarded them with respect. The drawings in his fourth show at Tibor de Nagy in 1956 comprised a series called *Hats* (though if these were hats, wrote Laverne George in *Arts*, they were "headgear unlike anything which even Hedda Hopper might devise"). The hats parodied the styles of Braque, Picasso, and Miró, and included among them in the same constellation of regard was the *Portrait of Rupert Barneby, Esq. (botanist)*. Dwight's Picasso wore a cross-eyed woman on his head, his Braque wore a Cubist salad on his head, and his Rupert wore that flowerpot on his head: three drawings to suggest what was *in* each head as well. It requires no stretch of the evidence to conclude that Dwight—linguist, poet, botanist, et cetera—admired in Rupert the single-minded pursuit of *Astragalus* and, later, *Dalea*. In one of his unpublished stories the characters are called Manfred and Rupert. The names hardly need to be unpacked. "Besides I tell you, Rupert, I have an idea," says Manfred. "It is so long now that I have had an idea worth speaking of that I am very fond and proud of it. I am no longer bored by the buzz of my own vacuity. You can hardly realize what that means, you whose mind is always occupied with your absurd weeds."

Dwight did have an idea, one that finally would bring his interests together in a single focus of contemplation, and that idea was how to use the colored pencil. In this he showed foresight and considerable self-confidence as well, because if there was no language for wit and nonsense in an age of anxiety there certainly was no language for the colored pencil. "Colored pencils can be used to decorate wood," wrote *Art News* in a column about new materials in 1955. "Plates, lamp bases, coffee tables, chests and so forth can all be colored in a technique which might be easier than paints for beginning craftsmen." Each time Tibor de Nagy Gallery devoted its space during the 1950s to Dwight's drawings, it was probably the only gallery in New York to be treating colored pencil as a primary medium for an adult artist. And each time, John Myers probably thought that the gallery was doing the medium, if not the artist, a

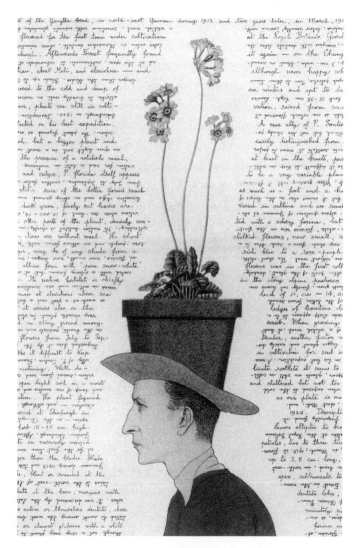

Dwight Ripley,
Portrait of Rupert Barneby, Esq. (botanist), *1955*

favor. In 1964 the magazine *Art in America* sponsored an exhibit of contemporary drawings at FAR Gallery that included the work of fifty-three artists, and not one drawing—even though the managing editor of *Art in America* by then was Dwight's friend Tony Bower— was in colored pencil. The ceramist Ken Price used colored pencil to make drawings of his ceramic cups in 1967; Joe Brainard used it in 1975 for a self-portrait and for his Dwight-like parody *If Nancy Was a Painting by de Kooning;* and Cy Twombly used it with graphite and ballpoint as a kind of calligraphic medium as early as 1960. Probably the best-known drawing in colored pencil to be made in the decade after Dwight died was David Hockney's 1974 portrait of Andy Warhol, best known because it was sold by Sotheby's in 1988 for $330,000. This was a record for colored pencil, even if it was the association and not the medium that was so highly coveted. In the meantime, a professional language for colored pencil was being developed thanks largely to the practicing artists themselves. You lift colored pencil to lighten value, you burnish it to deepen value. You layer it to change the hue. Sometimes these colored pencil techniques are used to produce the illusionistic "fine art" effects that can make a drawing look, paradoxically, still more amateur. An explanation for the paradox can be found by looking back to another influential article by Clement Greenberg, "The New Laocoön," which followed "Avant-Garde and Kitsch" in *Partisan Review.* "The arts, then, have been hunted back to their mediums," wrote Greenberg. "To restore the identity of an art the opacity of its medium must be emphasized." This was a simple but eloquent insight that would continue for years to resonate through the arts (a sculpture that confronts the pedestrian with an insurmountable wall of steel restores the opacity of its medium; poetry that presents an insurmountable wall of words has restored the opacity of its medium), and there is no way that Dwight, with Jean Connolly and Greenberg at his side in galleries and museums, could have escaped its significance. He *liked* pencils as a medium; he had been using them since childhood in botanical and zoological drawings. He liked his pencils so much that he regarded them, too, with fond dismay. He called them "pills." As he began seriously to draw, he also had before him on the farmhouse walls the constant example of his "Constellations" and his oils by Miró. One lesson to be taken from Miró was to resist the temptations of modeling, or even the discrete recessions of Cubism for that matter. "Modelling prevents shock and limits movement to the visual depth," is how Miró himself explained it. Combine these two insights—Greenberg on opacity plus Miró on modeling—and you have a formula for the application of opaque prospects of pigment, fearlessly stylized to hide your "fine art" techniques. On the occasion of his *Bomb* show, Dwight had been praised by Margaret Breuning in *Arts Digest* for "producing areas of glowing light and intricate networks of colored ribbons (one can imagine with what rubbings and scrubbings)." And yet the course of his artistic development was to master such techniques, then progressively subordinate them to the patient, stroke-by-stroke accumulation of unmodeled color. This was an achievement that added to my confusion when the drawings came one by one that midnight from the trunk. They were too dark for pencil drawings, too uniformly colored, too stylized, and too abstract. They looked too much like paintings to be drawings. Only later would I discover how Dwight himself described his work. "I am radiantly happy," he wrote, "& painting with all the aplomb, if not the technique, of Tintoretto."

Rupert could not tell us how long Dwight continued to support the Tibor de Nagy Gallery. I assume, from the twenty-fifth anniversary statement made by de Nagy, that Dwight wrote his last scheduled check sometime in the final months of 1956. The gallery's early ledgers at the Archives of American Art are for the years 1951 and 1953 only, but there is painful evidence to corroborate the de Nagy account: after Dwight's *Hats* closed, in March 1956, John Myers did not offer him a new show at the gallery for another six years. In each of the three preceding years Myers had sponsored a party in Dwight's honor, held not at his openings but at a date in midshow. "Last night, a party at Herbert Machiz' for millionaire dilettante Dwight Ripley," recorded Malina in her diary on January 14, 1954. "The de Nagy painters Jane Freilicher, Al Leslie, Grace Hartigan, Larry Rivers, Harry Jackson (sic!) & Joan, de Koonings Bill & Elaine. Willard Maas who turned all discussions to sex. Marie Menken with whom we talked at length about Ezra Pound in the kitchen where a shy colored maid was abashed by our vulgar vocabulary. I in black lace, Marie towering over me in lamé." A similar party, this time for *Hats*, took place in 1956 at the apartment of librettist John Latouche. Even Rupert had to admit that Dwight, whose first line of defense on social occasions was too much alcohol, was not a happy or an attractive figure at these events. "He was a loud and obnoxious drunk," remembered Harold Norse. "He insulted maître d's. At galleries he made disparaging remarks about paintings in the presence of the painter. I wondered why he wasn't pounded to a pulp." Budd Myers, later a good friend to Dwight and Rupert both (and no relation to the gallery director John Myers), remarked once that Dwight seemed to have "no core," which sounds like a phrase that Dwight himself would plant to ward off sympathy. It agrees with the assessment made by Malina at the time. "We drink with Dwight Ripley," she told her diary. "There is no real contact with him, no actuality, no human touch, yet he pours himself out towards us, yet he is so actual & so appealingly, appallingly human." Dwight—this will be no surprise—had a perspective of his own. "Do I scare people?" he asked Rupert. "Yes, of course. But it's odd nonetheless to find them getting nervous in the divine presence. They fidget & smoke & jump about & *never* look one in the eye." Among Dwight's letters to Rupert, Frank and I found a suggestive, if unpronounceable poem that he made from the word for oriole in eight languages plus Latin. The languages were English, Romanian, Russian, German, Spanish, Czech, Italian, and Polish. The spellings are Dwight's.

> The oriole, grangur, ívolga,
> Goldamsel, oripéndola,
> Zhluva, rigógolo or wilga,
> Galbulus sobbing day or night within the golden hedge;
> Here are no hidden fires. I have none.

It is probably witless to observe of artists, writers, or actors that they seem to be most themselves when painting, writing, or acting, but when separated from their work their personalities threaten to disintegrate. "Dwight is not a griever or a whiner," Rupert told John Myers. "Gone are the snows of yesteryear." Perhaps; although I suspect that the grief and the whining were melted not by time but art. Dwight's most engaging drawings had been fueled by a kind of pictorial dialogue with his critic friends, Connolly and Greenberg. Lives change, however, and when Greenberg was married in May 1956 to Janice Van Horne, Dwight marked the occasion by presenting him with a watch from Cartier. The critic was offended, on the defensible grounds that a wedding present should be given to Clem and Jenny both. He wore the watch, even so, for the rest of his life. You can see it in the later photographs. Van Horne remembered arriving with Greenberg at a party given by Dwight at 416 East Fifty-eighth Street. Dwight—who had pushed his way across the room calling "Clem! Clem!"—proceeded to kiss her husband, not glancingly, on the mouth. Greenberg, accepting the challenge, kissed Dwight as forcefully back. It was a crowded, noisy party in which Rupert was nowhere to be seen. After Greenberg inquired, he and Van Horne were led by Dwight to an adjoining room, where they found Rupert peering intently through his microscope at a plant. Rupert believed (the snows of yesteryear aside) that Dwight experienced Greenberg's marriage the way he experienced Jean's to Laurence Vail: a loss not to a rival world but, worse, to advancing time. Only the year before, Greenberg had summed up the artistic excitement of their wartime and postwar years in a retrospective article that was published as " 'American-Type' Painting" in *Partisan Review*. He made the point there that the Abstract Expressionist painters had challenged the idea of a picture as a luxury object that you frame and hang on a wall. Even when he was advising Dwight to buy his 1949 Pollock oils, the critic was known for the provocative opinion that Pollock had brought the easel picture to a crisis because his paintings came close to decoration, "to the kind seen in wallpaper patterns that can be repeated indefinitely," as Greenberg observed, beyond the frame. It was an opening that Dwight could no longer resist.

In the summer that followed Greenberg's marriage, Dwight began a series of drawings based on patterns—stripes and interlocking diamonds—that might indeed be repeated like wallpaper beyond the frame. On these patterns he superimposed the representations of framed pictures: his own shyly perspectival renderings, or capricci, of the best-known Baroque churches in Brazil. He had seen G. E. Kidder Smith's photographs of these churches in *Brazil Builds,* an architectural survey that was sponsored by the Museum of Modern Art in 1943. The show was devoted largely to Modernism; it traveled to forty-eight cities in the Americas over a period of three years and helped to legitimize Modernist architecture wherever it went. Dwight remembered the Baroque churches instead, especially those in the state of Minas Gerais which are associated with the work of a single sculptor, O Aleijadinho, or "The Little Cripple." Aleijadinho, whose real name was Antônio Francisco Lisboa, lost the use of his legs and suffered the amputation of his fingers and toes sometime around 1777, when he was still in his thirties. Using tools tied to his wrists, he went on to sculpt the medallions, doorways, and statues that make Minas Gerais a rich center of the

Brazilian Baroque. His most famous works are the twelve soapstone statues, representing prophets of the Old Testament, that front the church of Bom Jesus de Matosinhos in the town of Congonhas do Campo. Dwight's homage to Aleijadinho was combined with his nostalgia for the dialogues with Greenberg to result in a series of drawings—I call them *Churches;* so far we have found only four—in which the commentary seems burned away, and only an affectionate, apprehensive irony remains. When he put frames around his churches, Dwight made them seem to hang on their wallpaper backgrounds like museum artifacts released from history and geography. The extra-historical effect was heightened by the inclusion of images from other stylistic eras. On the same striped wallpaper with the *Baroque* edifice in Congonhas do Campo, Dwight placed a *Victorian* pleasure balloon (though it appears to wield a wrecking ball) and a *Modernist* work from his own collection (it was painted by the Italian artist Afro Basaldella in 1944). Years later, an art that posed the moral and aesthetic equivalence of styles would be called Postmodernist. Dwight also tagged his capricci with updated versions of a classical symbol for the migrant soul, the butterfly. His church at Congonhas do Campo is visited by an eastern swallowtail and a monarch butterfly. In a second drawing he did for this series, two churches in Ouro Prêto (it means black gold in Portuguese) were likewise visited: this time by *Icterus galbula,* a brilliant black-and-gold Baltimore oriole.

Dwight had the DTs, according to Willard Maas, when Menken filmed *Dwightiana* at the Fifty-eighth Street apartment in 1959. She even made the film, Maas later insisted, to take Dwight's mind off the people he believed were watching him from the street. With-

Dwight Ripley, Churches: Congonhas do Campo, *1956*

drawal had made him paranoid, but he was distressed further by the condition of his face. It was no longer a gardenia-peony-gardenia trick. Now it was "my Ivan Le Lorraine Albright thing," as he called it in reference to the Magic Realist painter best known for having created the grotesquely aging portrait in the 1945 motion picture *The Picture of Dorian Gray.* Malina recorded her opinion that Dwight, "by willing himself a monster," had brought his condition on himself. "His slim figure protruded, his skin broke into a sickly mass of splotches, his expression, disfigured by a discolored nose & watery eyes became one of disgust & disdain." By this description she had identified a problem not of character, of course, but of rosacea, an advanced case of which will result in the appearance made famous by rosacea sufferer W. C. Fields. Because of Fields, people mistakenly assume the condition is caused by alcoholism. Instead there is a link between rosacea and how frequently, and how severely, individuals blush. Drinking, unfortunately, can make the symptoms worse. Although Dwight scarcely needed an excuse to drink, a good one had presented itself in May 1956, when Peter Watson was found drowned in the bathtub of his apartment in London. Watson and Norman Fowler, the young American who replaced Hansen, had been reported quarreling. Fowler, who stood to inherit the bulk of Watson's fortune, was widely regarded as unstable. Friends thought the circumstances were suspicious enough to warrant investigation; the police, because the bathroom door was locked from the inside, and because the case involved cohabiting males, did not. A minor bequest in Watson's will went to Brian Howard, who had continued trying to find a place where he and Sam Langford could live together. With their French visas restored, they intended to settle at last near Nice. They arrived when their house was under renovation; a contractor had neglected to reconnect an exhaust vent, and, in chilly January 1958, Langford turned on a gas heater and was asphyxiated as he slept. Howard stopped eating. He purchased twin burial lots, planned a double funeral, and on the fourth day following Langford's death he took a drug overdose and died. That same winter a blizzard in Dutchess County caused a power interruption, the heat went out in the greenhouse at the Falls, and every plant in the collection was frozen and killed. Dwight spent much of the ensuing year drunk. "His drinking got so bad," remembered Hartigan, "he couldn't carry on a coherent conversation—and sober he was brilliant and witty and charming." In October he canceled a fiftieth birthday party because, as he apologized to the Effrons, "I'm on a convalescent kick, & the dreary thing is, if I get off it for just one l'il evening, I'm *perdu.*" He stuck to his resolve, and in the spring was so ill that he believed from the examples of Watson and Howard that he, too, was in danger of premature death. In a search of lost time, I suppose that Louise Ripley's jewels would be still under her five-year-old's bed. Menken encouraged Dwight's fears, in the hope, according to Rupert, that she might marry him herself. "She told him I was going to put his head in the oven and he was so sick by then I think he almost believed her!" Eventually, Dwight was admitted to Vassar Hospital, where he had recovered from the auto accident ten years before. As his strength returned he began again to draw. "Rupert told us that the trusty pencil is back in your hot little hand again," wrote Lee Effron in the autumn following. "You can't keep irrepressible and irresistible Dwight down—and a good thing it is too!" The new drawings could not have been more suggestive; one alluded to Kandinsky, another to Delaunay (both painters were known for their color theories). A third was of a yellow, egg-shaped bird surmounted by a refractive fountain of a tail in red, orange, yellow, green, blue, and violet. This drawing even was signed, and above the signature Dwight put the caption LIROGON. "What is *lirogon?*" I asked Rupert. "Oh that," he replied as if it was nothing special, "that is lyrebird in Polish."

I T WAS NEVER A SECRET to Dwight that his avant-garde friends thought he was a dilettante. Anyone who traces the references to him in memoirs and reviews will discover how persistent was the formula—linguist, poet, botanist, artist first planted with the *New York Times* by Peggy Guggenheim. The biographer Jacqueline Bograd Weld repeated that formula forty years later in *Peggy: The Wayward Guggenheim*, but with a writer's instinct for making it sting. "Ripley," she wrote, "was a gifted dilettante—botanist, linguist, poet. He occasionally painted." Dwight seemed sometimes to surrender to this view himself, particularly in the weeks following an exhibit at Tibor de Nagy Gallery of the new drawings he had made at Stirling House, the decaying mansion he and Rupert purchased in Greenport, on the North Fork at the east end of Long Island. This house was located on five acres with its back to Long Island Sound. Here Dwight walked daily to the shore ("our *plage*," he reported happily), collecting shells and pebbles as he had at Venice Beach in California and, before that, on the coast of Spain. Influenced by the shore, in part by Rachel Carson's *Silent Spring*, which first appeared in the *New Yorker* in 1961, he produced thirty mixed-media drawings for an untitled series I have called *Marines*. Each drawing began with gouache and colored inks that were dripped or puddled on artboard to create Pollock-like skeins; over these Dwight fixed cutouts of fish, shells, marine birds, ships, and

houses. The cutouts were enhanced further with colored pencil. In
description, this procedure suggests another replay of the old argument with Connolly. The effect, as the gouache and inks seemed to
trap lifeforms, ships, and houses alike in webs of systemic danger,
was of ecological foreboding instead. John Myers, persuaded by the
complexity of the new drawings, dropped hints about a show at the
gallery; but for several months this outcome was not assured. "Miss
Parsons is after me now," wrote Dwight to Jesse and Lee Effron in
the autumn of 1961, "& Johnny Myers is so unpredictable & capri-
cious that I'm seriously thinking of switching to her (tho' I don't
like her personally)." The *Marines* were finally displayed at Tibor
de Nagy for three weeks during April 1962. It was the year in which
Pop art triumphed at the galleries (Lichtenstein showed at Castelli,
Rosenquist and Oldenburg at Green, Thiebaud at Allan Stone,
Warhol at the Stable Gallery that fall) and, as Clement Greenberg
later remarked, "Abstract Expressionism collapsed very suddenly."
When Lee Effron suggested a follow-up show at the Three Arts,
Dwight was adamant. "Once again I risk our Friendship Forever by
saying *Não, nem, nyet, ochi, nein* or even plain *No!* Reason: I've
decided quite definitely that my 'career' (ha!) as an artist is Over."
He turned his attention to his old friends, other languages, and concentrated on the project that was to become his unpublished *Etymological Dictionary of Vernacular Plant Names*. By the time of his
death the manuscript measured 1.6 linear feet. He had planned a
cumulative index, but even as it stands the dictionary provides for
any species its common names in the principal European languages
and dialects, together with an indication of their derivations and
meanings. Myers surely had the *Etymological Dictionary* as one

example in mind when he observed of Dwight, "The word poly-math took on new meaning." A dealer today might find a savvier term for an artist who was, after all, a displaced national devoted to threatened languages, overlooked species, and unorthodox media. Partial responsibility for Dwight's eventual image must be borne, however, by autodidact Rupert. His influence can be detected on the tax return for Dwight's estate, where Dwight is listed as "amateur philologist and botanist," and in the biography *Peggy Guggenheim and Her Friends*, where Dwight is identified as a part-time artist with "an amateur passion for plants." Rupert had refused to understand that the word "amateur" does not mean in America what it meant in eighteenth-century England, and it would be a *solecism* to apply it to a George Bentham, say, or to himself. Dwight did understand, and he expressed his amusement in high style. Among his unpublished stories we found a single untitled sentence that was sufficient to be a story on its own. "Hervé le Saindoux had at the age of 26 already published three books: 'Au Large', a stirring saga of life aboard a windjammer; 'En Marge', an acrimonious study of the contempo-rary scene; and 'Barge', the autobiography of a godwit."

Even as he was saying no to Lee Effron in six languages, Dwight had begun to establish at Greenport the conditions that would enable him to make the three hundred drawings I discovered that midnight in the trunk. "The New Life is off to a good start," he reported, "with no booze at all (not as easy as it sounds—for a dyed-in-the-wool alcoholic); how genteel & dull can you get?" Dull, no doubt, but the improvement soon was noticed by his friends. Guggenheim returned briefly to New York in 1961 (she was suing Lee Krasner in regard to Pollock's last contract with Art of This

Century), and Dwight met her at the Auberge for lunch. "Peggy in Venice commented on how marvellous you looked," wrote Julian Beck after a trip later that year to Europe, "better than ever in the past." As an aid to recovery, the removal to Greenport had promised a refuge from the world of the avant-garde that the combination of the Falls and Fifty-eighth Street could no longer provide. In the two decades since "Avant-Garde and Kitsch" the prospect of belonging to such a world had become so seductive that its very definition was now seen as a prize. Tom Hess, the influential editor of *Art News,* declared in that magazine in 1958 that the Avant-Garde, when capitalized and defined as a group, was a relic of the previous age. Harold Rosenberg proposed in *Art in America* the existence of a Vanguard Audience instead. Henceforth, he predicted, the artist's "struggle with his environment" would be conducted from within the society and not from Bohemia. When *Art in America* asked a panel of artists if *they* thought there still was an avant-garde, Larry Rivers responded, "Is there anything else?" For certain of the painters and poets associated once with Tibor de Nagy Gallery, this line of thinking seemed to culminate in the observation, as made by John Ashbery in his address "The Invisible Avant-Garde," that the solution was to proceed even in the face of approval. Ashbery framed his insight earlier in more practical terms. "The calm and the isolation of exile," he wrote, "work together to accomplish this perilous experiment which, when it succeeds, can result in an art that is independent of environment, as art must be in order to survive when the environment has been removed." Exile was chosen by a number of artists who moved to Europe; examples frequently cited were Cy Twombly in Italy and Joan Mitchell in France. Likewise

Building the enclosed garden

courageous was exile in a place of no tourist appeal. Grace Hartigan moved to Baltimore and established her studio in a district of abandoned factories. At Stirling House, Dwight and Rupert created an atmosphere that Jesse Effron characterized at the time as "exotic but controlled, Victorian but classic, and quite suitable even for those who like a temperate climate." If this wasn't exile, it nonetheless supported a calm in which Dwight could draw, and during which

Rupert felt free periodically to make the long drive to the Bronx for work on *Astragalus* at the Botanical Garden. Howard Irwin, later the garden president, recalled one such trip as his first meeting with the future Dr. Barneby. "I soon realized that Rupert's shy, self-effacing manner masked a powerful intellect," he said, "an awesome capacity to analyze and sift detail, and a total devotion to his science." Irwin never knew, perhaps, that the powerful intellect was ticketed repeatedly on the Long Island Expressway during these trips, and always for the same offense: failure to maintain the minimum speed. A happy omen of the new life in Greenport appeared in November 1961, when Miró, revisiting the United States, surprised Dwight by sending a sketch he had drawn on Hotel Gladstone stationery. This sketch, a self-portrait of the artist as a stocky square, with stick legs, triangular feet, and a broad smile, is at the Archives of American Art in Washington, D.C. Frank saw it there. It is signed "per Dwight Ripley, afectnosament Miró." Dwight called it the *regalito*, the little gift, and he hung it on December 9 at Stirling House.

Under the combined impact of expenses for the new house and the decline in his fortune, Dwight could not afford to subsidize his eccentric friends as he had in the decade before. Apparently he was too proud to tell them, although in fairness there must be few of us who believe an annual statement of net worth should be filed with our friends. Within a year of the move to Greenport, Menken and Maas requested $14,000 to buy a house of their own—"the *copycats!*" pronounced Dwight—on Staten Island. They were not likely to know that Dwight's debts, listed in his pocket diary as a schedule of payments due to various creditors, amounted that year to more than $19,000 ($120,000 in current terms) or that, even so, he had loaned $4,000 to Tony Bower. In September 1961, Julian Beck requested $500 from Dwight to reopen the Living Theatre. "He was so proudly aristocratic," remembered Malina many years later, "that he never hinted to us that he was anything but wealthy—and he did make contributions to our work throughout his life." In October, Maya Deren suffered a series of strokes, and on Friday the thirteenth, aged forty-four, she died. She was survived by her impoverished young husband, Teiji Ito, the composer of the *Dwightiana* soundtrack. Menken immediately asked for money on Ito's behalf. It was Menken and Maas who had suggested Dwight come to the aid of Dylan Thomas's widow when Thomas died in 1953. At that time he responded with a thousand dollars, only to discover he had exceeded his income and would have to borrow funds himself. This time he refused. Maas, writing for the Maya Deren memorial issue of *Filmwise*, reacted angrily. "Marie had written a rich friend who shall be nameless out of respect for the days before he became a camel," complained Maas. "He chose to misunderstand Marie's letter, being guilty of his wealth as the rich always seem to be, and wrote back, 'And am I now expected to give the widower a thousand dollars?' This crude cruelty made me think of Maya and her frequent rages against the rich, and I wished she were here to give me words to express the scorn and hatred his letter engendered in me." The *Filmwise* had not been published (it was mimeographed) when Ito received a substantial sum from his father's estate and was no longer in need. Then the *Filmwise* appeared. During the two years that followed her making of *Dwightiana*, Menken had referred to that film as *Dwightiana for Dwight Ripley*. The drawings she used as flats amounted to a mini-retrospective of Dwight's work, and the film received a Creative Film Foundation Award in 1959. "Marie was one of the first," observed Warhol, "to do a film with stop-time." Now she made its filming sound like therapy. "This little animated film was shot in a few evenings," she said, "while watching over an ill friend whom I tried to entertain. He recovered." Maas told the same story, but added, "Dwight recovered and was never fun again."

Stirling House, at nineteen rooms, was a dramatic change from the farmhouse at the Falls. "It's probably all a big mistake," wrote Dwight to the Effrons, "but we were both getting fed up with that little house & its thousand-and-one disadvantages, & something Drastic had to be done before we went cuckoo." The new spaciousness reminded both men of the Spinney, and one more time Dwight withdrew to build a world of forms and colors that would be very much their own. It was, he admitted, a "half-crazed" thing to do. "For to be independent you have to damage yourself," he wrote. "It's all wrong and anti-social and the social machine resents it, claims its pound of flesh, so to speak." This sounds to me like a rationalization or perhaps a self-fulfilling prophecy. It was the defensive pattern repeated in each new house that the two men owned. Apparently it also worked. "Oh God am I glad to be away from those empty bird-cages," confessed Malina after a visit earlier to the Falls. Maas, once so frequent a presence in the two men's lives, was never to visit Stirling House. Menken was there three times. A wider audience soon made the acquaintance, albeit at some remove, of that unusual husband-and-wife pair. They were identified by playwright Edward Albee as his nearest models for the quarrelsome

Enclosed garden at Stirling House

George and Martha in *Who's Afraid of Virginia Woolf?* The play, which opened at the Billy Rose Theatre in October 1962, ran for more than two years. When it was made into a motion picture, the characters inspired by Menken and Maas were played by Elizabeth Taylor and Richard Burton. Another audience saw Menken and Maas themselves onscreen, but again without knowing it. Menken is the mother who harangues Gerard Malanga throughout one reel of

Warhol's film *Chelsea Girls*. She is Juanita Castro in *The Life of Juanita Castro*, and she appears with Maas, Malanga, and Edie Sedgwick in *Bitch*. Menken's active, expressionist camera was said to influence Warhol, by contrast, to an impassive camera that did not move, while her meticulous editing (she hung her film in strips and cut virtually frame by frame) prompted him, likewise, to let the reel itself determine the continuity of a film. "One can more clearly define the art of film in America since 1950 by saying 'Willard and Marie,' " declared Brakhage, "than by the terms 'avant-garde,' 'experimental,' and 'underground' and/or all of them together." Dwight and Rupert, meanwhile, did not know for months that their refusal to aid Ito had alienated Menken and Maas. It must have been painful to be apprised, in an intimate journal like *Filmwise*, that your long and definitive friendship was now at an end. In Greenport, Dwight turned to the garden and the pleasant burden of his *Etymological Dictionary*. When Rupert wrote to describe the garden to Peter Davis, who was by then a professor of botany at the University of Edinburgh, Dwight added a postscript. "The only real menace is crickets," he observed, "which lurk under rocks and come after dusk to munch contentedly on our favourite buns. But, the Lord be praised, no slugs."

A traditional virtue of exile is to permit a clear view of the interior subject. For Dwight, that subject first entailed travel, and in this regard an event as significant as the removal to Greenport occurred when he and Rupert returned, after an absence of twenty-eight years, to Spain. Rupert's appointment as honorary curator at the Botanical Garden, a certificate from the Department of Defense to document his service in the Ground Observer Corps, the impending completion of his work on *Astragalus*, and the changed political climate that accompanied the Kennedy administration all contributed to make the two men feel secure in traveling again outside the United States. They celebrated New Year's Eve with Tony Bower in his apartment at 54 East Sixty-sixth Street, and arrived January 15, 1962, at Gibraltar. "Can't *tell* you how thrilling it was to return to the Peninsula," reported Dwight. For ten weeks they herborized through Portugal and Spain. They even got out to Mallorca. Along the way Dwight made, as always, a record of their finds and collections. By late March they had reached the northeast *vertiente*, or slope, of the Torcal de Antequera. There they were seeking a plant that Dwight called "beautiful beyond belief," the *Linaria anticaria*. The flowers of this species are mauve—"or rather, not mauve at all," he explained, "but white, with a multitude of hair-thin violet lines ruled all over them as precisely as any shirt or ledger. It is as superior to any linaria now in gardens as Brahms to Mendelssohn, or Camembert to St. Ivel; and oh, what a distracted ass was I not to have collected seeds of this on a certain spring day years ago!" The *Linaria* was collected at last, but after ten weeks it was still difficult to leave, particularly since the two travelers had missed their visit to Cazorla, where Dwight hoped to pay his respects to *Viola cazorlensis*. Home in Greenport, he could not stop thinking of what they had, or hadn't seen, and he began as if from necessity to draw. The result was his series of *Travel Posters* for botanists, a concept, realized decades before ecotourism, that would be noteworthy in itself. Ten of these *Travel Posters* were in the trunk, and another three were located by Rupert the year before he died. The defining feature of all thirteen is their incorporation of botanical nomenclature as a

constituent, almost painterly element; the characteristic aspect of
each place has been configured from the scientific names of its in-
digenous plants. The *Travel Poster* for Cabo de Gata thus broadly
depicts the beach and headland, but it also contains, in small letters
that meet the eye at the shoreline, the binomials *Cichorium spi-
nosum, Erythrostictus punctatus,* and *Apteranthes gussoneana.* Defining the road to the headland is Sandwith's *Antirrhinum charidemi*
(the Romans called this cape Charidemus), while barely visible on
the rock itself is the name *Dianthus charidemi.* Dwight even made a
poster for Cazorla. The least pictorial of the thirteen, it nonetheless
has its own specific interest: each binomial was inscribed in the
flower color of its species, so the name *Viola cazorlensis* appears, for
example, in the pink of the bullfighter's thighs. A persuaded biographer might hope that Dwight recognized in these *Travel Posters*
the breakthrough drawings that united his polymath interests—
linguist, poet, botanist, artist. In Spain he carried his camera and for
the first time exposed only color film. "As Cecil B. once told me," he
reflected, "it doesn't matter a damn, dear, *what* sort of camera you
use, & to hell with filters, etc. What Counts is the Subject!!" Along
the left edge of the *Travel Poster* for Cabo de Gata he placed a sub-
title, EL PARAISO DE LOS BOTANICOS.

　　Although the drawings in the trunk were not titled or dated, the
prospect of sorting them was smoothed by Dwight's practice of
working in series. John Myers artfully slighted that practice when he
recalled the series *The Bomb* that was shown at Tibor de Nagy in
1955. "Having accidentally spilled some green ink on white paper,"
ventured Myers, "Dwight added *palazzi* and gondolas tossed to the
sky and called this drawing *The Bomb Hits Venice,* a sly reference to

his one-time fiancée, Peggy Guggenheim." By subject, color, and tone, the drawings that came from the trunk separated so clearly into groups, however, that even as I sorted them for the first time it became evident that Dwight was responding in each series to an emotional or technical problem he could resolve only by putting color to paper. In *The Bomb,* Myers to the contrary, he must have been dealing with *fear* through color. This was a strategy he returned to with greater success in the *Nuclear Suns,* which followed his *Travel Posters* in 1963. I call them *Nuclear Suns,* though individually these drawings appear to be sunbursts, because they were accompanied in the trunk by an unfinished collage of a mushroom cloud pasted above the legend "*Cymopterus ripleyi,* Yucca Flat." The Cuban missile crisis in October 1962 had raised again the threat of nuclear war. Dwight, by way of response, dissolved the satire of his *Bomb* series into the more durable power of ambiguity. His *Nuclear Suns* revealed the sun, or some other sun, for what it is: a nuclear explosion not the less spectacular because it too would prove, up close, to be annihilating. Technically, these *Nuclear Suns* represent also a realization in colored pencil of the painterly luxury that Dwight had been reaching for in the earlier series. A recurrent weakness of colored pencil is the pigment-deprived surface that results if the medium is used, intuitively but incompletely, as a pencil—in the expectation that atmosphere will be achieved by lighter strokes, or values deepened simply by pressing harder. Dwight's color in *Nuclear Suns,* and in the work that followed, was velvety, dense, and rich. Proof that his skill as a colorist had matured was provided by *Cabins,* a series of stylized landscapes he began in 1964 subsequent to the first trip he and Rupert made in search of *Dalea* in

Mexico. These drawings (they were among Rupert's favorites) are structured by their advancing and subsiding pinks, violets, oranges, browns, and the occasional scarlet. Due in part to the gouache-like matte he obtained with colored pencil, Dwight's colors could be unexpected without being cloying or repellent, and he successfully combined some that might, like *Viola cazorlensis,* be the despair of aunts with taste. A lifetime of attending to color in the patient, tangible manner demanded by a garden, or by collecting in the field, conceivably made of him what the art historian John Gage has called a "non-standard observer" of color. In Dwight's novel, *A Sunlit Scene,* the character Charles is discovered looking out on the harbor at Taormina. This, he thinks, must be the most beautiful spot on earth. He would rather be somewhere else, however, and the explanation he offers would have come easily to Dwight. "One has to have a quite unimaginative nature, or at any rate a placid one, to guzzle the *panorama splendide:* a vivid mind is more likely to be fired by the imperfect and the incomplete, by marshes and flat horizons, or empty, orange Utah."

Dwight, while he was making the best drawings of his career, never had another public show. Each evening as Rupert came in from the garden to fix dinner he found Dwight's work from that day laid out on the refectory table in the dining room where he could inspect it. The two men ate together in the kitchen, and afterward went to the dining room to discuss the work. Budd Myers, the younger friend and fellow rock-garden enthusiast who visited frequently until the end of Dwight's life (Dwight called him "Mr. Sunshine"), described similar exhibits that were held for small groups of friends. Myers had been a student of Willard Maas at Long Island

University, and Menken and Maas soon added him to their entourage. An editor later for *The National Cyclopedia of American Biogra-*
phy, he was married to the off-Broadway actress Trinity Thompson.
"Dwight would bring his drawings out, sometimes forty at a time,
and line them up along the shelves in the library," remembered
Myers, "and we would be ushered up for a show. Rupert would be
required to come too." On other occasions the audience included
Tony Bower. In the portrait that Dwight commissioned from Glyn
Collins, Bower was given a bitter expression, although Isherwood
recalled of him in *Down There on a Visit* that "his impudent, attrac-
tively comic face keeps breaking into grins." As managing editor at
Art in America, Bower sometimes wrote for that magazine. The
April issue in 1964 carried his positive reappraisal of painter Florine
Stettheimer. Awkwardly written, this article nonetheless praised
Stettheimer for having recognized the 1920s as "the one brief
moment in our history when pleasure was considered a laudable
goal." Others in Dwight's private audience were artist friends from
the east end of Long Island who comprised, with Bower, a remain-
der of the old Upper Bohemia: Lee Krasner in Springs, Alfonso
Ossorio and dancer Ted Dragon at their estate, the Creeks, in East
Hampton, and Theodoros Stamos, who, with his younger lover
Ralph Humphrey, lived nearby in a house he had built in East Mar-
ion. Stamos and Humphrey sometimes brought Mark Rothko; when
Frank and I asked for a comment on these historic visits, Rupert's
response was "They didn't know how to sit in a chair!" Humphrey
had a show of all-black paintings at Tibor de Nagy in 1959, and his
subsequent shows at that gallery were likewise in close-valued
monotones. A concern prevalent among younger artists at the time

Dwight, Theodoros Stamos, and John Bernard Myers at Stirling House

was to avoid color juxtapositions that might suggest one color required, or ever took precedence over, another. Stamos responded to Humphrey's example by restricting the color range in his own work. The red-versus-white standoff of *Ahab for R. J. H.*, now in the collection of the San Francisco Museum of Modern Art, was painted in homage to Humphrey. Dwight had its color ideology in mind when he remarked of Stamos, "I'm beginning to wonder if that one is quite 'all there'—over-influenced by his boy-friend who is *ob*viously deranged."

In the archives of the Ossorio Foundation, in Southampton, New York, is the typescript of a statement in which Ossorio praised

Dwight's mixed-media *Marines* for their "limpid complexity." We can only wonder what he and the others found to say about the *Travel Posters, Cabins,* and later drawings. Not so solemn as Abstract Expressionism, or even Pop art, these keenly personal works must have seemed the sort of art that people commonly tend to call idiosyncratic. An alternative label to the same effect was supplied by each of the four critics who, on four earlier occasions in *Art News* and *Art Digest,* decided to call Dwight's work "whimsical" instead. Perhaps they took his accent as their evidence. Rupert himself was careful to warn me as I began my inquiry into Dwight's life that I would discover his humor was not the norm. "He belonged to a generation who thought poems incorporated both meaning and music," advised Rupert, "but the meaning could be buried incomprehensibly deep and the music included rude and 'camp' sounds." He didn't need to be so gentle. I had got over my fear of Firbank, and had come to recognize in Dwight's brand of fond dismay an attitude that deserved, and deserves still, I think, to be admired. Any malice that was detectable in black-and-white long since had dissolved in color, as Dwight's wit became more visibly receptive and affectionate. We can all think of artists who exemplify kinds of wit. There is solemn wit and puzzle wit, scatological wit—indeed, there is sacerdotal wit—and these are employed by artists who don't always recognize the humor in humans' having an attitude. There is also a custodial wit, like Stettheimer's (in poetry one thinks of Marianne Moore), or Trevor Winkfield's, or, for that matter, like Miró's. It is humor characterized by a combination of affection and frolic foreboding, and its nonfrivolous message is that we don't even *see* without prior advantage of wit. Dwight's *Nuclear Suns* took their

shape from the places they were imagined to destroy: the sun over
Mexico bursts in the form of a marigold, the one over Fuji is a tidy
parasol. Perhaps these drawings were not so ambiguous, after all.
To propose the destruction of a place in terms of its irreplaceable
beauty is, surely, to make the argument against ever destroying it.
Nowhere was the quality of Dwight's wit more evident, however,
than in his *Travel Posters* and later *Language Panels*. Each *Language
Panel* was divided, cartoon fashion, into quadrant panels in which
typically two or three stick figures deploy Polish, Czech, or Russian
terms (these represented in the word balloons) as they attempt to
identify various plants and animals. The stick figures were not so
much personalities as sites. They are sites where language intersects
matter to organize life. They might be systematic botanists or ety-
mologists. All the *Language Panels*, in fact all Dwight's later drawings from the *Travel Posters* on, may be characterized as allegories of
discovery and classification. Even his premonitions of cosmic doom
were transfigured in the *Botanist UFOs* to include aliens that have
arrived to explore *this* undiscovered planet. Modest enough one by
one, the drawings that came from the trunk seemed to comprise an
outlook on evolution itself—the long wit that makes time, and
species, visible. On occasion, Dwight folded into his writing this
same deep sense of time. "The Croatian *slap*, 'a waterfall,' " he
wrote, "is from the Latin *lapsus*, a cool Vergilian surprise in that
tongue's dark labyrinth of consonants, and a most elegant metath-
esis to boot." I should not have been surprised at how affirmative
Dwight's wit turned out to be. The romance with Rupert was fueled
in the first place by their shared love of naming the plants in Latin.
Rupert, of course, was renowned among students and scientists at

Dwight Ripley, Language Panel: Pstruh! (trout), *1968*

the New York Botanical Garden as their resident expert in Latin. Eventually he placed his Latin dictionary in the garden's library, where it could be used by everyone. Douglas Daly, when he went there to consult it, was amused to find that this dictionary had been supplemented with aggrieved corrections that are penciled into the margins. "Oh no!" said Rupert when confronted, "those are Dwight's."

Several years had elapsed in our friendship with Rupert before I realized the importance of the explorations he undertook with Dwight in the American West, and then it made me uncomfortable.

The problem was timing. I wondered if these two privileged exiles from Blighty had stolen an opportunity from American youths who were absent, of necessity, fighting a war. I am not the only one to have wondered this. As I learned since, however, the two men were not wanted in the army, and many of the plants they identified were plants they located just in time, in a West that rapidly was betrayed to misuse, development, and invasive species. Twenty-one species of American *Astragalus* alone are endangered or threatened with extinction as of this writing, and the American government has been in no hurry to defend them. Given that treasonous record, I might better conclude that Dwight and Rupert had as good claim to be American, because they loved the country, as any of their draft-aged American contemporaries who, as soon as they returned to it after the war, lost little time in drilling, stripping, bulldozing, and, in Nevada, even bombing it instead. "We have to hurry, hurry, hurry and find out what's there before it's gone," remarked Rupert to his interviewer from the *New York Times*. Dwight's opinion may be read in his drawings, but his articles for the Alpine Garden Society were spiced with contempt for the relentless human campaign against the earth. Writing of *Ptilotrichum pyrenaicum*, a rare alyssum from the eastern Pyrenees, he noted that fewer than half a dozen plants were known to exist—"perhaps none at all now," he added, "if the visiting German botanists, with national thoroughness, should have carried their policy of *Vertilgunskrieg* to its logical con-clusion." In the summer just after the war, he warned his readers of the destruction that the Americans had brought, by ostensibly peaceful means, to their own irreplaceable heritage. "I won't waste the reader's time," he observed of the coast at Eureka, California, "by describing either the coast itself, which is unattractive, or the flora, which is on the way to extinction, or the European weeds which have largely replaced it, or the ruthless regiments of wool a-tinkle and a-baa on every other bluff." Noel Sandwith, reading this sentence at Kew, had responded with a cautionary delight. "The style is certainly not infected with the austerity of our age," he wrote. "Who else would dare to write 'a-tinkle,' 'a-baa'?"

Dwight's youthful hyperboles would be finally unpersuasive if it were not for the context of Rupert's science and his own later drawings. His *Travel Posters*, for instance, were precipitated by shock at what tourism was doing to Mallorca and the coast of Spain. "A beach is close by," explained a guidebook that he purchased in Barcelona, "and, subsequent to the rise of the tourist industry which Franco, in order to get foreign exchange, propagates and promotes intensively, summer villas, hotels, restaurants, bars shoot up in the rock-solitude." That guidebook was a translation (perhaps you suspected) from German, but the real irony was not lost on Dwight. He and Rupert, Cyril Connolly and Jean, Tony Bower, Hope and Harold Chown, had been the first wave of tourists in their youth, and if their presence was innocent and nondestructive then, it appeared in retrospect that this was because their numbers had been few. On his plant-hunting trips with Rupert, Dwight learned to savor the exchange between their botanical expectations and the unmediated realities they encountered in the field. His *Travel Posters* glow with this same conjunctive energy. They advertise the romance most tourists expect to enjoy, while in fine print they index the details that comprise the romance—details the tourist is apt to obliterate rather than see. Here was the disabused perspective both men

Dwight Ripley, Travel Poster: Monte Gordo, Fuentebravía, *1962*

would share with a new friend, the Spanish artist César Manrique, who first came to visit them in Greenport when his work was included in an exhibit at the Guggenheim Museum in 1965. Born on Lanzarote in the Canary Islands, Manrique was unhappy in New York, and he was gratified to be welcomed in Greenport by his own language, the Spanish plants in the garden, his hosts' personal knowledge of his native islands, and the works Dwight owned by Manolo Millares and Manuel Rivera, two prominent Informalist artists in a reawakening Spain. Manrique stayed sometimes at Stirling House while Dwight and Rupert herborized in Mexico, and his own work soon joined the Millares and the Rivera on its walls. Back in Lanzarote ("César se marcha," recorded Dwight in his diary),

Manrique dedicated himself to preservation of the island. "When I returned from New York," he explained later, "I came with the intention of turning my native island into one of the more beautiful places in the planet." He built a model dwelling to demonstrate how modern materials could be used in accord with traditional island architecture, and he was instrumental in obtaining legislation to contain tourism with zoning and construction codes. Lanzarote, which was designated a reserve of the biosphere by UNESCO in 1993, has been called his most significant work of art. A similar concern for an aesthetic to be realized through nature was supported meanwhile in the friendship between Dwight and Rupert in Greenport and Ossorio and Dragon at the Creeks on Georgica Pond. There, with Rupert's ongoing counsel, Ossorio created a combined sculpture-and-conifer landscape that he came to regard as living art. Arborists considered it one of the outstanding conifer collections in the world. According to Robert Fincham of Coenosium Gardens, it was Rupert who convinced Ossorio to plant evergreens for year-round color and foliage. Rupert recalled traveling by private plane to select specimens at distant nurseries. Mature trees were transported to the Creeks by helicopter. Eventually the arboretum became Ossorio's primary canvas and its major features were named as if they were paintings in a series. These features largely disappeared after Ossorio's death when the Creeks was sold and the new owner, Ronald O. Perelman, began to clear the sculptures and the trees. The view to the American flagpole had been called Barneby's Vista.

A mystery in Dwight's later life that I can't explain is why, during the politically tumultuous August of 1968, he disappeared for two weeks in Mexico City. Certainly Mexico meant a great deal to him. If the return trip to Spain had liberated his mature drawing, then by analogy it was the trips to Mexico that sustained it. For three springs in a row he traveled there on his own in search of rock-garden species for Greenport and Daleas for Rupert. From Puerto Kino, Sonora, he brought home the fresh specimens Rupert would need to describe *Erraȝuriȝia megacarpa* (the name honors the family of Eugenia Errázuriz, patron of painter Christopher Wood and, before that, Picasso). This year, however, Dwight departed in the heat of mid-August, two weeks into a general strike that had been called by students to protest an incursion by the Mexican army on the grounds of the national university. Dwight boarded his train in New York on the evening of the day that protesters first filled the Zócalo, the plaza before the presidential palace in Mexico City. From Laredo he went straight to the capital. He arrived Sunday, August 18, but kept no record of his daily whereabouts or activities. It was Wednesday of that week that Soviet tanks first entered Czechoslovakia, and it was the following Monday that the Democratic National Convention opened in Chicago, to be followed by a police assault the same night on demonstrators in Lincoln Park. Dwight was still in Mexico City the next day when three to four hundred thousand students and their supporters marched on the presidential palace, directing their soon famous chant *(¡Sal al balcón, chango hocicón!)* to President Gustavo Díaz Ordaz, who, they believed, was subservient to American corporations and supine regarding U.S. policy in Vietnam. With the autumn Olympics imminent in Mexico, Díaz Ordaz was said to be especially angered by the insult to his authority. Two days after the demonstration Dwight resumed his record. He reentered the United States, and in four days more was exchanging currency on Fifth Avenue. He would never need pesos again. That autumn, on Wednesday, October 2, 1968, a mixed force of soldiers, police, and undercover agents surrounded a mass meeting called by students at Tlatelolco Square in Mexico City and opened fire. Official estimates of the dead ranged around thirty; historians place the number at more than three hundred. The massacre shook Mexico and further radicalized students in Europe, the United States, and throughout the Americas. Among Dwight's drawings I found one of a bullet-wound sun (it is the color of blood with a green center) suspended between two purple volcanoes. The volcano to the left is restive like Popocatépetl; the one to the right, like Iztaccíhuatl, is quiescent. At the foot of the volcanoes Dwight drew a lavalike flow of color whose red base was held down by the successive layers of color that are stacked above it. Two of these he checkered in the manner of finish-line flags at the Olympics. One layer has been labeled COCA-COLA, the other DIAZ ORDAZ. Compressing the whole stack from the top are the patterns of military camouflage. Even without my speculation on its origins this drawing had a kind of noir urgency, like an extraterrestrial's view of a dangerous planet. Spain in the civil war, the Spinney, Nevada, Mexico—all the places with which Dwight had identified—became targets of military violence. You might not need to be paranoid to take this personally. In one of the *Language Panels,* Dwight drew a missile in the shape of a nose cone that appears over a desert basin populated by stonelike plants. The plants, clearly frightened, seem to curse in an unknown language (there are angry symbols in their word balloons), while the missile cruises toward them towing a banner that reads, in Russian, "We Are Friends."

Clement Greenberg wrote memorably of Miró that he had rescued pleasure, meaning he rescued it from the decay of styles and politics. Of course he also rescued it in the real sense that he carried the first ten "Constellations" off from Varengeville in a suitcase, to escape the advancing German army. Miró used suitcase-sized paper (the "Constellations" are roughly fifteen by eighteen inches), supposedly because he knew that the series had to be transportable, something you could take with you in a hurry, not something to be installed in an institution. Dwight used mostly inexpensive papers that were not larger than eighteen by twenty-four inches; the *Language Panels* are eleven by fourteen. Budd Myers remembered that he worked on a flat table, in a small room off the upstairs library, where he could bend over the paper as if he was writing in color. Given his wealth and privilege, Dwight might have kept his money to himself and lived as the dilettante his beneficiaries presumed him to be. Instead he trained himself (intentionally perhaps, but more likely by fate of temperament) to combine the affection of a gardener, the attention of a scientist, the dismay of a sophisticate, and the nonstandard responses of a colorist in drawings that surprised me as they came from the trunk with their unexpectedly philosophical view. Together, they made a witty variant on the perspective we knew and valued once as *sub specie aeternitatis,* the long disinterest of eternity. But the surprise was sharpened by a sense of loss, by the sudden reminder in these drawings of how rare that perspective has become, how gravely threatened it is by the resurgent fictions of sal-

Dwight at fifty-seven

vation, and hypocrisies of intellect, that seem always eager to betray the work of perception in favor of their own evaporating vanities. Dwight's drawings, however, never hector you. Because he *enjoyed* his wealth and sophistication there was nothing starved or resentful to eventuate in his art. Rupert, in the "Atlas of North American

Astragalus," explained that its taxonomic system was meant to express his vision of "the course that evolution may have followed in bringing forth to the observer's grateful and astonished eye the marvelously diverse *Astragali* which decorate the hills and deserts of the North American continent." In his room off the library, leaning over the table to draw, Dwight called to paper this same evolution-ary view. During the spring of 1947, as Peggy Guggenheim returned to Europe, he had been scaling cliffs with Rupert in Red Canyon, Utah. In a subsequent letter to Peter Davis, he left the kind of evidence I was looking for: a holotype, in words, that could iden-tify his art, Rupert's science, and the lives of both.

> Two days later we set off for Loa to hunt for the *Gilia caespitosa,* found only once by Ward back in 1875. His specimens were over, so no one knew the color of the flowers, but presumably they were lavender or whitish, in view of its affinities. Rupert found it almost as soon as we reached the first sandstone cliff. I was raid-ing the thermos for some Adam's ale when a faint cry, like that of some stricken bat or a poetess at a cocktail party, came to me on the wind, and a few minutes later R. appeared bearing a large green football. His mouth was dry, his eyes feverish. For the football glittered like crystal with the unnumerable grains of sand lodged there on its glandular leaves, and from it stuck out, as pins from a pincushion, hundreds of long-tubed flowers of PUREST SCARLET.

Dwight had predicted he would leave no anecdotes (was he *seri-ous?*) because, he said, he was antisocial. Like many people who are thought antisocial, he was not aloof because he was indifferent or antipathetic, but because he was so profoundly affected by others that he could not easily locate the boundaries between their expectations and his own. As a result he was explosive in public, inhibited by his blushing, and shaken by the misfortunes that overtook his friends. He put Jean and Clem and John Myers into his stories and poems. He put an Ossorio, modeled after that artist's "Congregations" series, into one of his *Language Panels*. Among his *Botanist UFOs* there is one that looks like a Rothko that has landed. But when Rothko died by suicide late in February 1970, the effect on life at Greenport was immediate. Stamos, for whom Rothko was both friend and mentor, broke down and had to be briefly hospitalized. The following year Stamos was sued, along with the other executors of Rothko's estate, for conflict of interest and conspiracy to defraud the estate in favor of the Marlborough Gallery. The allegations overwhelmed him, and he suffered anxieties that made his friendship unavailable. In the meantime Dwight witnessed at a distance the decay of Marie Menken and Willard Maas. After an ill-fated experiment with LSD, Maas too had attempted suicide. He was hospitalized temporarily at Payne Whitney, the psychiatric unit of New York Hospital. When he returned home he was taking lithium. Nevertheless he and Menken continued to drink heavily, perhaps competitively, every day. "Marie's drinking," reported Brakhage, "finally killed her." Menken died, aged sixty-one, on December 29, 1970. Four days later, Maas, fifty-nine, followed her. Maas's obituary in the *New York Times* attributed death to a heart attack, but colleagues assumed that it was suicide. Dwight, despite the estrangement, was visibly upset by the fate of his two old friends. "I can only answer for what I accept," he had written in *A Sunlit Scene,* "just as Evelyn accepts God, and Dwight, poor sweet, *l'anéantissement total.*" (*L'anéantissement* is annihilation.) A further shock was delivered July 3, 1972, when the body of Tony Bower was found in his new apartment at 160 East Sixty-fifth Street. He was shot in the chest. Bower had published four years earlier an article in *Art in America* that explored fraud and forgery in the art world. He even named dealers who were the sources of suspect paintings. He then left the magazine to become a dealer himself, first at the Knoedler Gallery and next at his own gallery in the Hyde Park Hotel. The police reported that Bower knew his murderer, robbery was not the motive, and the case soon would be solved. No arrest ever was made. Of the four couples in Pansyhalla, only Dwight and Rupert remained. With Bower, their last link to the young Jean Connolly was gone. It was barely two months later that Dwight responded with a conspicuous, and I believe telling, parenthesis to Virginia Dortch, who was preparing her biography of Peggy Guggenheim. "Had I not met her (through Jean Connolly, a dear friend now defunct and the wife of Cyril Connolly)," he wrote, "I doubt whether I would have become interested in modern art." Budd Myers recalled that it was not clear when Dwight began drinking again, or whether he sometimes was abstaining and sometimes not. But the drinking at the end was uninterrupted, and it did not take long to kill him. Dwight Ripley was sixty-five when he died of cirrhosis of the liver, early Monday morning, December 17, 1973, at the East Long Island Hospital in Greenport, New York. Even as he declined he continued to draw, inscribing a kind of color etymology into the final drawings I have called *Glyphs.* These were geometric abstractions whose thick chunks of color seem to emerge from their afterimages. Bravely (and it seems a persuasive courage for someone whose blushing was a lifelong embarrassment), he had identified life with the contravention of good color taste. He equated taste with death. In Granada, on the isolated peak of Dornajo at six thousand feet, he and Rupert in their youth admired *Echium albicans*. Observed Dwight: "In death the coral-coloured flowers exhibit perfect taste, for after their little day of pink triumph is over they fade insensibly through tones of strawberry and purple to a deep ink-blue."

Frank and I thought Rupert, the latter-day stoic, was not sentimental and certainly not superstitious. He once suggested I cut down a tree to widen a lawn, and when I mentioned that the birds seemed to use that tree he responded, irrefutably, "They only use it because it's there!" We had known him five years, however, when one autumn evening as he approached the door to his loft an oriole landed on his shoulder. Orioles make difficult cage birds, but this was an immature Baltimore oriole. Dwight had closed his long poem, *Spring Catalogue*, with the sudden autumn appearance of a *vhla*, which is Czech for bee-eater and—by the sort of linguistic duplicity that delighted him—Slovak for golden oriole. The Polish equivalent, *wilga*, he explained in his notes to the poem, is also an oriole. He went to "Oriel" College. Because the bird would not leave, Rupert took it inside, made it a home in one of the antique birdcages, and cared for it daily. When he went botanizing in the West, we cared for it. A fussy bird, it required its orange slices on a tiny Spode dessert plate and its water in a hand-painted porcelain bowl. We last kept it for Rupert in 1983. That autumn in his loft the oriole escaped from its cage, flew twice around the room, headed straight for an open window and disappeared outside. Rupert destroyed that particular cage. During the memorial program at the Botanical Garden, Noel Holmgren described how Rupert talked to himself as he composed sentences in his office and then refined them in the hallway. He talked to *Dwight* when he came to stay with us. Three years after Dwight's death the wife of botanist Duane Isely also died, and Rupert wrote to him in sympathy.

One must never pity the dead, who have escaped the torments of flesh and the treadmill of time, but one's heart is wrung for those left behind, exposed to that most powerful and corrosive anguish of loneliness. At first there seems to be no way out of it; there is darkness all about. They say that Time heals wounds, but that is a pious hoax; time simply accustoms one to live with them. But that can be done, and you who have such an abundant gift of vital force and momentum toward the good and the beautiful should find it less hard than most. In crises of this sort, when one's course is suddenly and inflexibly altered by the inscrutable gnome who plots our brief passage through the looking-glass, the only thing is to pick up one's battered valise and plod dutifully forward. Somewhere over this hill, or perhaps, the next or the next one, the meadows are still in flower. You'll get there, I know.

In the spring that followed Dwight's death, Rupert returned to Spain to visit the site of *Viola cazorlensis,* pink like the bullfighter's thighs. He sent two *Language Panel* drawings to Peggy Guggenheim in Venice. He gave the Miró *regalito* to Dillon Ripley, who passed it on to the Archives of American Art. Six species were named for Dwight: *Aliciella ripleyi, Astragalus ripleyi, Cymopterus ripleyi, Eriogonum ripleyi, Omphalodes ripleyana,* and *Senna ripleyi.* Eventually the trunk of drawings came to us. This perhaps was a plan; it was Rupert who had suggested a house in the country and Rupert who further suggested where. "The country around Honesdale, PA is rather pretty, and not too fashionable at present, so (I assume) not ruinously expensive." We buried his ashes there in Smith Hill Cemetery (U.S. Route 6 to Cliff Street in Honesdale, north on Cliff Street continuing on Daniels Road a total three and two-tenths miles, right on Smith Hill Road six-tenths of a mile). I burned one of Dwight's unfinished drawings, collected the few ashes from that, and next to Rupert's ashes we buried those.

Notes

CITATIONS FOR THE SOURCES I found repeatedly useful are given fully in the schedule of Dwight's exhibitions, the list of publications by Rupert and Dwight, or the selected bibliography. Very little of the research required by *Both* would have been accomplished if I had been left to imagine it on my own. My model was Frank, who was plant information officer at the Botanical Garden for only two years after we met Rupert. He went on to become university librarian at Rutgers, the State University of New Jersey.

page 5   "Rupert, the gentle one": This observation was recorded June 17, 1956, and published by Grove Press in *The Diaries of Judith Malina* at page 407. The references to Rupert and Dwight in Malina's unedited manuscript diaries are more revealing, and sometimes more extensive, than in the published version. Malina may have thought her original entries were not sufficiently polite (in the unedited entry for June 17 she described Rupert and Dwight as "forlorn losers"), but I was grateful for everything about the two men that she chose to record. I relied therefore on the manuscript, which is in the Billy Rose Theatre Collection of the New York Public Library for the Performing Arts. The corresponding entries in the Grove Press edition may be found by their dates or by consulting the index of names.

page 13   Sandwith, who died unexpectedly: A biographical sketch by J. P. M. Brenan appeared with a bibliography of Sandwith's publications at pages 245–55 of *Taxon* 15:7 in 1966.

page 15   The suffix *oides:* The standard guide to botanical Latin is William T. Stearn, *Botanical Latin*, originally published in 1966 and reprinted in its fourth edition by Timber Press in 1995. Gardeners, and the nurseries that supply them, are frequently exasperated by changes in the Latin names of their favorite plants. Taxonomists are equally exasperated by names that prove to be inaccurate, and they itch to revise them. As new evidence of a plant's evolutionary position becomes available, the species is likely to be moved from one genus, e.g., *Statice,* to another, in this case *Limonium.* The name of the genus is not really "changed," because the genus *Statice* still exists for other species. Even the most ruthless taxonomist will try, meanwhile, to preserve the specific epithet, which here was *asparagoides.* Of course it is possible, when replacing one term but not the other, to produce some anomalous Latin. The botanist James Reveal recalled that "Rupert would review my Latin—as he did for numerous others—and comment dryly about my effort to get it right. He admired Stearn for what he had done to help the Latin illiterates like me."

page 17   Once, while I was turning pages: The party group is pictured in Clive Fisher, *Cyril Connolly: The Life and Times of England's Most Controversial Literary Critic* (Macmillan, 1995; St. Martin's Press, 1996), where it faces page 147, and in a slightly different exposure in Jeremy Lewis, *Cyril Connolly: A Life,* where it precedes page 239. The same group, but with Dwight and Jean Connolly cropped from the picture, appears in Michael Shelden, *Friends of Promise: Cyril Connolly and the World of Horizon,* and in Francis Wheen, *Tom Driberg: His Life and Indiscretions* (Chatto & Windus, 1990). Dwight is nowhere identified, and Tony Hyndman is identified only by Lewis. The biographies of Cyril Connolly were useful sources for understanding the attitudes and ambitions that would be transplanted by Dwight, Jean Connolly, and their friends from England to the United States. Shelden's concise and focused *Friends of Promise* was especially important in this regard. Likewise indispensable was Cyril Connolly's own youthful journal, edited and presented in the context of a lucid memoir by David Pryce-Jones in *Cyril Connolly: A Journal and Memoir.*

page 20   "a primrose wrapped": Dwight gave this description in his long poem, *Spring Catalogue,* and observed in a note to the poem that the *Maurandya* was "perhaps the most extraordinary plant in the entire West." In his article "The Limestone Areas" he explained that the genus as a whole

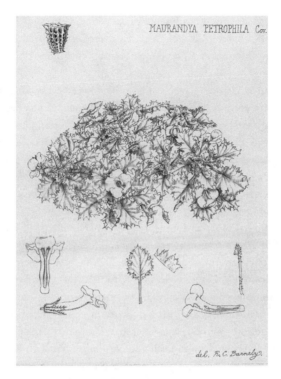

Rupert Barneby, Maurandya petrophila

tends to flop or twine, but *M. petrophila* sits tight in a dome of prickly leaves while its flowers "peer from the stiff rosettes like sumptuous primroses—primroses just opening with the flowers still a little crumpled, of a serene and candid yellow, lighting the grottoes and the echoing solitudes of rock with moonlit pallor." The plant is a *Maurandya,* however, no more. Following a modern analysis of its DNA, it was moved by the botanist Wayne Elisens to a new genus, and since 1985 it has been properly called *Holmgrenanthe petrophila.*

page 22   *"Yo-gee!": "Yo-gee! Whee!!"* wrote Dwight to Rupert in 1940. "Heard apparently 'levitates' (if that's the word) up to the ceiling. Well,

Norman can do that on a couple of brandies. I promise I won't allow myself to be roped in to such degrading intellectual jinks. The spectacle of Aldous doing a Lauri Devine before breakfast must be sump'n wonderful—"

page 22   Prince Paul of Greece: The prince became the king of Greece. There are references to his relationship with Fouts in Shelden, *Friends of Promise,* at page 57; in Gore Vidal, *Palimpsest: A Memoir* (Random House, 1995), at page 180; in James Lord, *Some Remarkable Men: Further Memoirs* (Farrar, Straus & Giroux, 1996), page 193; and in Michael Wishart, *High Diver* (Blond & Briggs, 1977), at page 52. Wishart was enamored of the later Fouts and devoted a chapter of his book to the influence Fouts exercised on his life.

page 25   "Mr. Barneby, an Englishman": Howell and Alice Eastwood are defining figures in the history of the California Academy of Sciences. Eastwood was one of those indomitably Emersonian women—she reminds me of Willa Cather or even Gertrude Stein—who brought American culture safely forward into the twentieth century. She was also, like so many great Americans, Canadian. Curator at the time of the San Francisco earthquake in 1906, she entered the partially collapsed academy, negotiated the ruined stairs to the herbarium on the sixth floor, and succeeded in lowering most of the type specimens by string to the street below before the advancing fires overtook the building next door. She was eighty-two when Rupert first arrived at the CAS herbarium. "I believe that we enjoy no other visitor," she wrote him soon after, "as we enjoy having you." The official biography is Carol Green Wilson, *Alice Eastwood's Wonderland: The Adventures of a Botanist* (California Academy of Sciences, 1955), and a more recent account is in Marcia Bonta, *Women in the Field: America's Pioneering Women Naturalists* (Texas A & M University Press, 1991). Howell was profiled by Gladys L. Smith in "John Thomas Howell: Peripatetic Botanist," pages 11–19 in the journal *Fremontia* 17:1 (1989), and by Arnold Tiehm in *John Thomas Howell,* Occasional Paper No. 7 (1996) of the Nevada Native Plant Society, P.O. Box 8965, Reno, Nevada 89507. Howell's recollections of Rupert were written for the festschrift, Hester et al., "Barneby Dedication," published in *Brittonia* in 1981.

page 26　　Look under *Lepidium nanum:* The Archibalds' seed list is available from Jim & Jenny Archibald, 'Bryn Collen', Ffostrasol, Llandysul SA44 5SB, Wales. The Arrowhead Alpines catalog, written with considerable zest by owner Bob Stewart, can be ordered at www.arrowheadalpines.com or by writing to P.O. Box 857, Fowlerville, Michigan 48836. Both sources sometimes stock the bluish-leaved, pink-and-yellow-flowered columbine, *Aquilegia barnebyi,* which was discovered by Rupert and Dwight in 1948 in Colorado, and named for Rupert by botanist Philip Munz.

page 30　　Rupert once told an interviewer: A profile on Rupert by Douglas C. Martin, "After England and Hollywood, Beans Win Out," appeared in the *New York Times,* April 18, 1992, in the Metro L section at page 23. Rupert dismissed this profile as being "thought up by the Garden's promotion department," but he made sure Frank and I had an extra copy in case we wanted to pass one along.

page 37　　"Dwight Ripley, a millionaire": Greenberg's letter was written March 2, 1942, as part of a youthful correspondence with his friend Harold Lazarus. Greenberg's widow, Janice Van Horne, collected the candid, ambitious, anxious but fearless, and finally redeeming letters of this correspondence in Clement Greenberg, *The Harold Letters, 1928–1943: The Making of an American Intellectual.*

page 38　　"Jean Connolly, Dwight Ripley": Lee Krasner was quoted by Jacqueline Bograd Weld in *Peggy: The Wayward Guggenheim* at page 313. Rupert's characterizations of Guggenheim were likewise quoted in Weld. They closely match the remarks he made in private, and I conclude that he meant them. Weld's book is comprehensive, not deferential, has a good index, and was a valuable guide when I was ready to learn more about the roles played by Dwight's friends and acquaintances in the wartime art scene in New York.

page 39　　"Letter to R": The sonnet, which is pretty dreadful, can be found in Oscar Williams, ed., *The War Poets* (John Day Company, 1945), at page 178. "Hand / I hold against my heart, forever hold me," pleads the poem.

page 40 "the dismal cult of personality": This example of Barnebian wisdom graduated to the Web after it showed up in his obituary, Douglas C. Martin, "Rupert C. Barneby, 89, Botanical Garden Curator and Expert on Beans, Is Dead," *New York Times* (December 10, 2000), page 67. It is all my fault, because I let the comment loose. Rupert included it in a letter to Frank and me on January 26, 1999.

page 45 these discoveries: The final count of new species that Rupert and Dwight discovered in the United States and Mexico remains to be determined by historians of taxonomy. James Reveal has credited the two men with the discoveries of *Cryptantha barnebyi, Lepidium barnebyanum,* and *Mirabilis pudica* in addition to those I found in Dwight's *Record,* while Arnold Tiehm credits them with *Arenaria stenomeres* as well. Reveal described the final era of botanical exploration in the United States in terms of four collector partnerships: Eastwood and Howell, Ripley and Barneby, Bassett Maguire and Arthur Holmgren, Reveal himself and Noel Holmgren. See his article "Botanical Explorations in the Intermountain Region" in Arthur Cronquist et al., *Intermountain Flora,* vol. I (New York Botanical Garden, 1972), at page 69, and his book *Gentle Conquest: The Botanical Discovery of North America with Illustrations from the Library of Congress* (Starwood Publishing, 1992), at page 156. Tiehm observed to similar effect of Rupert and Dwight that "their names are inextricably linked to Great Basin botany." Tiehm's biographical sketch of the two men appears in his clean, complete, and readable history, "Nevada Vascular Plant Types and Their Collectors," *Memoirs of The New York Botanical Garden* 77 (1996), at pages 32–33.

page 46 "I hope you won't desert the Mediterranean": Peter Davis became an expert on the flora of Turkey, a professor of botany at the University of Edinburgh, and with Vernon Heywood the author in 1963 of a standard work on systematic botany that would be required reading for students in the United States. During their long friendship with Davis, Rupert and Dwight derived pleasure from remembering him as a young friend of high ambition but not so much authority. "He's planning to write a flora of the Cyclades & Crete," wrote Dwight to Rupert in 1940, "which strikes me as

a weeny bit ambitious for someone who thinks Statices are Labiates."
There are recollections of Davis by Kit Tan and Thomas S. Elias at pages
x–xiv of *The Davis & Hedge Festschrift* (Edinburgh: University Press,
1989), and by Heywood and P. Harrison at pages 167–69 of the journal
Watsonia 20 (1994). A winning portrait was set down by Davis himself
in the words of his wartime letters to Rupert and Dwight, now in the
Archives at The LuEsther T. Mertz Library of the New York Botanical
Garden.

page 49   "Rupert," he reveals, "spent most of his day": John Myers's memoir, *Tracking the Marvelous; A Life in the New York Art World,* was the first
book from the art world in which I saw the names of Rupert and Dwight.
This inspired me to learn more, in part because it offended me. Myers was
transparently condescending, and even he, after years of accepting checks
from Wappingers Falls, couldn't spell Rupert's last name. It is Barnaby
throughout his book.

page 50   he named it *Astragalus agnicidus:* Rupert's genius for scientific
names was not infallible. Although *agnicidus* means lamb-killing, it is now
believed that the *Astragalus* was not the culprit after all, and a lupine is suspected of killing the Tostens' sheep. Once Rupert had collected the *Astra
galus* it was eradicated, however, and for many years was considered
extinct. A new population was discovered at the site in 1987; this has been
fenced, not to protect the sheep but to protect the plant.

page 51   William Buck has determined: Buck's bibliography, "An Annotated
List of the Publications of Rupert C. Barneby," *Brittonia* 53:1 (January–March 2001), is considerably more than a list. It appears to include the
name of every single species (I did not try to count) ever described by
Rupert in his publications.

page 54   Dwight once prepared a list: Dwight's list, "Native Species Growing at Wappingers Falls, N.Y.," is attached to a letter from Rupert to Mrs.
James V. Campbell, July 5, 1962, and is part of the Ripley Collection in the
Archives of the California Academy of Sciences. The collection is small
but useful. I presume that a more extensive collection of Barneby materials
waits to be catalogued.

250 Notes

page 54 *Penstemon desertipicti:* Dwight meant the small, mat-forming and purplish-flowered plant that is now considered a variety of another species, *Penstemon caespitosus* var. *desertipicti.* There is a fine photograph in Robert Nold, *Penstemons* (Timber Press, 1999) at plate 19. Nold called Dwight "one of my favorite garden writers," though he would not have known how Dwight privately described this North American genus when he first encountered it. "Pentstemon," wrote Dwight to Rupert, "is, in my opinion, considerably more thrilling than Digitalis and Antirrhinum put together."

page 58 Marcel Le Piniec Award: Lincoln Foster announced the award in the *Bulletin of the American Rock Garden Society* 32:3 (June 1974) at pages 107–09. Wrote Foster: "Dwight Ripley and Rupert Barneby through their long years of association formed an ideal symbiosis."

page 68 "By day a dowdy weed": Nested among the Latin descriptions in Rupert's *Astragalus* and *Dalea* monographs are handsomely honed passages in English. This quiet celebration of *Marina scopa* is in "Daleae Imagines" at pages 134–35.

page 73 "The many illustrations": Grady Webster's romp—*"Daleae Imagines,* by Rupert C. Barneby," *Madroño* 25 (1978), page 111—should be an inspiration to reviewers everywhere. The *Dalea* monograph took Rupert ten years, and Webster summarized its plot in five quotable lines.

page 74 sold to the art dealer: According to the receipt, Loria paid $38,000 total for the two Pollocks on March 24, 1975.

page 76 Porter resurrected a name: Porter's persuasive work was reported in *"Aliciella,* A Recircumscribed Genus of Polemoniaceae," *Aliso* 17:1 (1998), at pages 23–46. Billie Turner's warm and equally persuasive assessment of the interface between molecular systematics and traditional taxonomy appeared in the subsequent issue of that same journal. Billie L. Turner, "Plant Systematics: Beginnings and Endings," *Aliso* 17:2 (1998), pages 189–200.

page 76 "Indeed they will be in good company": A previous paragraph in Rupert's article *"Gaultheria* versus *Chiogenes"* seems to leave no doubt of his final opinion toward those who insist on custom over evidence. "Inertia in the face of change," wrote Rupert, "often supported by sentiment, ensures on all sides a second life, if not indeed a sort of immortality, to ideas which lost their stuffing years, perhaps centuries ago, like the antique Mesopotamian nonsense handed out daily, in the name of 'science,' by Hollywood astrologers."

page 79 In a series of publications: Citations to these studies may currently be found on the informative *Astragalus* Web site designed by Hu, Wojciechowski, and Sanderson. Go to http://ginger.ucdavis.edu/astragalus/astragalus_home.htm. The citations appear if you follow the menu to *Phylogenetics*. Among the other menu choices are *Classification and Taxonomy*, which leads to a short taxonomic history that has been summarized from Rupert's own introduction in the "Atlas of North American *Astragalus*," and *Pictures at the Exhibition*, which leads to a gallery of Wojciechowski's attentive photographs of *Astragalus* species in their native habitats.

page 85 Rupert had so many friends: Andrey Sytin, of the Komarov Botanical Institute in St. Petersburg, remembered Rupert as "the world's most charming botanist." Among the tributes that have appeared since Rupert's death are Richard Spellenberg, "Rupert C. Barneby: A Memoir," *Sida, Contributions to Botany* 19:3 (August 23, 2001), pages 745–51; Stanley L. Welsh, "Rupert C. Barneby (1911–2000)," *Taxon* 50:1 (February 2001), pages 285–92; and an anecdote by Noel H. Holmgren, "Rupert Barneby and the Discovery of the Holmgren Milkvetch," in *Wild Earth* (Spring 2002), page 84.

page 93 "Of course I have a feeling": The interview was conducted by Leslie Mandell, assisted by P. Adams Sitney, and it appeared in 1964 in the *Wagner Literary Magazine*, a student publication of Wagner College on Staten Island. It was republished by Sitney three years later in *Filmwise*. I used the *Wagner Lit* version of this, the most important interview that Menken ever gave.

page 94 "Except for Dwight Ripley": Although Rivers was not kind to Steinberg in his review, he seems to have meant the aside on Dwight to be a compliment. Larry Rivers, "Young Draftsman on Master Draftsmen," *Art News* 53:9 (January 1955), at page 59.

page 94   Nine of his drawings were sold: Grace Hartigan recalled her own sales from Tibor de Nagy Gallery during that same year. "[A]t my first show we sold one painting of mine for fifty dollars to a young man whose mother made him return it. In the next year we sold nothing." Hartigan's remarks, with likewise keen remarks by Hilton Kramer and James Merrill, are in Thomas Sokolowski et al., *A Memorial Service for John Bernard Myers* (Sea Cliff Press, 1988).

page 95   "Dwight," he wrote, "was an alcoholic": Brakhage's judgmental description of a benefactor he can scarcely have known seems to me morally witless, but his account of Marie Menken and her work in his book, *Film at Wit's End: Eight Avant Garde Filmmakers*, was the first I encountered and I am greatly indebted to it. The comment on Dwight appears at page 44. Brakhage died in 2003 and I never interviewed him.

page 96   He had an allowance: The trustees who administered Harry Ripley's allowance were his brother Sidney Dillon Ripley and the Knickerbocker Trust Company. Harry charged his brother with misconduct and sued for an accounting, but his case was compromised when his brother died while the suit was in progress. The court ruled against him. "Finds Sidney Ripley a Faithful Trustee," *New York Times* (July 30, 1905), page 7. Dwight was born three years later.

page 97   "COURT MAKES BABY": The headlines suggest that certain aspects of American life remain constant. "H. D. Ripley Left $989,000," *New York Times* (November 11, 1915), page 7; "Widow Gets Bulk of Ripley Estate," *New York Herald* (November 11, 1915), page 6:7; "Income of $1,000,000 Goes to Mrs. Ripley," *New York Times* (July 6, 1914), page 7; "Gets Income from $1,000,000 Estate," *New York Tribune* (July 6, 1914), page 7:4; "Court Makes Baby a Millionaire," *New York Herald* (July 6, 1914), page 8:5.

page 101   "any signs of intelligence": Beaton's judgment on Harrow was quoted in Martin Green, *Children of the Sun: A Narrative of "Decadence" in England after 1918* (Basic Books, 1976), page 214. Rupert never spoke of the school itself, or of his own student performance, but only of Dwight's reputation ("he was an eccentric") there. To complicate the perspective on Rupert's family, I should note that it was his brother Tom who, despite Dwight's reputation, introduced the two boys. The effect on Dwight can be seen in his two drawings that survive from Harrow. Both are of Rupert. It was Dwight, of the two boys, who was the better scholar. In 1926 he won the Cyrillus Norwood Prize (Cyril Norwood was headmaster at Harrow) and received not a plaque or a cup but Reginald Farrer's two-volume landmark, *The English Rock-Garden*, first published in 1919. After Dwight's death Rupert gave the Farrer to their friend and fellow rock gardener Budd Myers. It was Myers's belief that Farrer had a lasting influence on Dwight's own tastes and literary style.

Dwight Ripley,
Portrait of Rupert Barneby
at Harrow, *1925*

page 103   "The hard Hebroid scum": Although the quotation appears in full at page 233 of Green, *Children of the Sun,* I thought it couldn't possibly be this bad in context. If anything, it's worse. Byron's words are in *An Essay on India* (George Routledge & Sons, 1931), page 90. Byron was on his way to Egypt as a war correspondent when a German torpedo ended his life in the summer of 1941.

page 103   Brian Howard: Brian Howard was cruelly caricatured by Evelyn Waugh as "Ambrose Silk" in *Put Out More Flags* and as part of "Anthony Blanche" in *Brideshead Revisited.* He was portrayed somewhat less cruelly by Cyril Connolly as "Christian de Clavering" in the satire "Where Engels Fears to Tread" in *Condemned Playgrounds,* by Jocelyn Brooke as "Hew Dallas" in *A Mine of Serpents,* and by Nancy Mitford as part of "Cedric Hampton" in *Love in a Cold Climate.*

page 107   Connolly said of Jean: Connolly's sexy, funny first descriptions of
Jean are in his journal as edited by David Pryce-Jones, and they offer on
page 202 a possible insight into her peculiar powers over young male intellectuals. "She has all the good lesbian qualities—," writes Connolly,
"frankness, independence, masculinity and an interesting way of talking
about women's faults and figures, hates anything tartish."

page 111   Severe blushing can be corrected today: Contemporary treatment
for severe blushing was described by surgeon Atul Gawande in the "Crimson Tide" chapter of his book *Complications: A Surgeon's Notes on an
Imperfect Science* (Henry Holt, 2002). Gawande's account illustrates how
truly troublesome the syndrome is for those who suffer it. One patient,
interviewed after the still novel surgery, reported that he would have gone
through with the operation even if told there was a fifty percent chance of
death.

page 115   "You can't escape": Spender's open letter to Isherwood was
quoted by Shelden in *Friends of Promise*, page 66, to explain Spender's
decision to return to London despite the Blitz. Shelden gave no sense that
the letter was the latest in a series of similar public attacks on Auden, Isherwood, and other expatriates who might regard it as opportunistic moraliz-
ing by someone they had trusted as a friend. Isherwood's reaction to such
attacks can be gauged from the responses at pages 55, 83–84, 101, and
364–67 in his *Diaries, Volume One: 1939–1960*, which was edited and
enhanced with a chronology and a glossary of names by Katherine Bucknell. Dwight has been identified in a footnote to the U.S. edition as "English poet," and in a footnote to the U.K. edition as "English versifier,
painter and botanist."

page 115   "I shall always think": Spender married his first wife, Inez Pearn,
in 1936. His boyfriend, Tony Hyndman, felt abandoned, joined the International Brigade, and left England to fight for the Spanish Republic.
Hyndman had internalized Spender's attitudes and adopted his politics, but
he was disillusioned by the experience in Spain and ended up in prison,
where he was in serious danger of being shot as a deserter. Although
Rupert, and presumably Dwight as well, held Spender responsible for the

damage done to Hyndman, we should note in fairness that Spender himself was in danger when he went rather heroically to Spain and rescued Hyndman from prison. The passions and politics of this period in British intellectual life were recalled by Tony Bower's English lover, T. C. [Cuthbert] Worsley, in his novel *Fellow Travellers* (London Magazine Editions, 1971). The main characters in Worsley's book are Spender, thinly disguised as Martin Murray, and Hyndman, portrayed as Harry Watson.

page 116   When Neddermeyer was arrested: The grim episode was described by Isherwood in *Christopher and His Kind* (Farrar, Straus, and Giroux, 1976) at pages 273–81.

page 116   "So—really, I have no plans": Howard's declaration is at page 396 of Marie-Jacqueline Lancaster, ed., *Brian Howard: Portrait of a Failure* (Anthony Blond, 1968). Mrs. Lancaster's counterfactually titled and virtually unobtainable book is the only biography, but it was compromised by her grotesque presumption. "Unlike most normal young men," she observed while introducing her subject, "he did not consider that earning money could almost be turned into a pleasurable necessity heralding the joys of wife and family to come."

page 121   Keith Winter, a novelist: Winter was two years ahead of Dwight at Oxford. His novel *Other Man's Saucer* (Doubleday, Doran & Co., 1930) is the story of a class-crossed, romantic friendship that begins at Oxford and all too soon encounters the realities of tradition and power in an English country house. In other words, it anticipates scenes in Evelyn Waugh's *Brideshead Revisited*, published fifteen years later in 1945. When Waugh arrived at Metro-Goldwyn-Mayer in 1947 to consult on a motion-picture adaptation of *Brideshead* he found that the screenwriter assigned to the project was none other than Winter. The MGM film was never made. There is mention of this incident in Humphrey Carpenter, *The Brideshead Generation: Evelyn Waugh and His Friends* (Houghton Mifflin, 1990), pages 244 and 396. Winter wrote screenplays for *The Strange Affair of Uncle Harry* in 1945 and *The Red Shoes* in 1948, but Dwight and Rupert lost contact with him after they left California and I have learned nothing about his later life.

page 126   "*WE* have still done": Connolly's complaint is in the David
Pryce-Jones memoir at page 286. The marital difficulties of the Connollys
were fuel for gossip. "Dined at the Embassy on Thurs:" reported Nancy
Mitford on April 13, 1946, to Evelyn Waugh. "Stephen Spender—I suppose you hate him. He told me an awfully funny story about when Cyril
was living with Jean & Diana Witherby & caught them both out having
affairs with other people & said to Steve, almost in tears, 'It *is* hard, here I
have been absolutely faithful to 2 women for a year, they've *both* been
unfaithful to me.'" Charlotte Mosley, ed., *The Letters of Nancy Mitford and
Evelyn Waugh* (Houghton Mifflin, 1996), page 39.

page 126   "What pushing & pulling": This excited erotic inventory was
compiled for Lazarus on August 13, 1940. Like Connolly's journal, Greenberg's letters to Lazarus are witness of how it felt to be young and in love
with Jean Connolly. In fact *The Harold Letters* are compelling in this regard
and they place Greenberg in a light in which he glows.

page 127   "Denham came up from Pennsylvania": Dwight later complained
to Rupert that he was required to have dinner with Fouts, which was
"rather a bore." In his book *Cyril Connolly*, the biographer Jeremy Lewis
called Fouts "sinister" without giving any explanation beyond a succession
of prominent male lovers and a drug problem—a formula by which Marilyn Monroe might be called sinister too. Lewis compared Jean Connolly,
without quotation marks or attribution, to "a genial Red Indian squaw."

page 133   Some deferments seem inevitable: Pollock's 4-F classification was
discussed by Steven Naifeh and Gregory White Smith in *Jackson Pollock:
An American Saga* (Clarkson N. Potter, 1989) at page 363. John Cage's
deferment was noted by Calvin Tomkins in *The Bride and the Bachelors:
Five Masters of the Avant-Garde* (Penguin, 1976) at page 96. Auden's
response to his draft status was criticized by Isherwood, and by Greenberg
too, as an exercise in self-dramatization. Isherwood, *Diaries, Volume One*,
page 994; Greenberg, *Harold Letters*, page 226.

page 134   First she commended: Jean's comments on Pollock are in the
Nation, May 1, 1943, at page 643, and May 29, 1943, at page 786. Pollock's
letter to his brother Charles was quoted by Francis V. O'Connor in *Jackson*

Pollock (Museum of Modern Art, 1967) at page 28. Naifeh and Smith quoted this letter but omitted "the *Nation,*" making it appear that Pollock had referred instead to a male critic who mentioned him in the *New Yorker.*

page 135   *Jean Connolly at the Falls:* The painting behind Jean in the photograph is *Les portes tournantes,* 1936, by Yves Tanguy. Jean was described by Dwight in *A Sunlit Scene:* "Her enormous face was smothered in a deep orange powder that successfully hid any tan she might have acquired during the summer, while an object apparently from Yucatan clasped her throat in an uncomfortable embrace." It would be a mistake, however, to conclude from her independent income and the descriptions by her male friends that Jean was simply, as Greenberg called her, an "international glamour girl." In 1941 she began what was probably the first English translation of *Memoirs of a Revolutionary,* written in French by exiled Soviet dissident Victor Serge. The fragment she completed was published as "On the Eve" in *Partisan Review* 9:1 (January-February 1942) at pages 23–33. Art critics may recognize accents of Greenberg's own historical determinism in Jean's translation of Serge, an intimate coincidence that suggests why ideas can hardly be disentangled from the personal relationships of their time. "Few people have as yet this new sense which modern man is painfully acquiring, the sense of history," translated Jean. "Nevertheless, the people who fled with us along all the roads of France and in the last trains had to acknowledge in their stupor that 'it had to happen.' I suddenly recaptured the strongest and most heartening emotion of my childhood, the one, I feel, that will stay with me all my life: confidence."

page 137   Dwight promptly bought four: *Drawing, c. 1943–45* was reproduced in color in Bryan Robertson, *Jackson Pollock* (Harry Abrams, 1960), page 83; in color in Marlborough-Gerson Gallery, *Jackson Pollock* (Marlborough Gerson, 1964), plate 66; and in color in Italo Tomassoni, *Pollock* (Grosset & Dunlap, 1968), plate 26–7. The same drawing, renamed as *Untitled (1946),* was reproduced in color in Bernice Rose, *Jackson Pollock: Works on Paper* (Museum of Modern Art, 1969), page 60, where it accompanies a second Pollock drawing from Dwight's collection, likewise called *Untitled (1946),* which is illustrated in black-and-white at page 59. In

O'Connor, *Jackson Pollock,* the retitled drawing appears in black-and-white at page 95, to the right of yet a third Pollock work called *Untitled (1946)* from Dwight's collection.

page 137   The two Mirós: Dwight's former "Constellations" are illustrated in color in Carolyn Lanchner, *Joan Miró* (Museum of Modern Art/Harry Abrams, 1993). Number 1, *Le lever du soleil,* is at page 238 and number 5, *Femme à la blonde aisselle coiffant sa chevelure à la lueur des étoiles,* is at page 242. A facsimile edition of twenty-two of the twenty-three "Constellations" was published in an edition of 384 boxed sets by Pierre Matisse in 1959. The "Constellation" *Nocturne* was not included, which may help to explain the breathtaking price it brought at Sotheby's New York in 2001 when it was sold for more than $5.5 million dollars. The "Constellations" continue to inspire deeply felt response. Two recent examples are an unusual book by Paul Hammond, *Constellations of Miró, Breton* (City Lights Books, 2000), and a jazz tribute by Bobby Previte, *The 23 Constellations of Joan Miró* (Tzadik #7072, 2002).

page 137   "We were even 'engaged' ": In her book, *Peggy Guggenheim and Her Friends,* Virginia Dortch assembled a biography from the letters of reminiscence that she solicited from Guggenheim's friends and acquaintances. "Men would not think of making a book like that," responded Sonia Delaunay. Guggenheim's secret was identified convincingly in the letter from Matta, who observed: "She speculated in glamour." Dwight's response, at page 125, is one of the duller ones. Dortch's book contains photographs I have seen reproduced nowhere else, including a studio pose on page 145 of a very British-looking Dwight Ripley.

page 139   "Can't you just *see*": Dwight's idea of an effective joke on Cora Shadequarter would have been widely appreciated at the time. John Richardson recalled for a fashion feature in the *New York Times Magazine* in August 2000 that Guggenheim would never have slept with a gondolier, in part because gondoliers were known to work in their off-hours preparing corpses for burial.

page 139   their friend George Barker: According to Stan Brakhage, Barker's body figures in the film's geography too.

page 141   Dwight's friend Francis: Turville-Petre, like Brian Howard, may have suffered from a bad press at the hands of his literary friends. An archaeologist, he excavated the famous Galilee Skull from Zuttiyeh Cave near the Sea of Galilee when he was only twenty-four. He intended later to excavate a tumulus in Greece that he believed was the site where Iphigenia had been sacrificed. He rented an island opposite the site and proceeded to build his house there. The result was described by Isherwood in *Christopher and His Kind*, beginning at page 138, and in the "Ambrose" chapter of *Down There on a Visit*. Jeremy Lewis cited this Ambrose chapter in his book *Cyril Connolly* to characterize Turville-Petre's island household as "a bizarre homosexual establishment." Lewis also identified the island as Euboea, which would make it a very large establishment indeed. It was the island of St. Nicholas the Less in the strait between Euboea and the mainland. There is a photograph of the house and island in an intelligent article by Ofer Bar-Yosef and Jane Callander, "A Forgotten Archaeologist: The Life of Francis Turville-Petre," in *Palestine Exploration Quarterly* 129 (1997) at pages 2–18. Dwight's reference to his friend in a letter written to Rupert on March 12, 1941, was soon overtaken by events. "Then tomorrow evening I dine with Gilbert Sheldon," wrote Dwight, "whom I met in a bar on the wrong end of 42nd Street the other night & who knows Eddie [Gathorne-Hardy], Brian [Howard], Peter Davis, Francis Turville-Petre & most everybody we've ever met." Two weeks later the Germans invaded Greece. Turville-Petre escaped near the end of April on the last ship to make it safely from Piraeus to Alexandria. German pilots, assuming that his house hid gun emplacements, bombed St. Nicholas the Less and destroyed the house. Turville-Petre languished in a Cairo suburb and died there in August of the following year, having refused to go to a hospital unless it was run by Greeks.

page 142   "In the evening": Dwight's tribute to the West is in his article "Nevada 1944."

page 145   "We drove in on a mule track": Rupert's letter was quoted by Janice Beatley in "Ash Meadows: Nevada's Unique Oasis in the Mojave Desert," *Mentzelia* 3 (1977), pages 20–24. The hard-to-reach *Astragalus phoenix* was collected by Arthur Cronquist in 1966, too late for Rupert to describe the species in his "Atlas of North American *Astragalus*." Beatley and James Reveal made limited collections afterward and noted the plant's steady decline—"not from our collecting," reported Reveal, "but from the expanding agricultural activities in the Ash Meadows."

page 150   Tony Bower took Auden: Anthony Bower, who was at this time the North American agent for *Horizon*, turns up frequently in accounts of Connolly, Jean Connolly, Greenberg, Isherwood, and of course Dwight, as a supporting player. Connolly and Greenberg were critical of Bower's behavior, and Isherwood's portrait of him as "Ronnie" in *Down There on a Visit* was not wholly positive. Bower, meanwhile, put irreverent sketches of Auden and Isherwood into an arch satire on American life that he published under the name Antony Bourne as "Where Shall John Go? III-U.S.A." in *Horizon* 9:49 (January 1944) at pages 13–23. Rupert once took Bower along on a trip to hunt for *Astragalus*. "I enjoyed your acid description of Tony's trip into the mountains," admitted Dwight. "What a maladjusted little thing he is."

page 151   He has been called the father: Altmaier was honored on the fortieth anniversary of his death with a civic ceremony held in Flörsheim am Main, which is where he was born in 1889; a wreath was laid on his grave in the Jewish cemetery there. A biography by Christoph Moss was published by Boehlau in 2003. It has not been translated into English, but the title would be *Jakob Altmaier: A Jewish Social Democrat in Germany (1889–1963)*. Moss published a biographical essay on Altmaier in the June 2001 issue of *IWK* (Internationale wissenschaftliche Korrespondenz) 37:2, at pages 228–46, in which he gave almost no information about Altmaier's life between 1930 and his exile from Germany in 1933. He did locate Altmaier briefly in Sussex, however, and cited as his evidence a letter, dated April 12, 1931, that was written by Altmaier from a place called "The Spinney." The photograph of Altmaier reproduced in *Both* was taken in the Luxembourg Gardens in Paris in August 1930. On the back it bears the inscription "For ever. . . . To Dwight, 20/21.IX.30 Jakob." A second photograph, undated, is inscribed "To Rupert, in memoriam et in fe, Jakob."

page 155 "The Cliff House is a success": Ingwersen's report appeared in the *Quarterly Bulletin of the Alpine Garden Society*, No. 59, 13:1 (March 1945), at page 1. The Ingwersen nursery, which Rupert remembered fondly, continues to operate under the guidance of Ingwersen's son M. P. Ingwersen. Birch Farm Nursery, W. E. Th. Ingwersen Ltd., Gravetye Estate, East Grinstead, West Sussex RH19 4LE.

page 156 As a home remedy he bought two more Mirós: One of Dwight's Miró oils, *Femme et oiseaux dans la nuit* (number 2, 1946), turned up for auction at Sotheby's New York on May 11, 1993, and was illustrated as number 43 in Sotheby's catalog 6415, *Impressionist Paintings, Drawings and Sculpture, Part I.*

page 159 "thud heard round the room": Dwight appears briefly as himself and as the millionaire "Cyril Reed" in Norse's *Memoirs of a Bastard Angel.* The descriptions, as in this party scene at pages 185–86, seem reliably to flatter Norse but not Dwight. I have to admit that they contain recognizable elements even so. "Cyril spoke twelve languages and wrote light verse in all," remembered Norse. " 'Listen to my Croatian poem, dahling! It's about absolutely nothing!' "

page 160 It all came to an end on a winter evening: I suspect, though of course I can't prove, that Dwight's observation on this turn of events was recorded in *Spring Catalogue* the following year:

Winter is a time for razor-sharp retorts,
Flowers by wire, and sonnets cold as quartz.

page 161 "Dwight Ripley, a wealthy painter": Dwight's purchases were *Number 26, 1949,* and *Number 18, 1949.* The latter is presumed lost. Naifeh and Smith, *Jackson Pollock,* at pages 598, 883n.

page 164 Watson returned to London: The Institute of Contemporary Arts was founded by Watson, Roland Penrose, and Herbert Read. Others on the organizing committee were Frederick Ashton and Geoffrey Grigson. "It was their idea," recalled painter Michael Wishart in *High Diver*, page 78, "to make it the embryo of a London Museum of Modern Art, a scheme which, as a glance in its direction today will show sadly too well, came nowhere to fruition."

page 166   "penniless, with only a few pieces": De Nagy's daughter recalled in a tribute to her father ("Tibor de Nagy, 1908–1993," New York: The Hungarian Consulate, April 25, 1994) that he arrived in New York in 1948 and met John Myers in 1949, a sequence that accords with the chronology of other events. Myers claimed in his memoir, *Tracking the Marvelous,* that he met de Nagy one year earlier, but his dating was inventive throughout that book.

page 167   named Rupert his sole heir: Dwight and Rupert never questioned that financial and testamentary obligations would follow from the course of love. Indeed, this seems to me such an unexceptional and self-evident expectation that I can't understand why it surprises people. But it does. In the meantime they are capable of unexamined self-regard. One afternoon Frank found Rupert still seething from an encounter with a colleague who had approached him in his office to recommend that he leave everything in his will to the Botanical Garden. Rupert, being quicker under the circum-stances than I would have been, asked the colleague if that was what he intended to do. Came the reply, delivered in a tone that meant it should have been obvious: "I have a *son.*"

page 168   It was the next Monday that he took Myers: In her book, *Clement Greenberg,* the biographer Florence Rubenfeld placed the meeting of Dwight, Myers, and Greenberg in 1951. Her footnotes suggest she had the story from Greenberg but tried to fit it to the year given by Myers in *Track-ing the Marvelous.* Myers unaccountably wrote there that the gallery was founded in 1951 rather than 1950. He admitted the error, at least implicitly, when he was interviewed by Robert Mattison on August 12, 1985, in prepa-ration for Mattison's *Grace Hartigan: A Painter's World* (Hudson Hills Press, 1990). Reports Mattison at page 18: "In the spring of 1950 Myers was offered financial backing for an art gallery by the wealthy botanist Dwight Ripley and carte blanche in selection of its artists." In his memoir Myers also gave the gallery's address as 219 rather than 206 East Fifty-third Street, and this error has been perpetuated in further books and library abstracts.

page 170 "Clem Greenberg picked": Kootz's firsthand assessment of Greenberg was recorded by Jay Jacobs, "New York Gallery Notes," *Art in America* 54:6 (November-December, 1966), at page 109.

page 171 Dwight paid the rent: The gallery's rent was $85 per month, or $1,020 per year. In the gallery's first twelve months Dwight contributed $5,155 to its support. There are two ledger sheets in the Archives of American Art in New York that purport to show the gallery's finances for November and December 1950. According to the second of these, Dwight's contribution in the first twelve months was actually $5,705. The ledgers list six other contributors in that same period: Tibor de Nagy, $280; Jeanne Reynal, $250; Alfonso Ossorio, $100; XY, $100; Ellen McCoole, $25; and Babs Simpson, $25. After the gallery showed the antique lace collection of Marian Powys Grey in March 1951, the lace collector Jean Flagler Matthews—she is called "Mrs. Satterfield" in *Tracking the Marvelous*—began installment payments that totaled $5,002. But this was a purchase and not a contribution. (Marian Powys Grey was the sister of writer John Cowper Powys and known to Dwight from England. Jean Flagler Matthews, the granddaughter of Standard Oil magnate Henry Flagler, was an ardent horticulturist who was a member of the New York Botanical Garden and the founder later of the Flagler Museum in Palm Beach; her sister, Mary Flagler Cary, left the present Cary Arboretum to the Botanical Garden.) The Tibor de Nagy Gallery records for 1952 are missing. In 1953, Dwight gave $1,600, or three-fifths of the year's total contributions. The three other supporters that year were William Lieberman, $500; John Myers, $475; and Roland Pease, $80. The records for the remainder of the 1950s are also missing. There are later materials at the Archives of American Art in Washington, D.C.

page 171 Because Dwight seldom was seen: The founding of the Tibor de Nagy Gallery has been variously set forth by John Gruen in *The Party's Over Now: Reminiscences of the Fifties—New York's Artists, Writers,*

Musicians and Their Friends (Viking, 1972) at pages 134 and 186; by Grace Hartigan in "Oral History Review," conducted by Julie Haifley for the Archives of American Art, at www.artarchives.si.edu/oralhist/hartig79. htm; by Myers in *Tracking the Marvelous* at page 147; by Naifeh and Smith in *Jackson Pollock* at pages 883–84n; by Mattison in *Grace Hartigan: A Painter's World* at page 18; by Larry Rivers, with Arnold Weinstein, in *What Did I Do? The Unauthorized Autobiography* (HarperCollins, 1992) at pages 200–02; by Brad Gooch in *City Poet: The Life and Times of Frank O'Hara* (Alfred A. Knopf, 1993) at pages 197–99; by David Lehman in *The Last Avant-Garde: The Making of the New York School of Poets* (Doubleday, 1998) at pages 21 and 382n; by Rubenfeld in *Clement Greenberg* at pages 143 and 155; and by Karen Wilkin in *Tibor de Nagy Gallery: The First Fifty Years* at page 22. The Rivers account, with its extravagant descriptions of three alleged angels (none being Dwight), was the most creative. It was also insightful. Wrote Rivers: "Such were the humble yet noble beginnings of the careers of Tibor de Nagy, John Myers—and Larry Rivers. And Fairfield Porter, Jane Freilicher, Al Leslie, Nell Blaine, Neil Welliver, Grace Hartigan, et al."

page 172   "Those days were fruitful": Frankenthaler's evocative remark was given by Gruen in *The Party's Over Now* at page 187. Frankenthaler married Robert Motherwell in 1958 and left Tibor de Nagy Gallery later that year, but Dwight continued to keep track of her. "Did you see the Motherwells," he asked his friends the Effrons in 1961, "now cozily ensconced in Provincetown?"

page 172   "In the end they": Guest was quoted by David Lehman at page 24 of *The Last Avant-Garde*. Lehman's account of four avant-garde poets— John Ashbery, Kenneth Koch, Frank O'Hara, and James Schuyler—who were first published by Tibor de Nagy Editions is now the next best thing to being secretly in the group oneself. I confess that when Frank and I first met Rupert I was impressed, not because he had two Pollocks on the walls, or because he had revised the genus *Astragalus* of which I then knew nothing, but because he had a complete set of the unprecedented poetry chapbooks published by Tibor de Nagy Gallery.

at page 46.
was instruc-
e by twenty-
to Dwight.
e valuation
re eminent
enken was
's Museum
um. It was
ed job in
this was
lock, but

recalled
POP-
Charles
aas in
ga in
him-

Iazel
otel
een
an
rs
d,
te
e

placed in
ery cele-
with a
opened
hed for
ustrated
ry: *The*
the cata-
ne title by
en Wilkin.
garded the
gy Gallery as
American art,
in's essay one
hen the catalog
and I were sur-
ver a photograph
cage that we knew
t's loft. The photo-
ovember 1951, shows

Dwight Ripley,
Heron in a Cage, *1951*

ront from Fifty-third Street at night. Dimly visible below
ow is a sign that advertised the ice vendor who operated
level of the building. Plainly visible in the window is the
e beyond it one can see Alfred Leslie installing the Franken-
Dwight's drawings from *Birds, Fish, and Cages* are already

nken had a second show: If Menken had increased the size of
es and added broken crockery she might have been an art star
e 1980s. In her own time, however, the common verdict of the
d other artists was that she relied on "decorative" effects. Her
vere reviewed by Judith Kaye Reed in *Art Digest* 24:20 (November
) at pages 20–21; Bette Krasne in *Art Digest* 25:24 (February 15,
at pages 24–25; Mary Cole in *Art Digest* 25:27 (March 15, 1951) at page

27; and Robert Goodnough in *Art News* 50:2 (April 1951
Dwight and Rupert owned six of Menken's paintings, and i
tive to discover that one of these, *Dr. Coon's Ghar Hotu*, twelv
one inches, is included on an undated insurance policy issue
The Menken was insured for two hundred dollars, the sam
placed on a nine-by-twelve-inch gouache by the now mo
William Baziotes. Before she went to work at Time, Inc., M
employed as a secretary to Hilla Rebay at Solomon Guggenheim
of Non-Objective Art, the predecessor to the Guggenheim Muse
Menken who secured for a young Jackson Pollock his short-liv
1943 as custodian in the basement of that museum. At least
Menken's story. She is absent from Naifeh and Smith, *Jackson Po*
there is no evidence in their account to contradict her.

page 183   "The Maases were warm and demonstrative": Warhol
Menken and Maas with affection in Andy Warhol and Pat Hackett
ism: The Warhol '60s (Harcourt Brace, 1980), at pages 25–26. (
Henri Ford first took Warhol to a party given by Menken and M
1962, but the lasting connection was provided by poet Gerard Mala
1963. Malanga had been Maas's student at Wagner College before he
self began to work with Warhol.

page 184   the Medea of the Twentieth Century: On October 19, 1928, H
was alone with her two sons, aged one and four, on the roof of the H
Surrey on East Seventy-ninth Street in New York. Both boys fell thir
floors to a roof below, and were killed. The police determined it was
accident. Dwight listed Hazel among his collectors and her name appe
in his pocket diary, though never after 1958. In that year her boyfrien
Alexander Kirkland, got himself stranded in the south of France and wro
Dwight to demand a thousand dollars so he could return to Hazel in th
United States.

page 185   Menken's camera gate had not been cleaned: Scott MacDonald dis-
cussed *Glimpse of the Garden* at length in *The Garden in the Machine: A
Field Guide to Independent Films about Place* (University of California
Press, 2001), pages 54–61, and noted there that no other woman who had

so significant an impact on independent cinema remains "as little celebrated." His book should help to correct that situation. MacDonald has the venue of the film wrong—he places it in "the Long Island garden of Dwight Ripley" rather than in the garden at the Falls—but this is a minor mistake taken on faith from Brakhage and it doesn't interfere with his descriptions of the film. A more significant problem of interpretation ensues from his belief that it was Dwight who was the "ex-lover of Menken's husband, Willard Maas." This too was taken on faith from Brakhage, who presumably repeated what he himself had been told. One can imagine a number of reasons, not wholly ignoble, why Menken and Maas may have preferred to tell the story this way. The truth does compromise the psychological interpretation of *Glimpse of the Garden* offered first by Brakhage and then by MacDonald, but it does not alter the justice of MacDonald's conclusion that Menken's life "seems to beg for a biographer." In 2003 the filmmaker Martina Kudláček began production of *Notes on Marie Menken*, a documentary that is sure to focus attention on Menken's career.

page 186   In the spring she fractured: In the Menken file of the library at Anthology Film Archives is a letter from Menken to Lottie Rothbard, written on Rupert's and Dwight's "Wappingers Falls" stationery, Thursday (May or June), 1956. Menken had been commissioned by Rothbard to decorate a folding screen with one of her sand paintings, but she was behind schedule. "I left the screen for the colors to set," she explained, "and came away to rest up in the country." The screen was later donated to Anthology Film Archives by Rothbard's granddaughter, Kezia Gleckman Hayman.

page 186   "like, you know, a bomb has been dropped": Brakhage made these remarks as he screened *Glimpse of the Garden* for the Innis Film Society in 1992, and they are found in "Stan Brakhage on Marie Menken," *Film Culture* 78 (Summer 1992), at page 8. During the screening Brakhage again misidentified Dwight as Maas's former lover, which enabled him to conclude that "Dwight Ripley's flowers" made Menken feel "all the ironies" of her life. "And so she starts sparking with that camera in hand and she makes of the camera a musical instrument."

page 188   Jonas Mekas observed: The Mekas review was in the *Village Voice* 7:11 (January 4, 1962) at pages 11–12.

page 189   The young Joe LeSueur: LeSueur's review in *Scenario* 3:2 (East Rockaway: Film Publishers Workshop, March-April, 1962) was quoted in the program notes for *The Films of Marie Menken*, presented in the Midnight Showcase at the Bleecker Street Cinema, May 27, 1963. It was accompanied by Menken's acknowledgment, "Without those who love me and whom I love, these small films could not have existed." She named, among others, LeSueur and Frank O'Hara. LeSueur's later opinion that Menken's films were "pretentious home movies that were passed off as 'experimental' " was quoted by Wilkin in *The First Fifty Years* at page 23. LeSueur died in 2001. At page 184 of his posthumous *Digressions on Some Poems by Frank O'Hara: A Memoir* (Farrar, Straus and Giroux, 2003) he remembered Menken as "a talented but dilettantish artist" who made "grainy, dimly lit experimental films like Willard's." Dwight and Rupert were not mentioned in the memoir, although they owned a drawing, done in pencil by the highly regarded John Button, of the young LeSueur.

page 190   "Marie dashed off to Spain": Dwight's letters to Jesse and Lee Effron, which frequently begin "Dear Both," were a considerable resource when I was writing this book and I am in debt to the Effrons for bringing them to my attention. The Effrons kept one of Dwight's drawings, a Mondrian parody (it is brown, a shade Mondrian detested) that was done probably in 1953. The drawing could be titled, from a legend that appears in one pane of its Mondrian-like grid, as *Titus Canyon*. Dwight's letter about Menken and Anger in Spain was dated August 11, 1958. Menken filmed *Arabesque for Kenneth Anger* in Spain, but that film is usually dated in the literature as 1961. If the episode described by Dwight was part of its filming, then the accepted date of *Arabesque* may need to be revised.

page 191   "I must say that people": Beck was initially a painter, and he met Dwight when he too was part of the crowd that circulated around Art of This Century. His work was included in a group show there in 1945, when he was only twenty. Beck's early paintings, like Menken's, were curiously Pollock-like in imagery, though not in technique. An exhibition, "Julian

Beck: Paintings & Drawings, 1944–1958," was at the Ubu Gallery in the spring of 2001. Dwight owned Beck's painting *Mexican Dollar,* listed on his insurance policy at one hundred eighty dollars. Beck and Malina were married in 1948. They had made plans for the Living Theatre the year before, but their inaugural season onstage at the Cherry Lane Theatre at 38 Commerce Street in Greenwich Village was delayed until August 1951. The plays they presented that autumn were by Gertrude Stein, Paul Goodman, and Kenneth Rexroth. Norse's lover Dick Stryker composed the music for the Rexroth play. Early in the new year the Living Theatre presented John Cage's *Music of Changes,* an event that John Ashbery later recalled as "a kind of renewal." Beck died, at age sixty, in 1985. In the autumn of 2003 he and Malina were inducted into the Theater Hall of Fame in recognition of their lifetime achievement in the American theater. There are only a few draft letters from Beck and Malina to Dwight, together with notes from Dwight in response, among the Living Theatre Records in the Billy Rose Theatre Collection of the New York Public Library for the Performing Arts. The letter quoted here was dated August 12, 1956.

page 194 "I do not attempt to understand": Stanley Welsh included this remark in a letter to me the summer after Rupert died. He added: "I wish England had a boatload of such 'rejects' to send to the US."

page 198 In 1964 the magazine *Art in America:* The *New York Post* critic Charlotte Willard described the FAR Gallery show in "Drawing Today," *Art in America* 52:5 (October 1964), at pages 49–67. Her illustrated article included reproductions of Dwight's Motherwell, an untitled 1944 drawing in ink and wash, which appeared at page 56, and of Tony Bower's Rivers, a pencil study for *Washington Crossing the Delaware,* at page 67. Bower was managing editor of *Art in America* from 1957 to 1970.

page 198 Probably the best-known: Hockney's *Portrait of Andy Warhol,* 1974, was on view at Artemis, Greenberg Van Doren Gallery in New York in November 2001.

page 198 You lift colored pencil: Many years ago I worked as the writer on some commercial projects with the artist Bob Conge, who, I now realize, was a master of colored pencil technique. I was too uninformed at the time to appreciate what he had accomplished. For my present purposes, the best guide to the fundamentals of the medium turned out to be Bet Borgerson, *The Colored Pencil: Key Concepts for Handling the Medium* (Watson-Guptill, 1995). Borgerson's manual is unintrusive but direct and helpful. An example of the unexpected intensities that can be achieved with colored pencil was provided by Steve DiBenedetto in his show of complex, even troubling drawings at Derek Eller Gallery in Chelsea in the autumn of 2002.

page 199   "Modelling prevents shock": Miró's remark is in his book *Je travaille comme un jardinier* (Société Internationale d'Art XXᵉ siècle/F. Hazan, 1964) at page 45. The book was in Rupert's, and thus Dwight's, library.

page 203   O Aleijadinho, or "The Little Cripple": It was recently suggested that Aleijadinho is a mythical figure whose sculptures should be credited to the anonymous artisans at work in colonial Brazil. This view is not widely accepted. Dwight at any rate would not have known of it. There was a book in Rupert and Dwight's library by R. A. Freudenfeld, published in Portuguese in Brazil and called *O Aleijadinho: Mestre Antônio Francisco* (Edições Melhoramentes nº. 2650). The book had no publication date, but an inscription makes clear that Dwight acquired it in 1956, the same year he drew the *Churches*. Aleijadinho's disfigurement may have been caused by leprosy, as reported in some accounts, or by syphilis, as the Brazilian embassy in London is not too bashful to say on its Web site. Since the sculptor moved about in public and had many assistants, syphilis seems the more likely. Whichever it was, Aleijadinho might surely be the patron saint of any artist who feels that he or she works under an unjustly inflicted handicap. The work of Aleijadinho was included in "Baroque Brazil: Beyond Heaven and Earth" at the Petit Palais in Paris in 1999, and in the shows "Opulence and Devotion: Brazilian Baroque Art" at the Ashmolean Museum at Oxford and "Brazil: Body and Soul" at the Guggenheim Museum in New York, both in the winter season of 2001–02.

page 206   Peter Watson was found drowned: Watson's unexplained death in his bath troubled his friends. After a memorial service Cecil Beaton wrote in his diary, "I noticed that Cyril Connolly was weeping, and I loved him for that." Beaton, *The Restless Years: Diaries, 1955–1963* (Weidenfeld and Nicholson, 1976), page 45. Watson's death was noted by Charles Henri Ford in *Water From a Bucket: A Diary* (Turtle Point Press, 2001) at page 216, and by Isherwood in *Diaries, Volume One,* at pages 616–17, 618, and 623. The painter Anne Dunn has reminded me that Norman Fowler used part of his inheritance from Watson to acquire a resort in the Virgin Islands. The resort was called the Bath Hotel. In 1971, near the fifteenth anniversary of Watson's death, Fowler was found drowned in his bath.

page 209   "Ripley was a gifted dilettante": Weld's verdict is at page 340. I am certain that Dwight encouraged this perception in his friends. In his novel, *A Sunlit Scene,* the character Madge (the one who is said to be Dwight Ripley's sister) observed in good Edwardian fashion that "a true aristocrat never lets his talent get the better of him."

page 212   In the two decades since "Avant-Garde and Kitsch": Hess's declaration is in Thomas B. Hess, "Inside Nature," *Art News* 56:10 (February 1958), at page 65, and Rosenberg's diagnosis is in "After Next, What?" *Art in America* 52:2 (April 1964), at page 73. The Rivers remark is in Barbara Rose and Irving Sandler, "Sensibility of the Sixties," *Art in America* 55:1 (January–February 1967), pages 44–57. Ashbery's insights were reprinted in his *Reported Sightings: Art Chronicles, 1957–1987,* ed. David Bergman (Alfred A. Knopf, 1989), at pages 393 and 97 respectively.

page 215   Ito received a substantial sum: Ito's father, Yuji Ito, designed the costumes for the Tin Man, the Scarecrow, and the Cowardly Lion in *The Wizard of Oz,* and for many years he was the director of prop and scenery design for the Radio City Music Hall Rockettes. Teiji Ito was forty-seven when he died while visiting Haiti in 1982. Two collections of his music are available. The somewhat moody *Meshes: Music for Films and Theater* (¿What Next? Recordings WN0020, 1997) includes Ito's 1959 score for Maya Deren's film *Meshes of the Afternoon,* while the more humorous *King Ubu* (Tzadik 7036, 1998) consists of his 1961 score for the Alfred Jarry play. Neither disc includes the music from *Dwightiana.*

page 216   "This little animated film": Menken's nonchalant estimate of *Dwightiana* was quoted in the program notes for *The Films of Marie*

Menken at the Bleecker Street Cinema, May 27, 1963. There is a copy of this program in the Menken file at Anthology Film Archives. Maas's emendation appeared in Maas, "The Gryphon Yaks," *Film Culture* 29 (1963), at page 46. His earlier description of Dwight as an "avant-guardian angel" is at the end of his summary, "Toward the Film Poem: Gryphon Productions," reprinted in *Film Culture* 78 (Summer 1994) at page 11.

page 216   They were identified by playwright Edward Albee: Albee led the drama workshop at Wagner College on Staten Island while Maas was director of the writing program there. "He used to come here every time to eat and just sit and sit and listen while Willard and I argued," Menken told Roger Jacoby near the end of her life. Jacoby, "Willard Maas and Marie Menken: The Last Years," *Film Culture* 63–64 (1976–77), at page 122. Reported Albee's biographer, Mel Gussow: "If anybody inspired George and Martha, he said, it was Willard Maas, a teacher and poet, and his wife, Marie Menken, who was a documentary filmmaker." Gussow, *Edward Albee: A Singular Journey* (Simon and Schuster, 1999), at page 185.

page 222   "non-standard observer" of color: John Gage's discussion of the nonstandard observer is in pages 15–20 of *Color and Meaning: Art, Science, and Symbolism* (University of California Press, 2000). The history of color theory can be explored from an exemplary Web site, www.colorsystem. com, produced by Urs Baumann. I also enjoyed reading David Batchelor's provocative *Chromophobia* (Reaktion Books, 2000) and the response by mosaicist Emma Biggs, "Come on Down, Colour," in *Modern Painters* 13:4 (Winter 2000) at pages 51–53. Wrote Biggs of color: "I can't understand how anyone could claim to have an interest in it, or understand about how to use it, without noticing it has a system."

page 223   Humphrey had a show: Ralph Humphrey's works are infrequently seen. Dwight bought one of his paintings for three hundred dollars in 1960, but I don't know what became of it. "Ralph's vernissage 4–6 p.m. (T. de N.)," recorded Dwight in his pocket diary on February 2, 1960. Humphrey's later paintings were increasingly colorful, and he moved through a succession of galleries until Mary Boone Gallery scheduled two shows of his work in 1990. He died that year at the age of fifty-eight.

page 224   Stamos responded to Humphrey's example: According to Rupert, Stamos responded to Dwight's example as well. Stamos made the first lithograph of his career in 1964, and Rupert insisted that it was based on drawings Dwight made a year earlier. I did not much credit this loyal exaggeration when I first heard it. After Dwight's *Nuclear Suns* emerged from their storage in the trunk, I began to think Rupert perhaps was right. The Stamos lithograph shows a bloated red-and-orange sun nearly exploded over three angry dark swipes, one of cloud and two of ocean. Rupert had already died when I found in Dwight's pocket diary for 1960 the memo "Show R's drawings to Stamos."

page 225   An alternative label to the same effect: The four critics were James Fitzsimmons, Betty Holliday, Dore Ashton, and Kermit I. Lansner. Citations to their notices appear in the list of Dwight's exhibitions.

page 226   The stick figures: The cartoon figures in *Language Panel: Pstruh!* (*trout*) are Snuffy Smith in the lower right and Miz Smif in the upper left panel. Dwight took the Smiths from "Barney Google and Snuffy Smith," the venerable comic strip that was created by Billy DeBeck in 1919 and continued later by Fred Lasswell. Google inspired a hit song, "Barney Google (With Your Goo-Goo-Googly Eyes)," which I suppose was irresistible material for Dwight. "After dinner," recalled John Myers of evenings he spent with Rupert and Dwight, "we all went to the parlor, where Dwight, sitting at the Steinway baby grand, would play *his* outrageous repertoire of pop tunes."

page 229   "A beach is close by": The guidebook, by Eric Arendt and Katja Hayek-Arendt, was called *Islands of the Mediterranean,* and it was published by Edition Leipzig in 1961, the year before Dwight and Rupert made their last visit to Mallorca.

page 230   Back in Lanzarote: "Queridos Dwight y Rupert:" wrote Manrique. "Aqui estoy trabajando lleno de alegria con un estudio estupendo frente al mar. Preparo mi proxima exposicion en Catherine en abril. Felices Pascuas y un abrazo. *César.*" Manrique's first solo show in America was at the Catherine Viviano Gallery, 42 East Fifty-seventh Street, in January 1966. His next show was in April 1967. In the autumn of 2003, I accessed the Manrique site, www.cesarmanrique.com, and reached a collection of photographs by clicking on *Photo Album.* The photo with the pop-up label "Friends in New York" showed Stamos, Manrique, and John Myers. It was taken at Stirling House by Dwight.

page 231　　Barneby's Vista: Robert Fincham's account, "The Creeks of Alfonso Ossorio," was in *Bulletin of the American Conifer Society* 2:3 (Winter 1985) at pages 69–70. Barneby's Vista was noted by Mike Solomon in his essay "Arcadian Dreams: The Creeks Conifer Arboretum and Sculpture Park (1952–1990)," which appeared in the illustrated catalog *Alfonso Ossorio: The Creeks: Before, During and After,* published by Michael Rosenfeld Gallery in the summer of 2000. The occasion was an exhibition, held at the Ossorio Foundation in Southampton, New York, that paired Ossorio's youthful watercolors with photographs of analogous features realized later in the arboretum at the Creeks. One of Ossorio's large assemblages, or "Congregations," hung in the dining room near the refectory table at Stirling House. It never made the transition to Rupert's loft at the Botanical Garden. Ossorio replaced it with the gift of a smaller "Congregation" that incorporated a small broom and was titled *Broom* in honor of the Daleas, or *escobillas,* that Rupert and Dwight collected in Mexico. Because of a legal wrangle, the Ossorio Foundation was closed to the public in 2003 when I might have inspected the drawings by Dwight that director Mike Solomon discovered in storage there.

page 234　　Miró rescued pleasure: Greenberg's inspiriting remark is in his *Joan Miró* (Quadrangle Press, 1948) at page 42. In the spring of 2001, Dwight's "Constellation" number five, *Femme à la blonde aisselle coiffant sa chevelure à la lueur des étoiles,* was back in New York for a show at the Morgan Library. I saw it there. Greenberg might not have approved of my attaching historical reflections to a work of art; but the history of this fragile gouache, combined with my knowing that Dwight had sold it so that Rupert could continue to botanize and he to draw, made the emotion in Greenberg's "rescued pleasure" remark seem almost personal. For the first time I understood one of Dwight's own *Language Panels,* drawn in 1968. In the bottom right of this drawing are two stick figures that gaze upward at a configuration of stars in a midnight blue sky, while one figure exclaims to the other, GWIAZDOZBIÓR!, which is Polish for constellation.

page 237   The following year Stamos was sued: The Rothko case was complex and perhaps ineffable. In 1975, Stamos and the other executors were held liable for more than seven million dollars. Two years later the New York Court of Appeals raised the damages to more than nine million, but determined that payment was the responsibility of the gallery director and not Stamos. At the same time, the court awarded Stamos's house on West Eighty-third Street to the claimants to cover their legal expenses. The effect of the lawsuit on Stamos's artistic reputation was disastrous. When his reputation began to recover it would be too late, of course, for him to enjoy it. He died in Greece in 1997.

page 237   "Marie's drinking": In *Film Culture* 78 (Summer 1994) there is a haunting photograph at page 10 that was taken of Menken and Maas in 1970 by filmmaker John Hawkins. Maas, in particular, is shockingly aged. According to the *Times* he was not fifty-nine but sixty-four when he died. If this was correct then he was born in 1906 and was thirty-seven when drafted in 1943. Maas's Social Security record (098-16-9817) agrees with the *Times*, but one suggestion I have heard is that he lied about his age in order to qualify sooner for Social Security benefits. Maas gave his birthdate in *The War Poets*, and again in *Contemporary Authors* (Vol. I, 1975, page 395), as 1911. I accepted this date because it makes him a more plausible thirty-two when drafted.

page 238   Bower had published: "The Double Dealers," by Anthony Bower, appeared in *Art in America* 56:4 (July-August 1968) at pages 58–67. The news of Bower's murder was reported in "Art Dealer Is Found Slain in East 65th St. Apartment," *New York Times* (July 4, 1972), at page 5, and again the next day in "Police Say Slaying of Art Dealer Here Is Near a Solution," at page 79. "Within the art world," wrote the *Times*, "Mr. Bower was known as a highly social, witty and charming personality whose circle of friends included John Hay Whitney, Sir Ronald and Marietta Tree, Marya Mannes and Mrs. Marshall Field. Friends said he was a bridge partner of Mr. Whitney's, and often visited the Trees at their winter home in Barbados."

Dwight Ripley,
Botanist UFO No. 2, *1970*

page 238   Dwight Ripley was sixty-five when he died: There was no obituary for Dwight in the *New York Times.* A brief obituary by Lincoln Foster appeared in the *Bulletin of the American Rock Garden Society* 32:2 (April 1974) at pages 88–89. An even briefer one by Roy Elliott appeared in the *Quarterly Bulletin of the Alpine Garden Society* 176, 42:2 (June 1974), at page 115.

page 240   "One must never pity the dead": Rupert's letter to Isely, written August 24, 1976, is in the collection of Stanley Welsh, and we are in debt to him for sharing it.

page 241   He gave the Miró *regalito* to Dillon Ripley: In the autumn of 1950 Dwight was peeved, recalled Harold Norse, because the *New Yorker* published a profile of his ornithologist cousin, Dillon Ripley, but failed to mention him. "The least they might have done," complained Dwight, "was to write: 'Dwight Ripley, a first cousin, is an expert taxonomist, although he knows nothing about birds.' "

Exhibitions of Dwight Ripley Drawings

1946   December 3 to December 21. Art of This Century, 30 West 57th St. (With John Goodwin, David Hill, Kenneth Scott, and Charles Seliger.)

        Edward Alden Jewell, *New York Times* (December 6, 1946), 93.

1947   March 31 to April 30. The Three Arts, 77 Cannon St., Poughkeepsie.

1951   October 30 to November 10. Tibor de Nagy, 206 East 53rd St. *(Birds, Fish, and Cages.)*

        James Fitzsimmons, *Art Digest* 26 (November 1951), 59.

        Betty Holliday, *Art News* 50 (November 1951), 57.

        Stuart Preston, *New York Times* (October 28, 1951), 97.

1953   May 12 to June 13. Tibor de Nagy, 206 East 53rd St. (*Season in Review:* Drawings by Dwight Ripley, paintings by Harry Jackson, selected work by Hartigan, Leslie, West, Frankenthaler, Elaine de Kooning, Porter, Rivers, Freilicher, and Goodnough.)

        August 1 to August 31. The Three Arts, 77 Cannon St., Poughkeepsie.

1954   January 5 to January 30. Tibor de Nagy, 206 East 53rd St.

        Dore Ashton, *Art Digest* 28 (January 15, 1954), 27.

        Kermit I. Lansner, *Art News* 52 (January 1954), 65.

        Stuart Preston, *New York Times* (January 23, 1954), 11.

1955   January 11 to January 30. Tibor de Nagy, 206 East 53rd St. *(The Bomb.)*

Margaret Breuning, *Arts Digest* 29 (February 1, 1955), 22.
Eleanor C. Munro, *Art News* 53 (January 1955), 47.
Stuart Preston, *New York Times* (January 15, 1955), 11.

Through February. The Three Arts, 77 Cannon St., Poughkeepsie.

1956   February 28 to March 24. Tibor de Nagy, 24 East 67th St. *(Hats.)*
Laverne George, *Arts* 30 (March 1956), 62.
Ronald Vance, *Art News* 55 (March 1956), 55.
Dore Ashton, *New York Times* (February 28, 1956), 28:3.

Through April. The Three Arts, 56 Raymond Ave., Poughkeepsie.

1962   April 10 to April 28. Tibor de Nagy, 149 East 72nd St. *(Marines.)*
Stuart Preston, *New York Times* (April 15, 1962), x22.

Publications by Dwight Ripley and Rupert Barneby

Book by H. D. Ripley and R. C. Barneby

A List of Plants Cultivated or Native at the Spinney, Waldron, Sussex. London: Unwin Brothers Ltd., 1939.

Selected monographs by Rupert C. Barneby

"A Revision of the North American Species of *Oxytropis*." *Proceedings of the California Academy of Sciences,* Fourth Series, no. 7 (1952).

"Atlas of North American *Astragalus*." *Memoirs of the New York Botanical Garden* 13 (1964).

"Daleae Imagines: An illustrated revision of *Errazurizia, Psorothamnus, Marina,* and *Dalea*." *Memoirs of the New York Botanical Garden* 27 (1977).

"Sensitivae Censitae: A description of the genus *Mimosa* in the New World." *Memoirs of the New York Botanical Garden* 65 (1991).

Selected articles by Rupert C. Barneby

"Plants from Eastern Crete." *New Flora and Silva* 11:3 (1939), 202–10.

"A New Species of *Cymopterus* from Nevada." *Leaflets of Western Botany* 3:4 (November 6, 1941), 81–83.

"Pugillus Astragalorum Nevadensium." *Leaflets of Western Botany* 3:5 (January 23, 1942), 97–120.

"A Suffrutescent *Gilia* from Southern Nevada." *Leaflets of Western Botany* 3:6 (April 21, 1942), 129–32.

"Pugillus Astragalorum Alter." *Proceedings of the California Academy of Sciences,* Fourth Series, 25:3 (June 4, 1944), 147–70.

"*Gaultheria* versus *Chiogenes*." *Bulletin of the American Rock Garden Society* 31:3 (Fall 1973), 118–19.

"Botanical Journal [1944]." *Parenthèse* (Spring 1975), 9–26. Barneby is misspelled "Barnaby," and the journal is misdated 1942.
"Looking Back." *Bulletin of the American Rock Garden Society* 34:1 (Winter 1976), 23–25.

Complete works of Rupert C. Barneby

For a complete bibliography see William R. Buck, "An Annotated List of the Publications of Rupert C. Barneby," *Brittonia* 53:1 (January-March 2001), 41–57.

Books by Dwight Ripley

Poems. London: Elkin Mathews & Marrot, 1931.
Spring Catalogue: A Poem. With three black-and-white drawings by Dwight Ripley. New York: The Weekend Press, 1952.
Impressions of Nevada: The Countryside and Some of the Plants, as Seen Through the Eyes of an Englishman. Edited by Margaret J. Williams. Reno: Northern Nevada Native Plant Society, 1978.

Articles by Dwight Ripley

IN THE *QUARTERLY BULLETIN OF*
THE ALPINE GARDEN SOCIETY OF GREAT BRITAIN
"The Limestone Areas of Southern Nevada and Death Valley." No. 47, 10:1 (March 1942), 18–27.
"Rareties of Western North America." No. 48, 10:2 (June 1942), 73–80.
"Utah in the Spring." No. 49, 10:3 (September 1942), 168–72.
"Plants of Southern California and Adjacent Mexico." No. 52, 11:2 (June 1943), 65–76.
"A Journey through Spain." No. 55, 12:1 (March 1944), 38–52.
"More Western Americans." No. 56, 12:2 (June 1944), 65–74.
"Nevada 1944." No. 59, 13:1 (March 1945), 28–37.
"Searching High and Low." No. 67, 15:1 (March 1947), 18–32.
"A Trip through Oregon." No. 69, 15:3 (September 1947), 178–89.

"The Paunsagunt Plateau and Other Wonders of the West." No. 71, 16:1 (March 1948), 15–28.

"Three Days at Leadville." No. 75, 17:1 (March 1949), 26–30.

"Some Southern Belles." No. 79, 18:1 (March 1950), 38–40.

"Notes from Long Island." No. 169, 40:3 (September 1972), 182–87.

"Notes from Long Island" [II]. No. 172, 41:2 (June 1973), 125–31.

IN THE *BULLETIN OF THE AMERICAN ROCK GARDEN SOCIETY*

"Experiment in New York." 8:1 (January-February 1950), 1–4.

"Experiment in New York" [II]. 8:6 (November-December 1950), 92–95.

"Garden Notes, 1952." 10:4 (October 1952), 68–70.

"A Miniature Bog Garden." 11:4 (October 1953), 87–89.

"Ranunculus hystriculus." 13:3 (July 1955), 69.

IN OTHER PUBLICATIONS

"Thymes of the Iberian Peninsula." *New Flora and Silva* 38, 10:2 (January 1938), 90–94.

"Some Observations on the Polish Language." *Gwiazda Polarna*, Stevens Point, Wis. (March 13, 1943), 8.

"Whence *Madroño* and *Aliso?*" *Leaflets of Western Botany* 9:8 (November 1960), 127–28.

Selected Bibliography

Unpublished material

Barneby Interview. Barneby, Rupert. Oral history of systematic botany at the New York Botanical Garden, 1989. Archives, The LuEsther T. Mertz Library of The New York Botanical Garden, Bronx, New York.

Beck Correspondence. Correspondence of Julian Beck and Dwight Ripley, 1955–1961. Living Theatre Records, Billy Rose Theatre Collection, New York Public Library for the Performing Arts, New York.

Effron Letters. Letters from Dwight Ripley and Rupert Barneby to Jesse and Lee Effron, 1947–1962, with related materials. Collection of Jesse and Lee Effron, Poughkeepsie.

Malina Diaries. Judith Malina [manuscript] Diaries, 1947–1959. Billy Rose Theatre Collection, New York Public Library for the Performing Arts, New York.

Menken File. Marie Menken File. Library, Anthology Film Archives, New York.

Mertz Library Letters. Letters to Rupert C. Barneby and Dwight Ripley, 1939–1950, from Peter H. Davis, Alice Eastwood, M. L. Fernald, John Thomas Howell, Walter E. Th. Ingwersen, Noel Y. Sandwith, E. Tester, and others. Archives, The LuEsther T. Mertz Library of The New York Botanical Garden, Bronx, New York.

Miró *regalito*. Dwight Ripley papers relating to Joan Miró, [ca. 1945]–1961. Archives of American Art, Smithsonian Institution, Washington, D.C.

Ripley Collection. Special Collections, Archives, California Academy of Sciences, San Francisco.

Ripley Dictionary. Ripley, Dwight. An Etymological Dictionary of Vernacular Plant Names. With an explanatory note by Rupert C. Barneby, 1973.

Harry Dwight Dillon Ripley Papers. The LuEsther T. Mertz Library of The New York Botanical Garden, Bronx, New York.

Tibor de Nagy Early Records. Tibor de Nagy Gallery Records, 1950–1953. New York Regional Center, Archives of American Art, Smithsonian Institution, New York.

Tibor de Nagy Later Records. Tibor de Nagy Gallery Records, 1950–1987. Archives of American Art, Smithsonian Institution, Washington, D.C.

Otherwise uncredited letters, manuscripts, diaries, records, and materials relating to Dwight Ripley and Rupert Barneby are in the collection of Frank Polach and are quoted by his permission.

Published books and articles

Brakhage, Stan. *Film at Wit's End: Eight Avant-Garde Filmmakers.* Kingston, New York: Documentext, McPherson & Company, 1989.

Dortch, Virginia M. *Peggy Guggenheim and Her Friends.* Milan: Berenice Art Books, 1994.

Greenberg, Clement. *The Harold Letters, 1928–1943: The Making of an American Intellectual.* Edited by Janice Van Horne. Washington, D.C.: Counterpoint, 2000.

Hester, James M., et al. "Barneby Dedication." With contributions by Arthur Cronquist, Peter H. Davis, Noel H. Holmgren, John Thomas Howell, Howard S. Irwin, Joseph H. Kirkbride, Jr., Peter H. Raven, Stanley L. Welsh, Margaret Williams, and others. *Brittonia* 33:3 (July-September 1981), 261–74, 294–303.

Isherwood, Christopher. *Diaries, Volume One: 1939–1960.* Edited and with an introduction by Katherine Bucknell. New York: Harper Flamingo, 1997.

———. *Down There on a Visit.* Minneapolis: University of Minneapolis Press, 1999.

Lewis, Jeremy. *Cyril Connolly: A Life.* London: Jonathan Cape, 1997.

Maas, Willard. "Memories of My Maya." *Filmwise* 2 (1962), 23–29.

Malina, Judith. *The Diaries of Judith Malina, 1947–1957.* New York: Grove Press, 1984.

Mandell, Leslie. "Interview with Marie Menken." Assisted by P. Adams Sitney. *Wagner Literary Magazine* 4, Student Association of Wagner College, Staten Island, New York (1963–1964), 47–53. Reprinted as P. Adams Sitney. "Interview with Marie Menken." *Filmwise* 5–6 (1967), 9–12.

Myers, John Bernard. *Tracking the Marvelous: A Life in the New York Art World*. New York: Random House, 1983.

Norse, Harold. *Memoirs of a Bastard Angel: A Fifty-Year Literary and Erotic Odyssey*. New York: William Morrow, 1989.

Pryce-Jones, David. *Cyril Connolly: A Journal and Memoir*. London: Collins, 1983.

Rubenfeld, Florence. *Clement Greenberg: A Life*. New York: Scribner, 1997.

Shelden, Michael. *Friends of Promise: Cyril Connolly and the World of Horizon*. New York: Harper & Row, 1989.

Weld, Jacqueline Bograd. *Peggy: The Wayward Guggenheim*. New York: E. P. Dutton, 1986.

Wilkin, Karen. "The First Fifty Years." *Tibor de Nagy Gallery: The First Fifty Years*. New York: Tibor de Nagy Gallery, 2000.

Acknowledgments

FOR THEIR ENCOURAGEMENT AND ASSISTANCE I am grateful to Eric Brown of Tibor de Nagy Gallery, Lynn Chu and Glen Hartley of Writers' Representatives, Inc., Deborah Garrison of Pantheon Books, Jacquelyn Kallunki of the New York Botanical Garden, and Frank Polach. For courtesies, permissions, assistance, and insights I am indebted to Joan Abrahamson; Bobbi Angell; Andrew Arnot of Tibor de Nagy Gallery; John Ashbery; Ted Barkley of the Botanical Research Institute of Texas; Star Black; Sam Brewster of Brewster Design; Art Bryant; William Buck, Willa Capraro, Douglas Daly, Judy Garrison, Noel Holmgren, Patricia Holmgren, Kevin Indoe, Sondra Lebost, Michael Nee, Heather Rolen, Joy Runyon, Barbara Thiers, and Thomas Zanoni of the New York Botanical Garden; Steven Carpenter of Abbey Lane Laboratory; William Corbett; Rosemary Cullen at John Hay Library of Brown University; Ted Danforth and Jim Fredrikson of Sea Cliff Press; Sam Del Propost; Tom Disch; Anne Dunn; Jesse and Lee Effron; Walter Effron of the Three Arts; Derek Eller of Derek Eller Gallery; Germán Esparza; Mark Ford; Helen Frankenthaler; Susan Fraser, Marie Long, John Reed, Stephen Sinon, and Don Wheeler at The LuEsther T. Mertz Library of The New York Botanical Garden; Vicki Funk and Dieter Wasshausen of the Smithsonian Institution; Jonathan Galassi; Kancheepuram Gandhi of Harvard University; Judy Gardner and Francoise Puniello of Rutgers University Libraries; Robert Gillis; David Gitel; Fernando Gómez Aguilera of the Fundación César Manrique; James Grimes of the Royal Botanic Gardens in Melbourne; Maxine Groffsky; Robert Haller, Shannon McLachlan, Jonas Mekas, and John Mhiripiri of Anthology Film Archives; Grace Hartigan; Scott Heald, Melissa Luckow, and the late Harold Moore of Bailey Hortorium at Cornell University; Patrick Henrendeen and Jun Wen of George Washington University; Richard Howard; Paul Ingwersen of W. E. Th. Ingwersen Ltd.;

Howard Irwin; Eric Karpeles; Panayoti Kelaidis; David Kermani; Nathan Kernan; Joseph Kirkbride of the U.S. Department of Agriculture at Beltsville; Wayne Koestenbaum; John Koethe; Valerie Komor at the New York Regional Center of the Archives of American Art; David Lehman; Alfred Leslie; Rika Lesser; Jean-David Levitte; Gwilym Lewis of the Royal Botanic Gardens at Kew; Robert Lin and Jenny Lin of Visual Art Photo; Aaron Liston of Oregon State University; Alicia Lourteig of the Muséum National d'Histoire Naturelle in Paris; Stephen Maas; Marit MacArthur; Celia Maguire; Gerard Malanga; Judith Malina; J. D. McClatchy; Sarah McNally of Counterpoint Press; Patricio Mena Vasconez of EcoCiencia Proyecto Paramo in Quito; Budd Myers; Harold Norse; Jed Perl; John Pipoly of Fairchild Tropical Garden; Sir Ghillean Prance; Stuart Preston; James Reveal; Michael Rosenfeld of Michael Rosenfeld Gallery; Maureen St. Onge; Mike Sell; P. Adams Sitney of Princeton University; Thomas Spence Smith; Tony Smith; Mike Solomon of the Ossorio Foundation; Bob Speer of Sanctuary Bookshop; Richard Spellenberg of New Mexico State University; Amy Stackhouse; Robert Starkoff; Sylvia Stein; Andrey Sytin of Komarov Botanical Institute; Bob Taylor of the New York Public Library for the Performing Arts; Judy Throm and Caroline Weaver at the Archives of American Art in Washington; Arnold Tiehm; Billie Turner of the University of Texas at Austin; Michael Underwood of S. B. Horton Funeral Home in Greenport; Janice Van Horne; Brian Walker; Michele Wellck at the Archives of the California Academy of Sciences; Stanley Welsh of Brigham Young University; Karen Wilkin; Coney Wilson of the Alpine Garden Society; Trevor Winkfield; and Kristen Bearse, Kevin Bourke, Michiko Clark, Archie Ferguson, Dan Frank, Katharine Freeman, Janice Goldklang, Andy Hughes, Altie Karper, Ilana Kurshan, Suzanne Williams, and their colleagues at Pantheon Books. For support at critical intervals I am grateful to the John Simon Guggenheim Foundation; the John D. and Catherine T. MacArthur Foundation; the Mrs. Giles Whiting Foundation; and the National Writers Union, UAW Local 1981.

Index

Illustrations Credits

ALL ILLUSTRATIONS ARE BY PERMISSION of Frank Polach except the following:

endpapers: Cymopterus ripleyi var. *saniculoides.* By permission of the William and Lynda Steere Herbarium of The New York Botanical Garden, Bronx, New York.

page 43: Rupert Barneby, *Astragalus pterocarpus,* 1962. By permission of the Archives of The LuEsther T. Mertz Library of The New York Botanical Garden, Bronx, New York.

page 70: Rupert on the San Rafael Swell. Photograph by Noel Holmgren. Courtesy of Noel and Patricia Holmgren.

page 197: Dwight Ripley, *Portrait of Rupert Barneby, Esq. (botanist),* 1955. Photograph by Rudy Burckhardt. Courtesy of Tibor de Nagy Gallery, New York.

page 217: Enclosed garden at Stirling House. Photograph by L. Budd Myers. Courtesy of L. Budd Myers.

page 245: Rupert Barneby, *Maurandya petrophila,* 1938. Collection of Noel and Patricia Holmgren. Courtesy of Noel and Patricia Holmgren.

LATER DRAWINGS OF DWIGHT RIPLEY:
Language Panel; Cymopterus ripleyi, 1968 (p. 75); *Churches: Congonhas do Campo,* 1956 (p. 205); *Language Panel: Pstruh! (trout),* 1968 (p. 227); *Travel Poster: Monte Gordo, Fuentebravi'a,* 1962 (p. 230); and *Botanist UFO No. 2,* 1970 (p. 276). Photographs by Sam Brewster. By permission of Frank Polach.

About the Author

DOUGLAS CRASE was born in 1944 in Battle Creek, Michigan, and grew up on a nearby farm. He is the author of *The Revisionist*, a poetry collection that was nominated for a National Book Critics Circle Award and an American Book Award. A former MacArthur fellow, he lives in New York City and Honesdale, Pennsylvania.

A Note on the Type

This book was set in Fournier, a typeface named for Pierre Simon Fournier *fils* (1712–1768), a celebrated French type designer. Coming from a family of typefounders, Fournier was an extraordinarily prolific designer of typefaces and of typographic ornaments. He was also the author of the important *Manuel typographique* (1764–1766), in which he attempted to work out a system standardizing type measurement in points, a system that is still in use internationally. Fournier's type is considered transitional in that it drew its inspiration from the old style, yet was ingeniously innovational, providing for an elegant, legible appearance. In 1925 his type was revived by the Monotype Corporation of London.

Composed by North Market Street Graphics,
Lancaster, Pennsylvania

Printed by Berryville Graphics,
Berryville, Virginia

Designed by M. Kristen Bearse